CLOSED STORES

 TAXES ON EVERYTHING!

 ROAD CLOSURES

 CRIME

THE CALIFORNIA LEFT COAST SURVIVOR'S GUIDE

The California Left Coast Survivor's Guide
A Pacific Research Institute Handbook to Help the Rest of America
Avoid Making a Wrong Left Turn

By Kerry Jackson and Tim Anaya

August 2024

ISBN: 978-0-936488-22-6

Pacific Research Institute
P.O. Box 60485
Pasadena, CA 91116

www.pacificresearch.org

Images © www.Vecteezy.com, www.Shutterstock.com, www.Unsplash.com, www.iStock.com

THE CALIFORNIA LEFT COAST SURVIVOR'S GUIDE

A Pacific Research Institute Handbook to Help the Rest of America Avoid Making a Wrong Left Turn

BY KERRY JACKSON AND TIM ANAYA

DEDICATION

For Rowena Itchon, who provided the spark for this book and who shepherded this project from an idea in her head to an important contribution to the liberty movement

and

Dana Beigel, who constantly amazes us with her beautiful designs and whose limitless creativity brings this book to life.

CONTENTS

FOREWORD

Generations from around the world have moved to California for their chance at better, more prosperous lives for themselves and their families.

In a speech to Congress Hall in San Francisco in 1866, Mark Twain observed that, "multitudes of stout hearts and willing hands are preparing to flock hither, to throng her hamlets and villages; to till her fruitful soil; to unveil the riches of our countless mines; to build up an empire on these distant shores that shall shame the bravest dreams of her visionaries."[1]

Twain was a better prophet than Nostradamus because that's exactly what transpired. Those who rushed to California helped build the transcontinental railroad that united a young country, produced the most bountiful harvests the world has ever seen, formed business empires, used the inspiration of their surroundings to make incredible innovations in medicine and technology, established the world's best centers of learning, and launched creative ventures that have entertained and influenced the world.

Gazing upon the majesty of Yosemite or watching millions sail through the Golden Gate Strait in magnificent San Francisco Bay, how could anyone not be inspired to go big and bold in California, given all the advantages it has to offer?

Unfortunately, somewhere along the way California's leaders forgot the "golden dream by the sea"[2] that Gov. Arnold Schwarzenegger – one of California's most famous immigrants -- spoke about in his inaugural address. "California has always glimmered with hope and glowed with opportunity" he said. "Millions of people around the world send their dreams to California with hope their lives will follow."[3]

But in true Hollywood fashion, California policymakers acted like B-movie directors, turning the California dream into *The Empire Strikes Back – Again and Again.*

In this movie, freedom and liberty are being choked by the state. Government knows better than Californians how they should live their lives: where to send their kids to school, how to run their businesses, the food they should eat, the cars they should drive. Over the past four decades, politicians have set about dictating Californians' every move, exerting as much control as possible over the state's economy, this abundant land and its natural resources, and an education system that is failing its students.

This era of policy mistakes came to a head in 2019, when, for the first time in more than 170 years, the human stream that was set off by the discovery of gold at Sutter's Mill and brought tens of millions to the state suddenly shifted into reverse. The unattractive quality of life that was the inevitable result of poor public policy caused a population decline over a three-year period starting in 2020.[4]

Not to be outmatched for bravado and ability to double down in promoting a failed agenda, California Gov. Gavin Newsom has traveled the state and nation championing what he calls, "The California Way."

Hearing Gov. Newsom coming, one would expect that the rest of the country would make a quick U-turn from the California Way.

Perhaps the most famous native Californian in politics today – Kamala Harris – has taken the lessons she learned as San Francisco's district attorney, state attorney general and U.S. senator with her to Washington in setting the national agenda.

In a speech to Democratic state legislators in Sacramento in January 2024, she called California "a heartbeat of so much that happens in our beautiful state but has happened around the country historically and today" and boasted that "we have a state with a population of over 40 million people, and we take great pride in what we know we can have in terms of impact."[5]

Despite decades of policy mistakes that have crippled California, which the *Los Angeles Times* calls "the de-facto policy think tank of the Biden-Harris administration,"[6] the California Way is gaining traction in state capitals nationwide and in Washington, D.C.

Consider Assembly Bill 5, which has been termed one of the cruelest laws to ever be enacted. It imposes limits on the freedom of Californians to work in the gig economy. In the law's aftermath, at least 15 other states – either through legislation, regulation, or court action – are signaling their support for policy modeled on AB 5.[7] Congress has been pushing a national version of AB 5 known as the "PRO Act," while the Biden-Harris administration issued a new rule in January 2024 to impose AB 5-style limits on the ability of people to work as they choose.[8]

AB 5 is just one of an almost endless number of examples of bad ideas from California spreading east. To give Americans the facts, data, and analysis needed to push back on these ideas when they are promoted elsewhere, PRI has compiled *The California Left Coast Survivor's Guide.*

Given our 45-year history of having a front-row seat to the policymaking spectacle in Sacramento and across California, nobody is better positioned than the Pacific Research Institute to expose the defects of proposals that are routinely exported out of state.

Our guide is inspired by the handbooks that have been produced for decades to prepare eager young scouts and adventurers for surviving the wild. However, instead of teaching one how to avoid poisonous snakes, tie a good knot, or start a campfire, we provide lessons on how to survive the progressive wilderness creeping in from California.

Thumbing through these pages, you'll find an easy-to-read-and-digest manual that we hope will inform and inspire both the liberty-minded and the realists who are not still blinded by California's former luster. Within these pages are background, anecdotes and data – including PRI's original research – presented in short essays on topics ranging from crime to homelessness, that will arm readers with the knowhow needed to stop California ideology from taking root.

The authors are uniquely qualified to compile a survival handbook. Kerry Jackson is an independent journalist with decades of experience writing editorials, op-ed columns, studies and books analyzing and deconstructing California policies on a host of issues from housing to energy and environmental policy. Tim Anaya was a top Capitol staffer for nearly two decades. He saw up close some of the biggest California policy decisions of recent times through his work as a senior advisor to nine legislative minority leaders. He was also a speechwriter for that Austrian-born governor who saw the golden dream by the sea.

It is PRI's hope that Americans will be inspired by what they learn on these pages to help their states and communities avoid Left Coast mistakes and make the case for market-based policy reforms. Despite the resistance to free markets found in some parts of the country, it's proven that they provide the path forward to prosperity.

Like the tens of millions from around the world who came here on the initial migration to California, we at PRI love this state and we want to restore the opportunity for all forty million of our friends and neighbors to achieve the California Dream.

California is not done. Despite Sacramento's worst efforts, there are still those of us left with "stout hearts and willing hands" and who share "the bravest dreams of her visionaries." This book by PRI is a warning, but it's also a roadmap that brings us closer to the dream.

Rowena Itchon
Chief Operating Officer
Pacific Research Institute

CHAPTER 1
Lions and Tigers and Bears, Oh my!
Keep Your Neighborhood Safe

California is a state filled with danger. Much of it is natural. Earthquakes. Wildfires. Floods. Mudslides. Snow. Deserts. It can be a tough place to survive.

Left Coast visitors should be advised that some of the danger in California, too much of it, is man-made. And the world has seen it. The videos of thieves running from high-end stores with all the designer handbags they can carry have been viral marvels. Mobs have been known to use hammers, crowbars, and large garbage bags to help them complete their tasks.

Meanwhile, quality-of-life crimes such as aggressive panhandling, public drunkenness and public urination, camping in and blocking public spaces, and trespassing have famously gone unpunished in the name of criminal justice reform.

> " As San Francisco DA and then Attorney General of California, I was proud to be a part of a different approach. It's what we called the Smart on Crime approach and the Obama administration similarly adopted and championed reforms at the federal level."
> —Kamala Harris, Speech to Center for American Progress, May 2017

VISITING CALIFORNIA?

TRAVEL WARNING — CALIFORNIA'S RETAIL THEFT EPIDEMIC HAS STORES CLOSING

Visitors to California are advised to pack plenty of supplies as it may be difficult to replenish them while traveling across the state. The reason? The state's growing retail theft epidemic, brought about by public safety policy mistakes, is leading to stores closing right and left.

- Retail theft rates in 2022 in San Mateo County were up 54% compared to 2019. In San Francisco, the figures were up 24% compared to 2019.[1]

- Commercial burglary rates in 2022 were up 16% statewide compared to 2019. Rates were up 29% in Los Angeles and 54% in Orange County.[2]

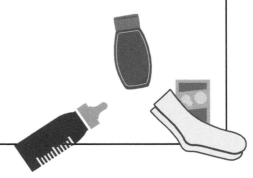

ITEMS YOU SHOULD PACK:

- Laundry detergent
- Deodorant
- Cold and Flu Meds
- Shampoo
- Toothpaste
- Socks
- Underwear
- Baby Formula
- Cosmetics

Retail theft has become such a fun and rewarding occupation for the criminally minded that stores have changed their strategy, which has evolved from just letting the larcenists, both the organized and wildcatters, walk away with their plunder, to locking their inventory behind acrylic sheets, which has infuriated the paying customers. Californians have become so fed up with brazen shoplifting that voters have even waited hours to sign a petition that would reform the one law that has been blamed for boosting retail theft.[3]

> **The $60 million the Raley's grocery store chain loses annually to retail theft, "is not available to lower prices so people can afford more food and is not available to pay people more. . .this is money for nothing."**
> —Keith Knopf
> President and CEO, The Raley's Companies[4]

Equally conspicuous have been car break-ins, which became so common in San Francisco that owners started "leaving notes on the windshields of their unlocked cars advising would-be thieves that there is nothing inside hoping they will return to not find their windows smashed," says PRI fellow Steve Smith.[5]

Less visible but no less serious is the piracy in the Oakland Estuary, increased violent crime all over, as well as a rise in crimes against property.[6] While people have taken to killing each other a little less often in recent years, violent crimes rose from 494.6 incidents per 100,000 residents in 2022 to 511.0 in 2023, an increase of 3.3 percent.[7]

Consequently, no one is surprised that someone would determine that four (Bakersfield 4th, Stockton 13th, Fresno 18th, San Francisco 21st) of the 25 most-dangerous places in the country are in California.[8]

It's clear that California has lost its survival skills. Rather than being tough on crime, which at one time was the case, policies of decarceration and decriminalization have created a new harsh, reality: mass victimization.[9]

Relatively speaking, the state became an unforgiving wilderness, thanks to decisions by policymakers and voters. The latter approved Propositions 47 and 57, while the former passed Assembly Bill 109. Officials also arranged an early release program during the COVID pandemic that might not have been the wisest decision, and prosecutors who have declined, refused really, to prosecute have manufactured conditions that are favorable for criminal activity.

PROPOSITION 47
FELONIES DOWNSIZED TO MISDEMEANORS

California's wandering in the badlands didn't start with Proposition 47. But the measure was nevertheless an ill wind. Prop. 47 was passed in 2014 by a large, 60 percent, and likely well-meaning majority. It has twice survived subsequent efforts to amend it through the ballot. A third attempt will be part of the November 2024 elections.

Once on the books, Prop. 47, misnamed the Safe Neighborhoods and Schools Act, reduced several felonious crimes to misdemeanors. When the "value" of a number of offenses, from shoplifting, forgery, petty theft and receiving stolen property does not exceed $950, the crime is classified as a misdemeanor.[10] Naturally this had an impact on retail theft.

BE SURE TO PACK YOUR MEDICATIONS — DRUG STORES ARE CLOSING IN CALIFORNIA

Prop. 47's reduction in penalties for retail theft has shoplifting on the rise and retailers hit the hardest closing their doors.

- Target closed three California stores in the San Francisco-Oakland market in October 2023 because "theft and organized retail crime are threatening the safety of our team and guests."[11]

- With CVS' announcement that it was closing a pharmacy in the Lower Haight area in December 2023, San Francisco had lost nearly half of its CVS stores over a two-year period.[12]

It has also allowed inmates convicted of offenses that were felonies prior to 2014 but were reclassified as misdemeanors by the measure to petition the courts to be resentenced at the lesser punishment.

Smith says that while "Prop. 47 looked good on paper. . . it was a policy Trojan Horse filled with misconceptions and danger."[13] It should surprise no one that criminals responded to incentives just as consumers do.

In the words of Nobel-winning economist Gary Becker, "The anticipation of conviction and punishment reduces the loss from offenses and thus increases social welfare by discouraging some offenders."[15]

Of course, Prop. 47 proponents say the law did not encourage crime, and even reference studies to back their claims. However, we've seen research from the Public Policy Institute of California that says there is evidence to the contrary, and noted that a study found "a rise in reported reclassified crimes that coincides with passage of Prop. 47" in Santa Monica.[16]

> "The minute you say, 'We're going to tolerate some level of crime,' you send a signal to criminals to test the system. The more success they have, the more emboldened they become."
>
> —Los Angeles developer and 2022 mayoral candidate Rick Caruso, in an interview with the *Los Angeles Times* on "a new breed of brazen takeover robbers hitting California luxury retailers."[14]

While Prop. 47 obviously explains some of the shoplifting sprees we've seen, it can't account for the widespread theft of luxury goods. For that, prosecutors who've shirked their duties bear much of the blame.

Faced with a growing demand by lawmakers, prosecutors and voters for Prop. 47 reform, Newsom tried to play political games in July 2024 when he pushed his own competing Prop. 47 reform measure in the Legislature and supported adding poison pill provisions to "sunset" an unrelated package of bipartisan retail theft legislation if voters approved the Prop. 47 reform measure proposed by prosecutors. In the end, voter and media backlash - and national political ambitions - caused Newsom to back down.

PROPOSITION 57
A GET OUT OF JAIL FREE CARD

Proposition 57, the Public Safety and Rehabilitation Act – also known as the get-out-jail-free card – was passed by voters two years after Prop. 47 by a 64-36 percent margin. The intent was to reduce sentence length for inmates convicted of violent crimes that were committed during California's 1990s "get tough on crime" era.[17] As described by Smith:

> It allows for early release for inmates deemed by the CDCR [California Department of Corrections and Rehabilitation] to be suitable through a variety of criteria. Where in the past individuals serving sentences for violent crimes were required to serve at least 85 percent of time served before they would be eligible for early release, CDCR's new rules allow for early release at just 50 percent of time served.[18]

NO IN-N-OUT FOR YOU ON
YOUR NEXT CALIFORNIA TRIP

Perhaps nothing is more iconically Californian than the In-N-Out hamburger. Hollywood stars often forsake lavish parties for a "Double Double, Animal Style" after award shows. Perusing social media, the first trip many Left Coast visitors make upon arrival is to the nearest In-N-Out.

But rising crime rates brought on by years of policy mistakes led to the January 2024 announcement by the California-based hamburger chain that it was closing its Oakland location, its first ever store closure. The restaurant was located in what PRI's Steve Smith calls a "crime triangle" of "what may be the most dangerous three roads in California."[19]

"We feel the frequency and severity of the crimes being encountered by our customers and associates leave us no alternative," company Chief Operating Officer Denny Warnick said in a media statement.[20]

Prop. 57 was also an attempt to reduce the state's prison population, save money, stop federal courts from indiscriminately releasing prisoners, and close the "revolving door" of crime by focusing on rehabilitation.[21]

Beginning in 2018, 1,136 felons were released under Prop. 57 guidelines, another 1,184 were set free in 2019, 1,234 in 2020, 1,424 in 2021[22], 1,259 in 2022[23], and 1,434 in 2023[24] for a total of 7,671.

Not every inmate that has been released early under Prop. 57 reoffended. But some did, and made names for themselves. Californians have to keep their eyes open in the likely event there are more Aariel Maynors and Smiley Martins out there. Smith:

> After his Prop. 57 early release Maynor committed a home invasion robbery in February 2022 in Los Angeles where he shot and killed Jacqueline Avant as she slept – later bragging after he was arrested that he would serve only 20-25 years. Maynor pleaded guilty and received a 140-year sentence. In October 2022, Smiley Martin, having just been released under Prop 57, allegedly participated in a mass shooting in Sacramento where he and his co-defendants shot 19 people – killing six.[25] (He would later be found dead in jail.)

Then there have been the "tragic stories of early release failures that resulted in more victimization, including a mass shooting in Sacramento, an early released felon killing a Selma police officer, an early released felon's murder and dismemberment of a local woman, and the tragic death of Sacramento's Mary Kate Tibbitts."[26]

CDCR has proclaimed Prop. 57 a success, that it has improved public safety. There are disagreements, though. "California is currently experiencing a notable increase in serious and violent crimes, often perpetrated by repeat offenders," says Elizabeth Berger[27] of the Criminal Justice Legal Foundation. Other critics have complained about a "lack of transparency" that "has led to confusion and distrust."[28]

"It is critical to public safety and, frankly, to the public trust, that CDCR be transparent in how it determines inmates that are suitable for early release," said Placer County District Attorney Morgan Gire.[29]

ASSEMBLY BILL 109 AND COVID EARLY RELEASE

Eager to clear state prisons of inmates so that the population didn't exceed 137.5 percent of the system's design capacity, a number set by a federal court, Sacramento made Assembly Bill 109 law in 2011. Some inmates were released back into civil life. Others were sent to county jails. In all, tens of thousands of non-violent, non-serious, and non-sex-offender inmates were moved. Those nearest the ends of their sentences got out first.[30]

As any sharp-eyed observer would have predicted, results were short of proponents' expectations. Following the implementation of AB 109 California homicides rose from 1,794 in 2011 to 2,361 in 2021. That's a 31.6 percent bump. Over the same period, aggravated assaults rose from 91,483 to 123,122 — a 34.6 percent increase. There were fewer than 8,000 rapes in 2011 but by 2018, there were nearly 16,000.[31]

The "crime reduction dividend" that was promised never materialized.

Meanwhile, Sacramento went on another inmate-release spree during the coronavirus pandemic.

> Beginning in July 2020 and running through December 2021, nearly 17,000 nonviolent, non-serious, and non-sex offender inmates were ordered freed under Gov. Gavin Newsom's emergency COVID-19 protocols.[32]

There were also three-week sentence reductions, which were granted to some of the worst offenders. Eligible inmates could have been convicted of "all Division 'A' through 'F' offenses, which include but are not limited to murder, rape, battery, assault, arson, escape, possession/distribution of contraband, possession of a cellphone, and gang activity."[33]

In May 2021, prison doors were opened wide, with 76,000 eligible to return to the streets, about three-fourths of the entire state prison population at that time. Of that number, 63,000 were convicted of violent crimes, including 20,000 serving life sentences with the possibility of parole. Repeat offenders, in a state with a recidivism rate of 50 percent, one of the highest in the country, were also included.[34]

These releases began just after homicides had increased over the previous year in Los Angeles (40 percent), Oakland (36 percent), San Francisco (17 percent) and San Diego (10 percent).[35]

Local jails also released inmates during the pandemic, notably in Alameda County, and in Los Angeles County, which released 1,700 inmates who had less than 30 days left to serve or were being held on bail of less than $50,000.[36]

Critics pounced on the early releases, again, arguing that the virus should not be used as an excuse for a get-out-of-jail-free card and pointing out that victims weren't receiving their due justice with so many lawbreakers walking free.[37]

Predictably, inmate advocates were not happy with the releases – they wanted even more to walk out before they had served their time.[38]

CHAPTER 2
How Not to Start a Fire and Other Critical Tips to Keep Nature Beautiful

A fire can mean the difference between survival and rescue and, well, a much worse fate. Those lost or stranded in the wilderness can use fire to keep warm, drive away varmints, provide a little light and signal searchers. The Boy Scouts of America considers fire to be "one of the most valuable aids to your survival."[1]

While fire can be a faithful servant, it can also be, if we may rework a phrase, a fearful master. A fire out of control is lethal, and none know this better than Californians. Wildfires consume hundreds of thousands of acres each year, and destroy hundreds of structures. They are far too often deadly. More than 150 lives have been lost to wildfires since 2017.[2]

Just a few years ago, in 2020, five of the 10 largest fires in California's modern history were all burning at the same time. More than 4 million acres were lost. Though the state makes up 4.3 percent of the U.S. land mass, that was more than half of the acreage burned in the entire country in that year.[3]

In 2021, the state's second-largest wildfire, the Dixie Fire, burned nearly one million acres, reduced to ashes more than 1,300 structures and caused one death.[4] It was started by Pacific Gas and Electric power lines.[5]

The August Complex Fire is the largest wildfire to burn through California, at least when man was watching and keeping records. Over the course of four months, it ripped through more than 1.03 million acres. One firefighter was killed and 935 buildings were destroyed.[6] It was the state's first "giga-fire," caused when dozens of separate fires that were started by lightning strikes joined into one big conflagration.[7]

The deadliest wildfire in California was the Camp Fire, which killed 85 in 2018,[8] and "all but wiped" Paradise, a city of 26,000, "off the map," says Brian Isom of the Center for Growth and Opportunity at Utah State University. The Camp Fire caused $16.5 billion "in recorded losses, with the cost of battling the fire estimated at $82.2 million."[9] It was also the most destructive in terms of structural damage, taking down nearly 19,000 buildings.[10] PG&E was again fingered as a culprit. One of the ignition sites was set off by faulty equipment.[11]

Wildfires are a natural event, part of the California landscape. Theirs is a critical role in forest ecosystems. Whether started by lightning or set intentionally through indigenous practices, fire has long been an important tool for clearing underbrush, boosting forest regeneration, and improving wildlife habitat.[12]

POLICY ERRORS PUT MORE CALIFORNIANS AT RISK OF DANGEROUS FIRES

Despite this knowledge, policymakers have chosen a path that over the last century has turned U.S. forests into "tinder boxes" that are highly "vulnerable to catastrophic wildfire." Our woodlands are overflowing with accelerants.[13] There are as many as 129 million dead trees in California.[14] This deadwood and uncontrolled brush "are packed together at up to five times their natural density."[15] Our unmanaged and mismanaged forests produce excess timber, which Republican Rep. Tom McClintock of Elk Grove, has noted comes out "one way or the other: it is either carried out or it burns out."[16] But then California no longer has enough lumber mills to process the timber. Their numbers "started declining in the 1990s," writes Pacific Research Institute board member Dan Kolkey.[17]

An unwillingness to perform controlled burns and cut fuel breaks also intensifies fires. Negligence – what else can it be called? – produced fires in 2020 (the year when wildfires hardly registered in Canada) that spewed more carbon dioxide into the atmosphere than all industrial emissions combined.[18]

California is plagued by a unique "arsonist" policy: Rather than use their scarce resources to update aging equipment that's been known to start wildfires and keep areas around power lines clear of accelerants, utilities have poured money into green projects. Could this be why the number of U.S. wildfires has remained constant since 1985 yet over the same time period they somehow grew in California?[19]

The laws in this state are increasingly influenced by environmentalists who, says Edward Ring of the California Policy Center, have "litigated and lobbied to stop efforts to clear the forests through timber harvesting, underbrush removal, and controlled burns."[20]

"Meanwhile, natural fires were suppressed and the forests became more and more overgrown," said Ring.

The battle waged by competing forces over the woodlands goes back for decades. Assembly Republican Leader James Gallagher says that on one side are California and the U.S. Forest service. They have adopted "the John Muir view of forestry," which he says, "is just preservation for preservation's sake – leave it alone, don't do anything in there." On the other side is the "philosophy of conservation . . . treating our forests as a resource you have to conserve. You have to utilize it," acting as stewards "for the long term so that resource remains." The former won and the result is "millions of acres of dead and dying trees, of overgrown forests that have become tinder boxes waiting for a match."[21]

And the victims aren't only human. Flora suffers tremendously when wildfires rage as does "the wildlife some of these proponents" of the John Muir approach "say they are trying to protect."[22]

Though he has sided with them, and given in to them on many occasions, it would be unfair to say Gov. Gavin Newsom is wholly owned by environmental zealots. He deserves credit for using his emergency powers in 2019 to approve removing dead and hazardous trees, clearing brush, cutting fire lines with bulldozers, and setting controlled burns. His order even suspended the environmental and regulatory reviews that had to be approved before fire-risk reduction projects could be started.[23]

DEFLECTING BLAME

Faulting man for California's wildfires has become standard procedure. It goes this way: Burning fossil fuels produces greenhouse gases which cause temperatures to rise and droughts to intensify, and under these conditions, wildfires burn hotter, bigger and longer. Geisha Williams, then chief executive officer of PG&E, said in 2018 "climate change is no longer coming, it's here . . . and we are living with it every day."[24] Former Gov. Jerry Brown opened his testimony before Congress in October 2019 swearing, presumably under oath, that "climate change is real, it's happening, and you and everyone else will recognize that." It is, he said, "a direct cause of California's increasingly dangerous wildfire seasons."[25]

The truth is almost the exact opposite. This state's recent wildfire seasons have been exacerbated by the politics of global warming. Here's how:

The state's regulated utilities, Pacific Gas and Electric, San Diego Gas and Electric, and Southern California Edison, have prioritized the transition to an all-renewables power grid over maintaining their systems and hardening them with fireproofing upgrades. PG&E, for example, has been responsible for thousands of wildfires, and a few years ago agreed to pay $1 billion to more than a dozen California cities, counties and agencies in compensation for losses resulting from deadly wildfires started by its equipment. It also paid an $11 billion settlement to resolve insurance claims over the Camp Fire and the Wine Country fires of 2017.[26]

It's been said before, but it can't be repeated enough: The rush to renewable energy, and the crusade to reduce and ultimately eradicate fossil fuels, have pushed utilities to allocate funds that should have been used for wildfire prevention to programs and projects conceived by politics.[27]

CHAPTER 3
Renewable Energy – Waste Not, Want Not

Renowned survival expert and adventurer Bear Grylls has said that "learning how to predict the weather. . .is a skill every Scout needs to know." An accurate forecast was also important to "farmers, sailors and others who lived and worked in the wild."[1]

But we don't need a weatherman to know that the sun sets in the evening and the wind doesn't always blow. Yet California policymakers believe, with a blind certainty, that solar and wind energy, both intermittent and unreliable, are the future. By 2045, due to a 2018 law which passed easily in the California Senate and Assembly, and was signed by then-Gov. Jerry Brown, "renewable energy resources and zero-carbon resources" are to provide "100% of retail sales of electricity."[2]

Under Senate Bill 100, the only sources allowed after the target date will be "biomass, solar thermal, photovoltaic, wind, geothermal, fuel cells using renewable fuels, small hydroelectric generation of 30 megawatts or less, digester gas, municipal solid waste conversion, landfill gas, ocean wave, ocean thermal, or tidal current, and any additions or enhancements to the facility using that technology."[3]

In practice, this will mean wind and solar. All those other sources won't add up enough to keep a Coleman lantern running.

Along the trail to this energy paradise are a few wayposts. By December 31, 2030, the dream is supposed to be more than half way fulfilled, with at least 60 percent[4] of the power sold in the state generated by the sources mentioned above. The mark to hit by December 31, 2026, is 50 percent[5], and then a full 90 percent by 2035[6].

Despite the grand ambitions, it's unlikely that California will have a zero-carbon power grid by 2045. If it does, then residents and businesses should expect blackouts, because there won't be enough electricity to meet demand, and the power that is consumed is going to be expensive.

CALIFORNIA'S COSTLY RENEWABLE ENERGY MANDATES GOING NATIONAL?

“ On the issue of climate, California has always been a leader. It has been leadership coming right out of this town – Sacramento. And because of the way that we know we should think about the future, (the Biden-Harris) administration has been able to . . . invest over $1 trillion in the next 10 years on addressing the climate crisis around resilience, adaptation, and a clean energy economy."
—Kamala Harris, speech to California Democratic legislators in Sacramento, January 2024

WIND POWER

State officials believe wind farms will generate a significant portion of California's power by 2045. Wind's contribution to the current power portfolio is 12 percent to 13 percent.[7] If there is to be enough wind power to offset the loss of natural gas and nuclear energy, contractors will have to build wind farms at the fastest pace in history, which in a state that can't finish a bullet train project on time or at cost is unlikely.

It might seem as if an eco-conscious state such as California would be able to site wind farm after wind farm, as effortlessly, efficiently and briskly as a mason lays bricks. It won't happen that way, though. The resistance to the buildout is already stiff and it's only going to harden.

Wind power is a massive land hog. The Nuclear Energy Institute says a wind farm needs as much as 360 times[8] more land area to produce the same amount of electricity as a nuclear site. So it's no surprise that locals are not cooperating, with voters rejecting noisy wind development projects[9] and residents taking their complaints to the courts because of "turbine syndrome," a condition that can cause headaches, insomnia, heart irregularities, depression, dizziness, tinnitus and nausea.[10]

WHEN INTERESTS COLLIDE — CALIFORNIA CLIMATE CHANGE FIGHTERS FIGHT WINDMILLS

The opposition is not found just "somewhere else" – it's in California, as well. San Bernardino County, the largest geographically in California and the size of West Virginia, has banned construction of renewable energy sites in unincorporated parts of the county, while Los Angeles County has also prohibited wind turbines in some of its unincorporated areas.[11]

The state is planning for 25 percent, or 25 gigawatts, enough to light 25 million homes,[12] of its power capacity to be produced by offshore wind turbines. Will the courts be able to keep up with the lawsuits that will be filed by environmentalist groups and locals who don't want their "view-shed" of the Pacific Ocean tainted by monstrous windmills?

The character of the California coast poses another problem for off-shore wind. Because of the way the ocean floor falls sharply just beyond the beaches, more than 95 percent of offshore wind turbines will have to be built on floating platforms. These structures are technological cu-riosities and there are only a few of them in the world. Those that do exist generate, according to the *MIT Technology Review*, "relatively little power." Furthermore, floating wind turbines are "a speculative and very costly technology," and will pose "a daunting geological challenge" for developers.[13]

NOT BLOWN AWAY BY DEMAND

"Electricity from wind is not cheap and never will be,"[14] author and science writer Matt Ridley wrote in the *London Telegraph*. "The latest auction of rights to build offshore wind farms failed to attract any bids, despite offering higher subsidized prices. That alone indicates that wind is not cheap or getting cheaper."

As an energy source, wind is notoriously unreliable. Some hours, some days, in fact, it just doesn't blow enough to keep the giant sails on the turbines spinning. Of course, some of the electricity produced by wind can be stored in batteries. But this creates another set of obstacles, from land use (batteries will require a not-so-small footprint) to disposal (like solar panels, they leak toxic chemicals). Mining for the raw materi-als needed to manufacture batteries is also a dirty job.[15]

SOLAR ENERGY

Like wind farms, solar sites also chew up large swaths of Earth. Just one needs up to 75 times more land than a nuclear plant, quite enough to stir local opponents who don't want rows and rows of photovoltaic arrays in their back yards.

That's while they're still useful. Eventually the panels run out of life and have to be discarded. Consequently, used panels are stacking up in landfills, where they leak selenium and cadmium. Those toxic heavy metals, primarily from utility-grade systems, can contaminate groundwater.[16] Residential panels contain lead, which is also toxic, its widespread use resulting "in extensive environmental contamination, human exposure and significant public health problems in many parts of the world," says the World Health Organization.[17]

That's almost an understatement. According to Bay Area organization Environmental Progress, "solar panels create 300 times more toxic waste[18] per unit of energy than do nuclear power plants."

"If solar and nuclear produce the same amount of electricity over the next 25 years that nuclear produced in 2016, and the wastes are stacked on football fields, the nuclear waste would reach the height of the Leaning Tower of Pisa (52 meters), while the solar waste would reach the height of two Mt. Everests (16 km)," says the group.[19]

Meanwhile, the intermittence of solar – the panels do nothing more than take up space at night – is another shortcoming that must be addressed. Again, batteries will have to be used to store energy. But they are expensive; have short durations, an average of 1.7 hours[20] for a utility-scale lithium-ion battery; and, yes, cause environmental headaches when they have to be discarded.

POWER LINES

New sources of electricity will need new power lines to move electrons to where they can be used. The California Independent System Operator says it will take 46 projects and an estimated $9.3 billion to get the job done. Well, lots of luck. The National Renewable Energy Laboratory estimates the U.S. would have to double the size of its transmission grid to be able to generate 90 percent of the country's electricity from renewables.[21] "At current growth rates," says energy author and journalist Robert Bryce, that would "only take about 140 years!"[22] Extending the grid by just 60 percent would take a mere 84 years.

What's more, land acquisition for the towers that support the lines will be a bear. The same fights over wind and solar farms will be repeated, if the projects ever get that far, several times over. Already a few states have passed laws that restrict the use of eminent domain for transmission lines.[23]

NUCLEAR

There is, says Bryce, a "notion that a global nuclear renaissance is, in fact, underway."[24] But California doesn't seem to be part of the world. Or maybe it's its own world. Nuclear power is renewable, reliable and land-sparing – in many ways all the things that wind and solar aren't. But it won't be considered a zero-carbon source of electricity in the new California and will be phased out by 2045. Sooner, actually.

As of 2024, there is only a single nuclear power facility remaining in California, the Diablo Canyon plant in San Luis Obispo County, generating "safe, clean, reliable energy since 1985."[25] It puts out roughly 17 percent of California's zero-carbon electricity and 9 percent of all electricity[26], says the California Energy Commission.

A CALIFORNIA U-TURN ON DIABLO CANYON, NUCLEAR POWER

Since the anti-nuclear heyday of the 1970s and Jane Fonda's famous film *The China Syndrome*, nuclear power has been about as popular as heating up leftover fish in the office microwave. But with concerns about climate change and energy reliability on the rise, attitudes are shifting.

- 56% of California voters in an October 2022 UC Berkeley Institute of Governmental Studies survey said they favored extending Diablo Canyon's operating life for another five years.[27]
- More Californians (44%) now support building more nuclear energy in California than oppose it (37%).[28]
- By comparison more than 60 percent of Californians opposed nuclear power during the 1980s.[29]

It was to be closed fully by the middle of the current decade, with the first reactor shut down in 2024, the second in 2025.

But when it was discovered that maybe this was being too hasty – after all, what was going to replace the lost power? – its execution date was delayed until 2030.[30] Even then it's still going to take about five years[31] to put substitutes in place. Wouldn't California be better off using the little more than five years of Diablo Canyon's life to build more nuclear power?

Taking advantage of new technologies would mean facilities could be built faster, at less cost and would be safer[32] (even as current nuclear plants have a safety record almost identical to those of wind and solar[33] when measured in deaths per terawatt hour of electricity production).

It seems, however, that more power isn't what California wants. It's easy to get the idea that the goal is to get by with less.

IS DIABLO CANYON KEY TO CALIFORNIA'S CLEAN ENERGY FUTURE?

Researchers say that if Diablo Canyon's "operating license was extended until 2035, it would cut carbon emissions by an average of 7 million metric tons a year—a more than 11 percent reduction from 2017 levels—and save ratepayers $2.6 billion in power system costs."[34]

CHAPTER 4
Energy Cents and Sensibility

Among the many merit badges that can be earned by Girl Scouts is one for "money choices." As they work toward their goal, Scouts "learn how to make smart decisions with the money."[1]

"When you've earned this badge," the *Girl Scout Handbook* notes, "you will know the difference between what you need and want, and you'll learn how to make choices about money."[2]

Left Coast survivors will have a tough time earning this badge in California when they see just how expensive things are in the state. After all, California has the nation's third-highest total cost of living, according to a recent ranking.[3]

But nothing can prepare people for the state's high energy costs. It will be a great challenge to those desiring the "money choices" badge to make smart choices while affording to drive a car or keep the lights on.

When driving around the state, motorists routinely pay among the nation's highest gas prices – and the nation's highest gas taxes.

On top of that, renters and buyers are routinely socked with some of the nation's highest residential electricity prices.

As will be explored in this chapter, the state's unaffordable cost of living and high energy costs are largely the result of bad government policy emanating from Sacramento. Government mandates and high state and local tax burdens drive up gas prices – and the cost of nearly everything else.

Meanwhile, green mandates, taxpayer-funded subsidies, and misguided climate change policies pushed by coastal elites are forcing more Californians to live in energy poverty as they are spending so much of their household incomes paying their electric bills.

Not only do these policies add to the cost of living, but they also impose huge costs on employers, hindering job creation and economic growth, and resulting in higher prices paid by consumers.

CALIFORNIA'S COSTLY AND UNREALISTIC GREEN AGENDA IS INFLUENCING GLOBAL POLICY

" The last international trips that I took were actually to Dubai to represent our country at (the) COP 28 (global climate change conference) and, of course, California has had a profound impact on the discussions that have happened at COP over the years."
—Kamala Harris, speaking to California Democratic legislators in Sacramento, January 2024

STATE GOVERNMENT IS THE REAL PRICE GOUGER — CALIFORNIA'S HIGH GAS PRICES

The Ordinary Traveler blog writes that "road trips in California are an adventurer's dream come true."[4]

"The moment I hit the open road, those feelings of (anticipation, excitement and nervousness) melted away, replaced by a sense of liberation and connection with the world around me," travel blogger Christy Woodrow writes.[5]

Unfortunately, Left Coast visitors won't be able to drive far without a small loan from their bank, thanks to the state's ridiculously high gas prices.

Gov. Gavin Newsom infamously declared that "oil companies are ripping you off" and proposed a "price gouging penalty proposal to hold 'Big Oil' accountable."[6]

When gas prices surpassed $7 per gallon in the summer of 2022, liberal legislative leaders including then-Assembly Speaker Anthony Rendon, created a special legislative committee to "investigate gas price gouging, with plans to question oil companies, regulators and economists to find out why California's gas prices are consistently the highest in the country."[7]

No investigation was needed — California's political elites need only look in the mirror to find the culprits of the state's astronomical gas prices.

Turns out it is state government that is "ripping you off." California motorists pay more to drive here thanks to state government imposing high taxes and fees and costly regulations that make gas prices much more expensive than virtually anywhere else.

DRIVER ALERT — WHY DO DRIVERS PAY SO MUCH FOR GAS IN CALIFORNIA?

Left Coast drivers beware — drivers in California routinely pay among the nation's highest prices for gasoline and the nation's highest gas tax burden. Here's how much taxes, fees, and regulations add to the price of gas in California:

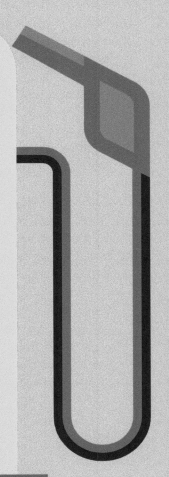

Cap-and-trade: ROUGHLY 27 CENTS PER GALLON[8]

Underground storage tank fee: 2 CENTS PER GALLON[9]

Low Carbon Fuel Standard: MORE THAN 22 CENTS PER GALLON[10]

State and local sales tax: 10 CENTS PER GALLON[11]

State Excise tax: 60 CENTS PER GALLON[12]

Federal Excise tax: 18 CENTS PER GALLON[13]

Considering all of the environmental fees levied by government on gasoline production and purchase – pegged at 51 cents per gallon – the California Energy Commission estimates that total government add-ons to gas prices in the state are $1.41 per gallon as of this writing.[14]

The figure is likely conservative and will certainly continue to grow higher.

Expanded requirements under the Low Carbon Fuel Standard will increase the annual production costs of a typical refinery from $93 million in 2024 to $1.22 billion by 2026 – an increase of $27.42 billion in operating costs by 2046 for the typical refinery.[15] This is expected to increase gas prices, according to the state Air Resources Board, by 47 cents per gallon relative to the baseline starting in 2025 and increasing even more in the subsequent years.[16]

If state government repealed these California-only laws that are driving up gas prices, Californians would save roughly $9.5 billion per year at the pump, according to PRI's research.[17] Not only would drivers save, but the state's economy would be boosted to the tune of a roughly 3 percent increase in average annual GDP growth and increasing the size of the state's economy by as much as $223 billion.[18]

FALLING PRODUCTION, RISING PRICES — CALIFORNIA'S WAR ON OIL AND GAS PRODUCTION

Aside from taxes, another factor impacting gas prices is supply.

Newsom appointed in 2023 an "oil czar," or more formally, a director of the Division of Petroleum Market Oversight for the California Energy Commission, whose job is to investigate market fluctuations in the oil industry.[19]

In his initial letter to Newsom following his appointment, Tai Milder asked why California experienced "a price spike on the gasoline spot market and at the retail level that was not explained by the supply-and-demand fundamentals" far in excess of the rest of the nation. The answer is California's oil and gas regulations.[20]

California requires unique gasoline blends and imposes stricter emissions standards on refineries than the rest of the nation. Due to these rigidities, prices in 2022 and 2023 spiked much higher in California and the higher prices lingered longer.[21]

However, instead of recognizing the state's role in creating this problem, the policy response from the Division of Petroleum Market Oversight was to pile on additional mandates on refiners. Now, in addition to complying with all the current requirements, refiners must also adhere to "minimum inventory and resupply obligations."[22]

The issue, of course, is not about potential supply. California has sufficient amounts of crude oil reserves to increase available supply — it has the fifth largest amount of crude oil reserves in the country, according to the latest data.[23]

Over the years, California's regulatory regime for oil and gas production has become extraordinarily complex, with many difficult regulatory hurdles and expensive taxes and fees imposed by state and local governments.

At one point, California was the nation's fourth-largest oil producing state, but crude production today statewide is about one-third of its peak in 1985.[24]

The Newsom administration has become increasingly hostile to oil production in the state altogether.

For example, Newsom directed state regulators to ban issuance of fracking permits in the state starting in 2024, though the issue has been subject to litigation, and additionally has called for an end to all oil production in the state by 2045.[25]

A recent ruling in a long-brewing legal feud between Kern County – the state's top producing oil region – and state regulators ruled against the county's approval of an oil and gas permitting ordinance, which could reduce the amount of oil produced in the state and oil supply available for consumption.[26] One company said the decision in the case could result in a 5 to 7 percent reduction in annual production and cuts to its capital investments.[27]

DRIVER ALERT – THERE MAY NOT BE ANY GAS STATIONS WHERE YOU VISIT

Aside from the Newsom administration's war on oil and gas production and affordable gas prices, local governments across the state are taking action to ban the construction of new gas stations in their locales.

- The Sonoma County city of Petaluma became the first in the nation to outlaw the construction of new gas stations.[28] It was soon followed by nine other Sonoma County cities and the county "following Petaluma's footsteps."[29]

- The city of Sacramento is the latest to propose banning new gas stations or upgrading existing stations, "unless of course you're adding electric vehicle charging," says Electrek.[30]

- Other California cities with enacted or pending new gas station bans include Los Angeles, Fairfax, San Anselmo, and Angels Camp.[31]

> "While progressives seek to wipe out Kern's blue-collar economy, they happily import oil from Saudi Arabia, which now supplies much of the state's fossil fuel energy."
> —Joel Kotkin, Chapman University[32]

Slashing oil and gas production in Kern County would be devastating for its economy.

About one in seven Kern County workers are employed by the oil industry or work in related fields, generating $9.2 billion to the local economy.[33]

As Joel Kotkin of Chapman University notes, the Newsom administration's war on oil production threatens about 366,000 high-paying jobs, largely blue-collar jobs, about half of them held by people of color.[34]

Facilitating the fracking revolution could, according to one study, generate more than $24 billion in additional tax revenue for the state.[35] Additionally, a recent Los Angeles County Economic Development Corporation study said the oil and gas industry "generates more than $148 billion in direct economic activity" each year.[36]

In addition to its economic benefits, fracking has helped the U.S. cut carbon dioxide admissions to its lowest levels since 1992,[37] and also enabled the U.S. to become more energy independent and see energy become more affordable.[38]

CALIFORNIANS ARE BEING ZAPPED! — ELECTRICITY COSTS IN THE GOLDEN STATE

Californians also pay significantly more than the rest of the country to keep their power flowing. As of May 2024, Californians pay the nation's second-highest average residential electricity rates and second-highest average business electricity rates.[39]

JUST HOW MUCH ARE CALIFORNIANS ZAPPED BY HIGHER ELECTRIC COSTS?

Thanks to misguided state government policies, Californians pay some of the highest energy costs in the United States.

- Californians pay $1,450 in average annual electricity bills.
- In several California counties, average annual electricity bills exceed $2,000.
- Californians pay 56% higher energy prices than the U.S. average despite using 34% less energy.[40]

Too many Californians are living in energy poverty each month — spending 10 percent or more of their household income on their power bills[41] — thanks to state government energy regulations, taxes and subsidies,

Among these misguided policies are the state's unrealistic 100 percent renewable energy portfolio mandates,[42] costly cap-and-trade regulations,[43] taxpayer-funded electric car subsidies — 79 percent of which are claimed by households making more than $100,000 per year[44] — energy efficiency standards that drive up residential and commercial building costs and the cost of living,[45] and net metering regulations that overcompensate homeowners with rooftop solar panels by paying retail rates for wholesale power.[46]

As will be discussed in the next section, electricity rates are on track to increase more thanks to the push by state government and utilities to address the impacts of global warming, and the need to replace aging infrastructure that poses a risk of wildfire danger to many rural communities.

> ❝ Californians are paying record-high electricity prices because bad policy choices made by state government are pushing more people into energy poverty."
> —Dr. Wayne Winegarden,
> PRI Senior Fellow in Business and Economics[47]

According to PRI research, if California were to repeal or reform the costly government mandates driving up electricity costs, households could save on average $517 per year in lower power bills. Residents living in the Central Valley, Inland Empire, and eastern regions of the state would save even more. Calaveras County residents would save up to $929.[48]

THE LATEST WOKE PROPOSAL? CHARGING FOR ELECTRICITY BASED ON INCOME

At the start of 2024, many California electricity households got a rude awakening. Customers of Pacific Gas & Electric, which serves 16 million Californians, saw their rates jump by 13 percent, which would add about $30 to $35 per month on average to their 2023 power bills.[49]

Immediately upon this rate increase taking effect, the utility announced plans to seek another increase adding an additional $12 to $20 per month to bills.[50] The plan is to "make its electric system safer and more resilient" after destructive wildfires that were allegedly triggered by faulty PG&E transmission and distribution lines.[51]

Meanwhile, San Diego Gas & Electric customers are expected to face a rate increase as the utility, which serves 3.7 million customers, seeks to "meet climate goals."[52]

Before the ink was dry on these rate increase proposals, the California Public Utilities Commission (CPUC) moved to approve what *CalMatters* calls "a controversial change to the way that millions of (California) households pay their utility bills."[53]

Under the plan, the state's investor-owned utilities – Southern California Edison, San Diego Gas & Electric, and Pacific Gas & Electric – will be able to charge their customers a monthly fee regardless of how much power they consume.[54] Most customers will pay $24 per month. Customers making under $62,200 per year, regardless of how much energy they consume, will pay less if they are eligible for other discounts.[55] Low energy users who make above the $62,200 threshold will pay the most under the new plan.[56]

The change is required by Assembly Bill 205, a budget "trailer bill" that passed with little fanfare in 2022 which requires a "fixed charge to be established on an income-graduated basis with no fewer than three income thresholds."[57]

The three utilities initially proposed income-based fixed monthly charges ranging from $20 to $34 per month for households making between $28,000 and $69,000 per year to $85 to $128 per month for households earning more than $180,000 per year.[58] The ensuing public backlash prompted several legislative Democrats who supported the bill to claim that they didn't know enough about the bill before voting on it, and that the initial proposal would "create an unacceptable burden for our constituents."[59]

A legislative proposal was put forward by a group of Assembly Democrats to cap the monthly charge at $10 per month – the bill was blocked in May 2024 by Assembly Speaker Robert Rivas[60] – and lawmaker pressure ultimately led to the lesser proposal enacted by the CPUC.

Despite the CPUC vote, it's probably not the last Californians will hear of the issue. Some legislators aren't buying the CPUC's estimated savings projections and fear additional increases. Members of the state Senate Republican Caucus sent a letter to the CPUC arguing that, "consumers will still face nearly $300 per year in increased charges" and noting that the CPUC has been granted "unchecked power" to increase the new charge at any time.[61] Legislation to revoke the fee increase in 2028 and limit any potential increases to inflation was defeated in the state Assembly in May 2024, when all but two Democrats on the Assembly Appropriations Committee failed to vote on the measure.[62]

CHAPTER 5
Watch Out for the Green Mobile

Left Coast survivalists need the skills to endure being stranded in remote, rarely traversed places if the vehicle they are traveling in happens to break down. If not, *The Scouting Guide to Survival* says, "the situation can become serious quickly."[1]

Running out of fuel accounts "for many stranded situations each year," the survival guide reminds us. "Plan the fuel for your trips on the one-third tank rule: one-third tank going, one-third tank returning, and one-third tank in reserve."

Why does this remind us specifically of California? Maybe because the state's electric vehicle mandate brings up images of EV drivers stranded with dead batteries.

A 2023 story in Wyoming's *Cowboy State Daily* had a little fun with "the driver of an electric truck from California" who "tried to go from Riverton" in the middle of the state to Rock Springs in the southwest corner "in his Rivian." He arrived, not behind the wheel, but with his EV perched "on the bed of a tow truck."[2]

"The Rivian driver had run out of juice" at a rest stop after he'd charged his truck for a 140-mile drive. Just "60 miles into the trip, he found himself running out of juice, well short of the next charging station."

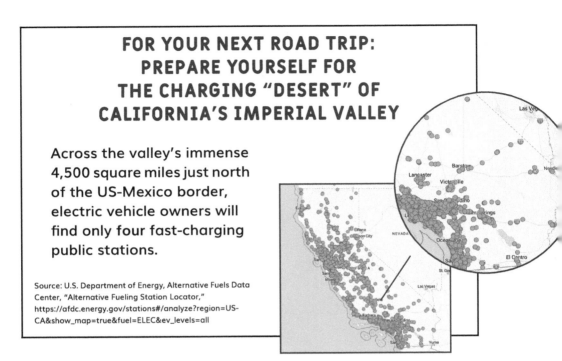

FOR YOUR NEXT ROAD TRIP: PREPARE YOURSELF FOR THE CHARGING "DESERT" OF CALIFORNIA'S IMPERIAL VALLEY

Across the valley's immense 4,500 square miles just north of the US-Mexico border, electric vehicle owners will find only four fast-charging public stations.

Source: U.S. Department of Energy, Alternative Fuels Data Center, "Alternative Fueling Station Locator," https://afdc.energy.gov/stations#/analyze?region=US-CA&show_map=true&fuel=ELEC&ev_levels=all

A few years earlier, the British *Daily Mail* recounted the story of a woman traveling through Kettleman City, California, who "stumbled across around 50" EVs "waiting in line for a recharge."[3]

"The stagnant procession reportedly spanned back more than half a mile."

"Bet they wish they had gas," one person quoted for the story "quipped." "But for the drivers stranded," the reporter writes, "it was no laughing matter."

In fact, it's quite serious, and would be even more serious if it were a school bus, which also have to be zero-emission vehicles (ZEVs) by 2035, filled with children. The last thing California parents need is an electric bus full of kids stranded with a dead battery at the farthest reaches of a route in one of California's "frontier school districts."[4]

To avoid the potential of "running out of battery" before they are able to find a charging station on the open road, EV owners have been known to rent conventional automobiles for long drives. It also makes for a faster trip. In some instances, a charge that will take a car a mere

300 miles can take six hours. But filling the tank of even the largest gasoline-burning car or SUV takes no more than a few minutes. The average fill-up is two minutes.[5]

"Be prepared" is not just a Scout motto, it's a must for EV drivers.

TO-DO LIST BEFORE AN EV ROAD TRIP

☑ Create a list of charging stations you can stop at along your route
☑ Have back-up options for if you come across out-of-order charging stations
☑ Add ample time into your itinerary for potential six-to-eight-hour charges at rural charging stations
☑ Map out your mileage in advance
☑ Turn off that air conditioner or heater and drive slowly to increase your range
☑ Be okay with having road trip plans ruined due to charging station maintenance issues

WARNING: ZEV MANDATES AHEAD!

In a little more than a decade, the sales of internal-combustion engine (ICE) cars and light trucks will be outlawed in California. In September 2020, Gov. Gavin Newsom, on his own without legislative checks and balances, issued an executive order "requiring sales of all new passenger vehicles to be zero-emission by 2035."[6]

"This is the next big global industry, and California wants to dominate it," Newsom said during the signing ceremony. The automakers that resist the zero-emission trend will emerge "on the wrong side of history," he said, and unable "to recover economically."[7] Less than four years later, Ford lost $130,000 on every EV it sold in the first quarter of 2024.[8]

The unelected California Air Resources Board approved Newsom's order in 2022.[9] This rule, Advanced Clean Cars II, does not specifically mandate electric vehicles, but there are, in reality, no other options that will meet the state's ZEV standard.

DEALER, DRIVERS REVOLT AGAINST EV PUSH

While Newsom and others dream of a zero-carbon dioxide world, EVs are being buried under a mountain of glitches. There has even been a revolt by car dealers. Nearly 4,000 – including 336 in California – have asked the Biden-Harris administration "to slow down your proposed regulations mandated battery electric vehicle (BEV) production and distribution."[10]

Other states followed Newsom's "lead," though one, Connecticut, abandoned its plan in late 2023.[11] Gov. Ned Lamont's "decision to withdraw the regulations is a reasoned approach to address the growing concerns raised by working and middle-class families," said Connecticut state Senate Republican Leader Kevin Kelly. "Adopting California emission standards which ban the sale of gas-powered cars is a substantial policy shift which must be decided by the General Assembly."

"There are too many questions regarding the capacity of our electric grid," Kelly continued, "the cost and location of grid improvements, and the negative impact on urban, rural and working poor families."

It might turn out to be of no effect, though. A 2021 executive order from the Biden-Harris administration set "a target that half of all new vehicle sales by 2030 will be zero-emissions vehicles, primarily electric cars and trucks."[12] In early 2024, the administration finalized its rule "that's expected to make a significant amount of the new car market electric or hybrid," *The Hill* reported.[13]

"Under the rule, 56 percent of the new vehicles on the market in 2032 could be battery electric, while an additional 13 percent could be plug-in hybrids. Under this scenario, just 29 percent of cars would be gas-powered, while an additional 3 percent would be other hybrids."

Critics, such as U.S. Senator Pete Ricketts, say the plan is delusional, foolish, "just plain wrong."[14]

"We lack the power generation, infrastructure, and domestic supply chain of critical minerals to make (the Biden-Harris administration's) mandate work," the Nebraska Republican senator said in a prepared statement. "The end result of this EV mandate will be higher prices, greater dependence on the Chinese Communist Party, and less choice for consumers. (The Biden-Harris administration's) actions today will make it harder for Americans to buy and maintain a vehicle. That's unacceptable."

Lawmakers introduced legislation in May 2024 to overturn the mandate.[15]

ELECTRIC VEHICLE SUBSIDIES MERELY WOLVES IN SHEEP'S CLOTHING

For all their alleged popularity, EVs have needed taxpayer money to keep sales at levels supporters could brag about. The goal has always been to stimulate the mass purchase of electric cars, as if the peddlers knew that EVs would never penetrate the market in any significant way on their own.

The subsidies have been as generous as $13,000 or more per consumer in states such as California. Manufacturing grants and loans at the federal level only have been valued at $40.7 billion over the lifetime of the programs, while consumers are being gifted $2 billion in federal tax credits to subsidize their EV purchases.[16]

But why? Most EV owners don't need the help. PRI senior fellow Wayne Winegarden figured out a few years ago that "79 percent of electric vehicle plug-in tax credits were claimed by households with adjusted gross incomes of greater than $100,000 per year," while "households with incomes greater than $50,000 per year claimed 99 percent of the credits." Remember, these numbers were compiled before inflation skewed income data.

Despite the poor optics of subsidizing luxury vehicles for the rich, EV zealots continue to pour taxpayers' dollars into their pet project. The 2022 federal Inflation Reduction Act included $400 billion in tax credits to nudge consumers into electric vehicles.[17] But even that might not be enough. EV sales have been dropping, even in California.[18]

Apparently, consumers are catching on. After all, who wants a vehicle that is exhausting to charge, referred to as an "external-combustion vehicle" due to its potential to catch fire,[19] costs a small fortune to repair,[20] is expensive to insure,[21] has an ecologically harmful manufacturing process, and is a threat to the power grid.[22]

THIS STATE'S WATER SUPPLY AIN'T THE ONLY THING WE'RE SHORT OF: CHARGING STATIONS

There are roughly 1.1 million EVs crawling around California roads as of this writing. To serve these vehicles, there are almost 15,000 charging stations. From 2016 to 2022, the number of EVs quadrupled in the state, while the number of charging stations merely tripled. There are now 75 EVs for every charging station, the second-worst ratio in the nation. In New Jersey, the ratio is 100-1, worst in the country; the national average is 55.[23]

Consequently, finding a station is cause for celebration.

"Anytime you can find charging, anywhere, it's great," Rodolfo Rodriguez told the *San Diego Union-Tribune* in 2018, when the EV-to-station ratio was not as wide as it is today.

> **❝I couldn't count on finding a charger that's functional or that doesn't have a line of cars waiting because only one of four chargers is working."[24]**
> —Doug McCune

The California Energy Commission says the state will need nearly 1.2 million public and shared chargers (stations tend to have multiple chargers) by 2030.[25] Is that even possible?

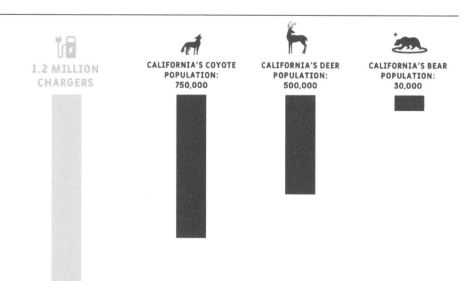

1.2 MILLION CHARGERS

CALIFORNIA'S COYOTE POPULATION: 750,000

CALIFORNIA'S DEER POPULATION: 500,000

CALIFORNIA'S BEAR POPULATION: 30,000

"California officials and energy analysts say it's doable," the *Washington Examiner* reported in 2020 (again, while EV sales were outpacing charger placements), "but it would require a massive overhaul of the state's infrastructure and policy."[26]

GET READY TO WAIT IF YOU HAVE TO CHARGE ON THE ROAD

It can take eight to 15 hours to charge an EV at what is called a "Level 1" station, used primarily for overnight, at home charging, and three to eight hours at a "Level 2" charging station while on the road. You could pitch a tent and take it all down 15 times in that amount of time!

Adding charging stations to multi-family housing, which about half of the state lives in, presents a particularly high hurdle. Fewer than 20 percent of charging stations in California can be found in apartment complexes, so there's a lot of work to be done.[27]

"Electrical upgrades at older (multi-unit dwellings, or MUDs) can be costly, especially when they require trenching to lay wiring," says Amanda Myers, a policy analyst at Energy Innovation. "Installing EV charging at existing MUDs can also trigger building code requirements in ways unrelated to EV charging, making a project financially infeasible, while utility interconnection approval can add cost and hassle."[28]

Myers also notes that "property owners often get little to no return on EV charging investments," which discourages incentives for adding stations.

Stations already built are often sources of great frustration:

A study released in early 2022 found that "27 percent of all EV charging stations in the San Francisco Bay Area" were "non-functioning." In most of those, the causes were unresponsive connectors, unavailable screens, payment systems malfunctions, charge initiation and network failures, or broken connectors. Other failures included cables being too short to reach cars' charging ports.

A few months before, a California Air Resources Board survey noted that 44 percent of EV drivers had experienced difficulties at charging stations "and considered operability and payment major issues to charging." Most EV owners—nine in 10—are satisfied with their cars, but according to a survey by the Los Angeles-based Plug In America, they are frustrated with the public charging infrastructure, "the most common issues being 'broken or nonfunctional chargers' or 'too few charging locations.'" More than a third of respondents said "this is at least a 'moderate concern.'" Drivers also griped about the long distances between charging locations, slow charging speeds and costs.[29]

STOCK UP ON YOUR HOUSE CANDLES: POWER SHORTAGES CAUSED BY ELECTRIC VEHICLES

There will be as many as an estimated 13.4 million EVs on California's roads when the EV mandate is in full effect in 2035.[30] The transition is going to sharply increase the demand for electricity. This will be especially evident a decade later, when the state has to complete its conversion to a net-zero power grid and nearly 22 million EVs will be prowling about. Will supply keep up with demand? There's little reason to be optimistic.

"Total electricity generation will be 21.1 percent short of projected demand," finds PRI's research study, *Sapping California's Energy Future*. "Assuming that other state residential electricity consumption remains flat—the trend since 2006—California will require a 20.2 percent increase in electricity generation to meet the EV mandates and increased charging demand."

To keep all those EVs' batteries topped off will require a 21-fold increase in the amount of electricity dedicated toward charging them. By 2045, an additional 56,530 GWh of electricity over the current electricity consumption projections will be needed.

Maybe Californians should start organizing "EV crews" right away. When these groups run their neighborhoods, they can set up "Roster Rotations," like a Melbourne, Australia suburb did a few years back. The local "crew" designates specific charging days and times and asks that during these periods non-EV-owning residents ration their electricity use. Everyone's air conditioners, washers, dryers, and other large appliances are supposed to be turned off so that the EV owners can charge their cars. It's just a "small sacrifice" needed to "help put an end to global warming and the associated issues."[31]

THE PROGRESSIVE, GREEN AGENDA DOESN'T STOP AT EVS

One of the virtues many associate with California is good health and a culture that promotes fitness and well-being. The keys are exercise and eating well.

There's even a Californian Diet, also known as the Sonoma Diet, based "on a coastal California way of living, blending simple and flavorful ingredients," says Healthfully.[32]

"The Californian diet promises a trimmer waist in just 10 days and allows you to eat a variety of foods but in strict portion sizes," the blog notes.[33]

State policymakers and the coastal elite have come up with a new diet that doesn't sound so great — the road diet.

One way to keep automobiles off the roads is to make "life more difficult" by halting "attempts to expand or improve our roads, even when improvements have been approved by voters," Chapman University professor Joel Kotkin wrote in 2016 when he coined the phrase "road diet."[34]

"This strategy can only make life worse for most Californians, since nearly 85 percent of us use a car to get to work. This in a state that already has among the worst-maintained roads in the country, with two-thirds of them in poor or mediocre condition."

"FEATURES" OF THE ROAD DIET INCLUDE:

☑ Reducing available parking spaces to change "urban residents' transportation behavior"

☑ Closing lanes, and sometimes entire streets, to automobile traffic

☑ Converting car lanes to bus and bicycle lanes.

The objective, says Kotkin, is "to force Californians to adopt the high-density, transit-oriented future preferred by" former Gov. Jerry Brown's "green priesthood."

How does this tie in to the "green mobile"? EVs are merely a step on the way to what that priesthood has in mind: A car-free California. Or as nearly car-free as possible. The lawmakers and the elites will still have their automobiles. But the average person will be expected to get around via public transit.

EVs are ideal for public displays of environmentalist bona fides. But as personal and family transportation, they create more throbbing headaches than ICE cars. The hassles, which also include a steep sticker price, a tax on an element necessary for building EV batteries (lithium), and maybe a slow walk in charging station construction will be enough for many to simply give up cars and ride the bus-and-train merry-go-round.

Eventually policymakers will begin to point out these annoyances, while acting surprised to find out that EVs aren't even environmentally friendly, and then proceed to offer public transit as the only alternative.

CHAPTER 6
Staying Hydrated

"Safe water," says *The Scouting Guide To Survival*, "is essential."[1] Survival expert and adventurer Bear Grylls reminds readers in *Do Your Best: How To Be a Scout* that "water is essential to almost every function of our body and without it we'll seize up like a car engine without oil."[2]

While these fundamentals seem painfully obvious, they appear to be unknown to most California policymakers. As PRI fellow Steven Greenhut wrote in *Saving California*, this state "is no stranger to water shortages and even to severe droughts."[3]

Harsh dry spells are as much of California's identity as earthquakes. A particularly brutal drought lasted from 2012 to 2016. "Other notable historical droughts," says the California Department of Water Resources, occurred in 2007-09, 1987-92 and 1976-77, with "off-and-on dry conditions spanning more than a decade in the 1920s and 1930s."[4]

"Paleoclimate records going back more than 1,000 years show many more significant dry periods."[5]

When the threat of yet another drought arose a few years ago, "the governor, Legislature and resource officials took few steps to plan ahead for the inevitable," said Greenhut. "There's been little commitment to bolstering infrastructure or clearing regulatory hurdles that delay desalination and other water projects."[6]

Proposals have been put forward, measures approved and billions in outlays of public money signed off on, yet California can't break free from its "crisis-to-crisis approach."[7]

Greenhut argues persuasively that "California actually receives enough water through rain, snowpack and groundwater to fully meet the needs of its (current) population."

"If the state's water wars were about numbers – how to store enough water to meet the needs of a specific population – rather than ideology, then California would have met its future needs long ago and water shortages would largely be a non-issue even during droughts."[8]

That ideology regards humanity as a threat to the natural environment if not a blight on all the Earth.[9] Its true believers, with the help of state and local policymakers, do all they can to stop growth and development, and even try to reverse much of the progress that's been made over the last century.

Farmers, those men and women who feed millions out of the fertile Central Valley and the many other bountiful agricultural regions in this state of varied climates and topographies, are a favorite target. This state is the breadbasket of the world. Yet lawmakers have wanted to fine farmers for using "too much" water during droughts,[10] as well as regulate their ability to pump water from their own ground.[11] Some policy "solutions" could mean that more than 500,000 acres of farmland could be lost by the early 2040s due to restrictions.[12]

The farm community has felt so frustrated for so long by policy that Interstate 5 and Highway 99 through the middle of the state are platforms for desperate messaging. Signs fulminating against the "Politicians Created Water Crisis" and asking if "Growing Food Is Wasting Water?" are common along the man-made dust bowl.[13]

The California Farm Water Coalition says the state has a "broken water system." If it's not repaired, there's a risk of permanent water shortages during even the wettest of years, and ever-escalating disaster during multi-year droughts.

Farmers aren't the only casualties in the water wars. Residents are also expected to curtail their consumption. Long showers, washing cars in driveways and watering lawns are considered to be excessive if not subversive.

HOW MUCH WILL THE GOVERNMENT FINE YOU FOR "OVERUSING" WATER?

Assembly Bill 460, which as of our publication date is still working its way through the California Legislature, would grant the state Water Resources Control Board the authority to levy penalties for violations of drought "relief orders."[14]

The bill would not target individual water customers, but rather "landowners, water agencies and districts that take water from rivers and streams," says *CalMatters*.[15] In other words, farmers growing the food much of the world relies on would be targeted, and the state water board would be granted significant new powers over long-standing water rights holders.

How much could Californians be fined if they "overuse" water and violate these orders? $10,000 for every day in which a violation occurs and $2,500 for every acre-foot of water. diverted in violation of the order. Inspections could be conducted without a warrant or consent if the state determines there is a public health and safety emergency.[16]

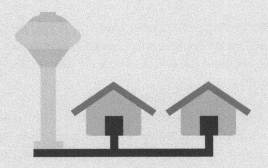

WHERE'S THE NEW STORAGE?

California has not built "any major water-storage projects since the 1970s, when California's population was roughly half of what it is today," says Greenhut.[17]

There's not been a shortage of proposals, nor an insufficiency of support. In 2014, two-thirds of California voters approved Proposition 1, with the understanding that $2.7 billion of more than $7 billion in bonds would be dedicated to storage, dam, and reservoir projects. But almost an entire decade later, "not much" had been built, says Edward Ring, co-founder of and senior fellow with the California Policy Center.[18]

The Sites Reservoir, one of the two largest projects to be funded by the bonds, however, is gaining momentum. Located in Glenn and Colusa counties north of Sacramento, the spot has been considered for storage since the 1950s. Late in 2023, Gov. Gavin Newsom announced that the project would be moving forward "under his streamlined infrastructure plan," according to CapRadio. The Bureau of Reclamation and Sites Project Authority have also certified the final environmental impact report.[19] The 1.5-million-acre-foot reservoir[20] is finally "inching forward," with construction "scheduled to begin in 2026 rather than the initial goal of 2024," says *Valley Ag Voice*.[21] It is "expected to be operational by the end of 2032."[22]

Meanwhile, the Temperance Flat Reservoir, the other large project, remains unfinished. Projected to hold nearly 1.3 million acre-feet of water[23] on the San Joaquin River, it is in fact "indefinitely on hold," says the Conservation Alliance, which blames "outrageous project costs" as well as "permanent damage to the landscape, wildlife and delicate habitat."[24] The organization boasts that it is "the 36th dam that

Conservation Alliance grantees have helped stop or remove,"[25] a statement that provides clear insight into why infrastructure is so difficult to build in California – environmental special interests have enormous clout in Sacramento and the local halls of government.

Both projects would be of immense help to the perpetually thirsty Central Valley (where 40 percent of the nation's fruits, vegetables and nuts, and about one-quarter of all domestic foods, are grown). But since neither project will be complete before at least 2030, if then, farmers, ranchers, their families, and the businesses that rely on the region's best-in-the-world agricultural output are expected to be patient and just make the best with the leftovers available to them.

Greenhut suggests an "all of the above" approach to water policy:

> There are many ways to feed more water into our state's 'plumbing' systems. Some are more politically feasible or cost-effective than others, but the goal should be a policy that creates water abundance, through a multiplicity of approaches. In most cases, simply building more surface and groundwater storage facilities is the least costly and most beneficial option – but it's also the one most fraught with political pushback from powerful environmental interests who almost always oppose storage projects, especially through building or expanding dams and reservoirs. We also desperately need more market mechanisms, such as a better means to price water.[26]

In some instances, the "projects that are less cost-effective are a reasonable choice because they face fewer political hurdles," says Greenhut. Nevertheless, "the end goal should always be adding water into the system," and while "more cost-effective projects always are better than less cost-effective ones," they ought to be "funded properly by end users rather than general taxpayers."[27]

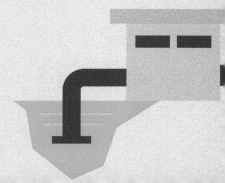

BRING YOUR OWN WATER WHEN VISITING THE LEFT COAST

Left Coast visitors traveling through California would be advised to bring an extra suitcase filled with bottled water. The reason? State regulators, at the behest of liberal lawmakers and the coastal elite, are crafting regulations that would impose strict limits of how much water Californians can use each day.

Senate Bill 1157, now the law in California, says that:

- Through the end of 2024, "the standard for indoor residential water use shall be 55 gallons per capita daily."

- Then on the first day of, 2025, and running until January 1, 2030, "the standard for indoor residential water use shall be 47 gallons per capita daily."

- On January 1, 2030, "the standard for indoor residential water use" falls to "42 gallons per capita daily."[30]

LIMITS ON RESIDENTIAL WATER USE

California residents use an almost insignificant portion of the state's water. About half of the water is for environmental purposes, while 40 percent goes to agricultural uses, leaving 10 percent for urban consumption, which is broken down into residential, commercial, industrial and large landscape applications.[28] Yet residents are expected to conserve water as if it were a luxury item rather than a necessity.

For instance, a ban on wasteful water uses has been extended through 2024. Under this regime, decorative fountains without a recirculation pump, washing vehicles without an automatic shut-off, and maintaining lawns rather than replacing them with "climate-appropriate vegetation" are considered practices of wasteful use.[29]

As it turns out, Californians have been mostly cooperative with officials' demands. They "stepped to the plate," says Greenhut, "and achieved stunning water-use reductions by exceeding Gov. Jerry Brown's aggressive conservation goals."[31]

Admirable though it might be, residents' commitment to austerity didn't make an appreciable impact on water supplies, since they use such a small portion. Nor has it appeased radical elements in the state. The efforts "never seem to be enough for the professional scolds," says Greenhut.[32]

CHAPTER 7
More No-Nos

Properly packed survival kits can save lives. Those wanting to survive the Left Coast would be advised to take with them into the wilderness a plastic tube tent, an emergency sleeping bag, a fire source, tinder, a signaling device, light, water, a knife, duct tape and a few other things. Altogether, the items will weigh about two pounds, can sustain life for 72 hours or more, and are compact enough to be stuffed into a reseal-able plastic bag.[1] Well, maybe not in California. Consumer-grade plastic bags have become prohibited goods.

Lawmakers initially banned the highly useful thin-gauge single-use bags in retail stores. They were replaced by bags that are four times thicker and are designed for multiple uses, good for garbage can liners, picking up pet waste, lunch sacks and in an emergency cheap luggage.

But then lawmakers went after those, too. Will they also ban resealable plastic bags? Given the zeal and impetuousness with which they and coastal elitists have tried to eliminate so many modern conveniences, it would surprise no one if they did. California policymakers are at war with plastics of all types, and while it makes for good politics, it doesn't make good sense.

California is the land of the banned. And plastic bags aren't the only products to be sacrificed on the steps of the green temple. Other items that are either restricted in some way or are entirely verboten include polystyrene takeout food containers, natural gas connections in new home construction, new gas stations, plastic shampoo and conditioner bottles in hotels, milk and juice cartons, condiment packages, plastic straws and utensils, and gasoline-powered lawn equipment. Some legislators wanted to chase CLEAR, a private document-verification company that operates at a number of California airports and takes some of the sting out of the security theater, out of the state.

WILL BANNING EVERYTHING SAVE THE PLANET? RESEARCH SAYS NO.

Even if all 50 states duplicated California anti-plastic statutes, there would be no noticeable improvement in the volume of plastic in the oceans, which tends to be the motivating factor behind efforts to regulate and outlaw consumer convenience products, because Americans aren't the problem. Neither are those in the industrialized nations that would most likely be "inspired" by California law. The Germany-based Helmholtz Center for Environmental Research has found that just 10 "rivers transport 88–95% of the global load" of plastic into the sea, and not one of them is in the U.S. Eight are in Asia, the other two in Africa.[2]

BANNING PLASTIC BAGS

CARRY ALL YOUR ITEMS HOME IN YOUR ARMS

Sacramento outlawed single-use plastic bags in grocery stores and pharmacies in 2014. Backlash followed, so a referendum was put before voters in 2016. They could either vote to keep the ban in place or vote to drop it. By a 53-47 margin, they approved the ban.[3]

Problem solved? No, another problem created.

Ten years after Sacramento outlawed single-use plastic bags, the never-dormant urge to ban struck again, with lawmakers advancing bills in 2024 that would prevent retailers from selling customers the multi-use bags that were supposed to be the solution to plastic bags building up in the garbage stream and "contaminating our environment," as Sen. Catherine Blakespear, the Encinitas Democrat who authored Senate Bill 1053, said.[4]

"California's original ban on plastic bags hasn't worked out as planned, and sadly, the state's plastic bag waste has increased dramatically since it went into effect," she said.[5]

The volume "increased dramatically" because the thin single-use bags were replaced by heavier multi-use bags, which are at least four times thicker.[6]

According to a report compiled by multiple organizations, one of them the Naderite U.S. Public Interest Group, "the amount of plastic bag waste discarded per person (by weight) actually increased in the years following the law's implementation to the highest level on record – proving the ban ineffective at reducing the total amount of plastic waste."[7]

DO PLASTIC BAG BANS REDUCE LITTER?

Two years after Austin, Texas, enacted a single-use plastic bag ban, residents were tossing heavy-duty reusable plastic bags into the garbage at a never-seen-before rate.[8]

Other plastic bag facts that lawmakers ignored, or merely didn't care about, when they passed the bans include:

- As a portion of visible litter, plastic bags are virtually *invisible*, responsible for only 0.6 percent of observable litter across the United States, the Reason Foundation reported when the first ban was working its way through the Legislature.[9]

- Thinner bags also consume fewer resources and have lower energy requirements in the manufacturing process than thicker plastic bags, compostable bioplastic bags, and paper bags.[10]

- Those reusable bags made of natural fabrics that customers carry into stores are not an eco-friendly alternative. They have to be used more than 100 times[11] before they register environmental benefits when compared to single-use bags.[12]

- The law of unintended consequences is always in effect. "When cities or counties institute plastic bag bans or fees, the idea is to reduce the amount of plastic headed to the landfill," says ScienceDaily. Yet a University of Georgia researcher found "these policies, while created with good intentions, may cause more plastic bags to be purchased in the communities where they are in place."[13]

BANNING GAS-POWERED LAWN EQUIPMENT

PUTTING MINORITY ENTREPRENEURS OUT OF WORK

Thanks, or rather due to, Assembly Bill 1346,[14] an executive order issued by Gov. Gavin Newson and a ruling by the California Air Resources Board, "Small off-road engines (SORE), which are used primarily in lawn and garden equipment," are being phased out. Newsom's order "directs the state board to implement strategies to achieve 100 percent zero emissions from off-road equipment in California by 2035, where feasible and cost-effective."[15]

If those last two words are taken seriously, then implementation might never be fully achieved.

The ban will be another costly burden on the nearly 8,300 landscaping businesses in the state, many of whom are minority entrepreneurs. It's the latest in a series of taxes, fees, regulations, and other mandates Sacramento has imposed over the years on entrepreneurs that make it so much more difficult for them to make a go of it in California.[16]

Lawncare and landscaping businesses have for some time been an affordable entry point for low-income and minority entrepreneurs to work their way into the middle class and provide more prosperous futures for their families.[17] But the barrier to entry is growing higher. The National Association of Landscape Professionals has pointed out that a gas-powered commercial riding lawn mower can cost from $7,000 to $11,000, while the zero-emission equivalents cost more than twice as much.[18]

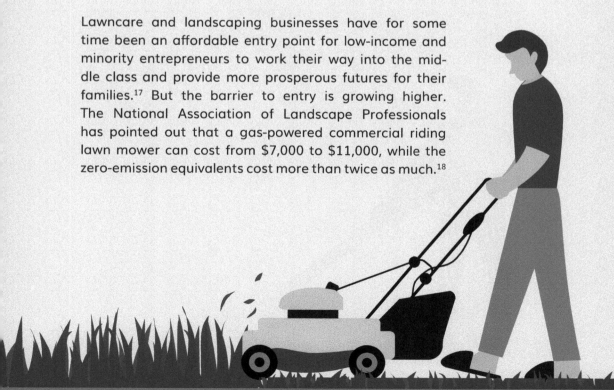

The Assembly's floor analysis of AB 1346 reports that "for commercial uses, there is very little market for zero-emission equipment as today's technology is relatively expensive and requires multiple batteries and/or frequent recharging and replacement."[19]

There is a time element, as well. Because electric motors are less efficient,[20] it will take more hours to do the same volume of work. Then there's the inefficiency of a three-person landscaping crew needing to carry 30 to 40 fully charged batteries to keep its equipment working over the course of a full day in the field.[21]

If they can locate the right batteries. *The Spruce*, a home and food publication, found that replacement batteries for some leaf blowers are hard to find.[22]

The burden placed on landscapers and companies could be enough to eventually push lawn-care companies to the point they decide to throw in the towel rather than comply with these government mandates from Sacramento.[23]

Some companies will no doubt decide to stick it out, but their customers can expect significantly higher bills.[24] They are already getting them in Florida, where one business placed solar panels on its vans — at a cost of $100,000 for each vehicle — to recharge equipment on the go and is charging its customers 10 percent to 20 percent more than its competitors.[25]

LIVING IN THE DARK IN AN EMERGENCY

It's helpful to have backup power in the event of blackouts (which are certainly in California's future, see Chapter 3). Generators can prevent food from spoiling, keep the heat and air conditioning on depending on the weather, and ensure that medical equipment and water pumps don't shut down during an emergency.

But beginning in 2028, emission standards for generators, as well as large pressure washers, must be zero.[26]

The average gas-powered generator can provide 10-12 hours of electricity to run lights, phone chargers, refrigerators, microwaves and more, with a simple refueling keeping them powered another half-day. Zero-emission power generators wouldn't work very well in lengthy power shutoffs as current models have the capacity to run only the lights, appliances and technology listed above for between 35 minutes and three hours.[27]

There are a couple of other points that show how odious the ban is.

One, zero-emission generators, which need batteries to operate, are particularly unreliable during outages. Their batteries "cannot be recharged during power outages without expensive solar panels or expensive spare charged batteries," according to a report carried on Business Wire.[28]

Two, the Senate floor analysis of Assembly Bill 1346 notes that "while portable power stations such as the popular Goal Zero Yeti can provide power without any associated noise or emissions from the unit, they are ultimately constrained by battery capacity," and "can also be five to twenty times the cost of fossil-fuel powered options."[29]

BANNING NATURAL GAS

CHEFS REVOLT AT
COOKING ON ELECTRIC STOVES

Beginning in 2030, new natural gas furnaces and water heaters in California will go the way of the incandescent light bulb. Not allowed.

This trend was fired off by Berkeley, which in 2019 was the first city in the country to bar natural gas connections on new home construction. Dozens of other cities and counties followed, outlawing or restricting new natural gas connections.[30] But a legal challenge led to Berkeley agreeing to "stop enforcing the policy while it goes through the legal process of repealing the ban."[31]

Meanwhile, the city of Palo Alto has ceased enforcing its 2022 building code amendment that requires that every new building within its borders to be all-electric.[32] It was the right choice but the city exposed its ban for what it was: a meaningless gesture. If natural gas were truly as dangerous as so many in this state claim it is, Palo Alto would have been negligent in backing off its original position.

California likes its celebrity chefs and it turns out that chefs, celebrity and short-order alike, don't like to cook with electricity.

"To say that an electric stove is as good as a gas one is misunderstanding the art of cooking," said George Chen, executive chef and founder of San Francisco's China Live.[33]

"If you get rid of the gas element, I don't think restaurants can do it unless you're like a coffee shop with a panini press. Whoever cooked up this idea should be reprimanded," said Matthew Dolan, executive chef and partner of restaurant 25 Lusk, also in San Francisco.[34]

Palo Alto's plan was doomed when José Andrés, baron of a vast epicure-an empire and one of the world's most admired humanitarians, threatened in 2023 to scrap his plans to open another of his Zaytinya Mediterranean-themed restaurants in the city's Stanford Shopping Center.

"Without a gas connection and appliances," Anna Shimko, an attorney for the property group that owns the center, wrote, "Zaytinya would be forced to alter its signature five-star menu, which it is unwilling to do."[35]

Prohibiting natural gas appliances is a gross violation of consumers' freedom to choose and increases the risk of shortages and blackouts as more appliances are connected to the power grid – not that California lawmakers ever give much thought to either.

YOU MAY HAVE TO BAKE YOUR OWN BREAD
(IN AN ELECTRIC OVEN, OF COURSE)

Policymakers and coastal elites are also targeting gas ovens used in commercial kitchens that make bread, baked goods, and other products for grocery stores and restaurants.

The South Coast Air Quality Management District – the unelected body given sweeping regulatory powers in the name of reducing air pollution in Southern California – has voted to outlaw commercial gas ovens by 2036.[36]

According to the district's analysis of the proposal, government overreach will be destroying about 3,200 jobs due to this costly new regulation.[37]

BANNING CLEAR

KILLING A BUSINESS THAT EXPEDITES AIR TRAVEL

For a modest fee, an entrepreneurial business will steer passengers around federal security theater chokepoints. Rather than having to wait in the document-confirmation line, members of CLEAR, a document verification company, are ushered directly past the security gridlock after their identities have been verified by biometric scans.

In addition to avoiding a travel hassle at nine California airports, members can also enjoy expedited entries at entertainment and sports venues. The cost: $189 a year.

This isn't acceptable to Sacramento's equity warriors. Democratic Sen. Josh Newman, who introduced Senate Bill 1372 in 2024, complains that the service CLEAR members' pay for is an "inconvenience and annoyance" to "travelers making their way through the security queue."[38]

Newman insists that "despite what some have said," his bill "doesn't seek to terminate the CLEAR concierge service at California airports." Instead, it simply requires "CLEAR and other third-party screening services operate separate lines for subscribers, eliminating the friction and frustration created by the current system."[39]

Yet he has publicly said that "when it comes to making one's way through airport security, the quality of that experience shouldn't be contingent on a traveler's income or willingness to pay."

That sounds like a statement that would please Karl Marx. It also ignores that TSA PreCheck, which expedites screening for fliers who have the "income or willingness to pay," also has a cost. But that's apparently OK because the Transportation Security Administration is a government agency.[40]

SB 1372 did not move forward in the 2024 legislative session, but we imagine that if it is ever on the books, the company would be justified in pulling its business from California airports. The costs it will have to pay to comply with the bill's demand that it operate separate lines could be enough to send it packing.

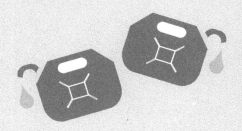

BANNING GAS STATIONS

MAKE SURE YOUR GAS TANK IS FULL BEFORE VISITING CALIFORNIA

Left Coast visitors are advised to make sure their gas tanks are full before crossing the state line into California. They may want to have a couple of extra gas cannisters filled up in their trunk just to be safe as gas stations are being pushed into extinction by local officials.

Just as Berkeley was the first city in the country to bar natural gas connections on new home construction, Petaluma was, in 2021, the first city in the U.S. to outlaw the construction of new gas stations. The zoning code change became the model for others to emulate.[41]

And it happened quickly.

"Less than a week after the Petaluma vote," *Motor Trend* reported that "one North Bay grassroots group leading the charge against new fossil fuel infrastructure in Sonoma County, the Coalition Opposing New Gas Stations (CONG), has managed to block the opening of three new stations."[42]

By August 2021, a number of other Sonoma cities joined forces "to follow in Petaluma's footsteps."[43]

At the time the bans were enacted, the media coverage treated the prohibitionists as selfless activists, forward-looking idealists, the smart set leading California – and the world – to a better future. And they likely think of themselves as such. But their policy pursuits aren't consistent with improving lives. [44]

For instance, limiting the options to buy gasoline raises prices. This won't bother the wealthy in Sonoma County, where the median household income is more than $81,000 a year, almost $6,000 higher than the state median income.[45] But it will hurt the residents who struggle financially, and the low-income workers from the outside who clean the wealthy's homes, mow their grass, trim their trees, repair their plumbing, and take care of all the other tasks needed to keep houses neat and in working order.

"You're creating an absolutely divided, racist society," says Todd Royal, co-author of three books on energy.[46]

"If the prohibitionists believe that in limiting the availability of gasoline they're cutting emissions because people will drive less, they're deluding themselves. Putting a lid on new stations will actually increase emissions," says Royal, because motorists are forced to drive farther to fill up.[47]

For all the good intentions of the activists who want to shut down gas stations, whose civic engagement "comes from a good place," says Royal, they are nevertheless misguided. They might celebrate their success in outlawing new stations, but their efforts are meaningless on any scale.

"If the United States shut down and ceased to exist," he says, "global emissions will still rise because India, China, and Africa won't stop using energy from fossil fuel sources."[48]

Famed Napa County didn't take long to join its slightly less famed neighbor. Now we have bans, according to Grist, "proposed in Los Angeles; Sacramento; Eugene, Oregon; and north into Kelowna, Canada."[49] Grist of course believes that eliminating gas stations is some sort of victory. But Californians (and Oregonians and Kelownians) who struggle with the financial strains that many are experiencing would disagree.

BANNING HOTEL ROOM PLASTIC

BRING YOUR OWN SHAMPOO WHEN VISITING

Some of us, actually almost all of us, are old enough to remember when hotels provided small bottles of shampoo, conditioner, body wash and lotion. They're handy. Make great souvenirs. They're also made of plastic, which is nearly a capital offense in California.

In addition to gas, Left Coast visitors to California are also advised to pack their own shampoo or soap as lawmakers and coastal elites have moved to outlaw the little plastic bottles.

No one lined up Molton Brown shampoo or Pharmacopia conditioner in front of a firing squad, but Sacramento decided that after Jan. 1, 2023, hotels could no longer provide "a small plastic bottle containing a personal care product to a person staying in a sleeping room accommodation."[50]

To enforce the law, the scolds of the bureaucracy will send out agents "with authority to inspect sleeping accommodations in a lodging establishment to notify lodging establishments of this requirement." Those who violate the directive could be cited and hit with penalties of up to $2,000 a year.[51]

Some guests have recoiled at the refillable dispensers that are used in place of plastic bottles, calling them "highly unsanitary" and unbecoming of a hotel of Marriott's stature.[52] On a European trip, one of this book's co-authors encountered bulk dispensers that did not seem fresh, inviting, or sanitary, even in the nicer hotels. In some, there was only one "shower gel" product offered, meaning it was intended for both body and hair.[53]

Using something that could allegedly pass as both soap and shampoo is rather uninviting.[54]

Concerns about cleanliness are legitimate. A study published in the journal *Applied and Environmental Microbiology* found that "bulk-soap-refillable dispensers are prone to extrinsic bacterial contamination," with one in four in public restrooms contaminated.[55]

DOES GOING WITHOUT HOTEL SHAMPOO BOTTLES REDUCE OCEAN POLLUTION?

Only about 1% of all plastic in the oceans is from the U.S.; California's "contribution" to the mess is negligible.[56]

While hotels can no longer set out personal care products for their guests, there's no law that says travelers can't bring their own, which means that in the end, we're not really going to reduce any plastic usage. But the ban does allow some people to feel good about making a political statement.[57]

BANNING FOOD CARTONS AND CONTAINERS

MILK YOUR OWN COW

With the volume of bans approaching absurd levels, it's not too much of an exaggeration to advise Left Coast visitors to aim their mouths under a cow's udder if they want to drink milk in the morning. That's because the latest target of prohibitionists are food cartons used primarily for milk and juice.

Politicians and the coastal elite are seeking to root out the aseptic container, those cartons found scattered across grocery stores that hold milk, juice, soup, broth, whipping cream, liquid eggs, tea and even wine. According to the West Contra Costa Integrated Waste Management Authority, this type of "packaging is a well-accepted technique for the preservation of liquid and particulate foods and has revolutionized the shelf life and shipping efficiencies."[58]

Needless to say, that makes it something that California wants to be rid of.

Under state law, one passed and signed in 2022,[59] aseptic containers might disappear from stores, as they are neither "potentially" recyclable nor compostable. The legislation also, according to a Senate floor analysis, "Prohibits producers of expanded polystyrene food service ware" – often known by brand name Styrofoam – "from selling, offering for sale, distributing, or importing in or into the state expanded polystyrene food service ware unless all expanded polystyrene meets a 25 percent recycling rate by January 1, 2025, 30 percent by 2028, 50 percent by 2030, and 65 percent by 2032, and annually thereafter."[60]

We won't know right away what happens to these products, since the deadlines for compliance are still months and years away. But what we do know is that the bill is a model for other states to follow.[61] Yes, companies will likely try to work around the law as best they can. That will come at a cost, though, to the businesses as well as consumers.

CHAPTER 8
Don't Spend it All at Once

From the time California became a state in 1850 during the Gold Rush era, millions flocked to the Left Coast seeking their fortune.

In the midst of the Industrial Revolution and the construction of the Transcontinental Railroad that brought visitors from back east to the train's terminus in Sacramento, Henry Wells and William Fargo and their famous stagecoach established the bank that bears their names – and the state as a global financial superpower.

Despite California's massive wealth, the history of the past forty years has been one of a state facing revenue volatility and massive state budget problems. Much of California's fiscal problems have been caused by poor political choices made by state politicians.

Two years after producing a $100 billion budget surplus, California in 2024 faces a massive budget shortfall – pegged at one point during the year by the nonpartisan Legislative Analyst's Office at $73 billion.

The largest deficit in state history is now on Newsom's watch, and it surpasses the $43 billion deficit the state faced in the 2008-09 budget crisis (though the crisis is smaller in percentage as state spending has more than doubled since then.)[1]

> "California is once again facing a fiscal crisis that will likely last for several budget cycles. This prolonged fiscal crunch is not due to revenues simply returning to 'normal.' It is a spending problem that requires fiscally sound solutions, not proposals that kick the can down the road in the hope that robust revenue growth will somehow return."[2]
> —Dr. Wayne Winegarden,
> PRI Senior Fellow in Business and Economics

The problem is largely caused by a lack of fiscal discipline. U.S. Census data indicate that the root cause of California's budget crisis is excessive spending. Excluding California, the total per capita expenditures for all other states is $6,325. California, on the other hand, spent $8,983 per capita, which was 42 percent more than the average of all other states.[3]

Perhaps this excessive amount of spending could be justified if Californians were receiving significantly better public services than residents of other states. But the state consistently ranks poorly in national rankings for the quality of its education system, infrastructure, and public safety.[4]

As PRI's Dr. Wayne Winegarden writes of the state's ongoing destructive budget problems, "the state's volatile economy and progressive tax system cause revenues to surge during good economic times, which politicians eagerly spend. This enables spending to grow faster than people's incomes and pushes expenditures to unaffordable levels."[5]

Among the high taxes levied by the state are state and local vehicle registration fees that add hundreds of dollars to the cost of purchasing and operating a car or truck and fees on cell phones that add nearly $9 per month – the equivalent of a 17.9 percent tax – to a $50 monthly phone bill.[7]

Things have gotten so bad in California financially that many individuals and businesses, tired of high taxes and ineffective public policy, are fleeing for the exits. California lost population due to domestic migration every year between 2012 and 2018, with residents fleeing the high cost of living that turns a 13.7 percent income premium versus the rest of the country into a 19.6 percent income deficit when you factor in taxes, fees, and bad policies.[8]

Money-hungry state officials are even trying to tax California refugees on their way out the door, which we'll explore later in this chapter.

TRAVEL ADVICE

MAKE SURE TO BRING LOTS OF CASH WHEN COMING TO CALIFORNIA

Left Coast visitors are advised to pack sacks full of money before making the trip out West as California politicians will be picking your pockets at every turn.

California has the:

- Highest state-level sales tax rate
- Highest state gas tax rate
- Sixth-highest state and local tax burden[6]

RIDE WIPEOUT!
THE CALIFORNIA REVENUE ROLLER COASTER

Many Left Coast visitors want to come to California to see some of the nation's best amusement parks – and the best roller coasters – at locations ranging from Magic Mountain in Santa Clarita to Knott's Berry Farm in Orange County and Great America in Santa Clara.

" California's public finances are at the mercy of an extremely volatile revenue system, one dominated by personal income taxes, especially those paid by high-income Californians on their stocks and other capital investments."[9]
—Dan Walters, CalMatters columnist

The colorful names of some of these thrill rides – Giant Dipper, Apocalypse, Gold Striker, Hangtime, The Joker, Twisted Colossus – could easily be the name of the politician-created roller coaster that towers over Sacramento, the state's volatile state tax system.

How did the state go from a $100 billion surplus one year to a $73 billion deficit a few years later? Politicians across the spectrum blame the state's fickle revenue collecting structure.

The bulk of California's tax revenue is produced by personal income taxes, accounting for nearly 70 percent of collections for the general fund.[10] This gives lawmakers great power to grant favors to friends and punish enemies, but a system based on steep income taxes on the rich is vulnerable to economic swings in the state and the stock market.

By being so heavily reliant on capital gains taxes, budget experts and economists have argued that even a modest recession in California could cause a big hit to state revenue due to the instability of a revenue system dependent upon the ups and downs of the stock market and investment earnings plus interest.[11] This is what the state saw play out in past budget crises in 2000-01, 2008-09, and its current budget mess.

MATH LESSON –
DON'T SPEND MORE THAN YOU'RE TAKING IN

California's budget roller coaster is driven by revenues, but it's also driven by overspending by politicians. That's how the state got into its current budget mess.

Between 2019 and 2022

Total state spending from all funds grew by **more than 51%**

Personal income tax revenue grew by **just under 18%![12]**

Why do policymakers like to ride on the edge? It turns out that California's revenue roller coaster has largely been created by the choices of politicians. The Legislative Analyst's Office explains why the state's personal income tax system encourages volatility – 40 percent of the volatility problem is due to the types of income taxes and 40 percent is due to the "progressive" nature of taxing higher incomes at different rates.[13]

Politicians from both parties decry the state's tax system, but efforts to reform it have gone nowhere. Recommendations from a bipartisan "Commission on the 21st Century Economy" convened during Gov. Arnold Schwarzenegger's administration – which included expanding the sales tax to services that are currently untaxed and flattening the tax to just two income brackets – went nowhere.[14]

To the contrary, Winegarden argues that California's budget volatility is the result of lawmakers breezily blowing through other people's money:

> The root cause of this destructive budget cycle is too much government spending that is enabled by a tax system that showers politicians with unsustainable revenues during good economic times. Since politicians eagerly spend all the money when the state's coffers are overflowing, expenditures surge to unaffordable levels during economic booms. When the economy slows, as it always does, the unsustainability of the spending spree is revealed by the crash in state tax revenues and the onset of the inevitable budget crisis.[15]

Gov. Newsom might actually agree with Winegarden that the issue is about spending – he just wants to spend more than the state currently allows. His solution to the budget volatility problem is to weaken the state's Gann Limit on spending to allow the state to "save" more.

His framing of the issue is challenged by State Sen. Roger Niello, vice chair of the Senate Budget Committee, who argues that, "the Governor and the majority party chose to spend the funds in other areas than building the reserves, despite two years of major surpluses."[16]

In the meantime, California taxpayers are once again riding the state's revenue roller coaster – Wipeout!

SOMETIMES, SPLITTING SOMETHING
IN HALF IS BAD

Left Coast visitors who have been paying taxes from morning 'til night may be surprised to notice one area where California has a relatively reasonable level of taxation – property taxes.

The nonpartisan Tax Foundation rates California 14th out of the 50 states and the District of Columbia for its property taxes, with number one being the state with the most competitive property tax system.[17]

The landmark Proposition 13, which was passed by California voters in June 1978, limits property taxes to 1 percent of a property's assessed value, though assessed values may increase no more than 2 percent annually to account for inflation.[18]

> **Proposition 13 was the political equivalent of a sonic boom."[19]**
> —Dr. Arthur Laffer

Economist Stephen Moore said Prop. 13 unleashed a "spectacular entrepreneurial and commercial explosion" in the first decade

after its passage.[20] Presidential Medal of Freedom honoree and noted free market economist Dr. Arthur Laffer said of Prop. 13 in his PRI book *Eureka! How to Fix California* that, "in the 10 years after the passage of Prop. 13, incomes in California grew 50 percent faster than the nation as a whole, and jobs grew at twice the pace."[21]

Even though Prop. 13 has been called the "third rail of California politics,"[22] and 65 percent of likely voters said Prop. 13 turned out to be mostly a good thing for the state on its 40th anniversary in 2018,[23] that hasn't stopped tax-hungry politicians from trying to gut the measure.

Special interest groups qualified a California state ballot measure (Prop. 15) on the November 2020 state ballot that would have partially changed Prop. 13 by creating a so-called split-roll property tax system.

Arguing that limits on taxing shopping centers, office buildings and factories "have starved funding for schools and local communities," Prop. 15 would have taxed residential property the same way since Prop. 13 went into effect in 1979.[24] However, commercial and industrial properties would no longer have been covered and therefore taxed at higher rates.[25] The added revenue, from a $12 billion tax hike, was supposed to be dedicated to education.[26]

Total education funding has grown sharply over the years, according to Laffer – even with Prop. 13 on the books.[27] The 2023-24 state budget spends $129.2 billion for all state-funded K-12 education initiatives.[28]

Split-roll supporters also vow to make changes to the state's tax system, demanding to "make it fair." As Laffer wrote in 2016, even though residential property owners pay nearly three-quarters of property tax revenue, less than 40 percent of that is paid by homeowners liable for the tax on their principal residence.[29]

Split-roll would negatively impact jobs and the economy, as well. A March 2012 Pepperdine University study that found that split-roll would "result in lost economic output and decreased employment," and "further undermine the attractiveness of the business climate in California."[30]

Calling a split roll property tax "the largest property tax increase in state history and the most direct attack on Proposition 13 in a decade," the co-chairs of the group Californians to Stop Higher Property Taxes, which was formed to fight the proposed weakening of Proposition 13, wrote:

A split-roll initiative would remove Prop. 13's protections for commercial and industrial property and raise their property taxes by billions of dollars a year. Businesses would have no choice but to pass those increased costs onto you and me, raising the prices on everything we buy, from gasoline to groceries, while also raising our utility and healthcare bills.[31]

Voters agreed and rejected Prop. 15 in November 2020 by a 52 to 48 percent margin.[32]

DOING THE SAME THING OVER AGAIN AND EXPECTING A DIFFERENT RESULT—WEALTH TAX

Left Coast visitors will experience California's massive tax burden firsthand virtually every day. Not everything is taxed, of course. Not yet, anyway.

Once Californians have paid their crushing state income tax burden every April 15, the astronomical gas taxes when filling up their cars, and the expensive state and local sales taxes every time they buy something, one may think the money that is leftover could be used to save and invest. They might even become successful in building a nest egg to pass on to future generations.

One California lawmaker wants to challenge the proposition that the state doesn't tax everything.

Benjamin Franklin once famously said that "nothing can be said to be certain, except death and taxes." California can add a third certainty to that list – the annual effort of liberals in the state legislature to find new ways to tax people.[33]

WEALTH TAXES HAVE FAILED WHEREVER TRIED

Some California policymakers are moving full steam ahead to try and enact a wealth tax, despite the fact that previous attempts at imposing wealth taxes were unsuccessful.

- Before its wealth tax was repealed, France lost 42,000 millionaires between 2000 and 2012,[38] showing that revenues raised from wealth taxes are inevitably disappointing.[39]

- Just four of the 14 members of the Organization of Economic Cooperation and Development countries that taxed wealth in 1996 do so today.[40]

- Rice University researchers who analyzed Sen. Elizabeth Warren's wealth tax from her 2020 presidential campaign found that it would "have deleterious effects, reducing labor productivity and thus wage income as well as economic output."[41] The Rice scholars note that just "a 1 percentage point increase in the wealth tax rate reduces the economic growth rate by between 0.02 and 0.04 percentage points."[42]

State Assemblymember Alex Lee, a self-described Democratic Socialist, wants to impose a "wealth tax" on Californians.

He has proposed a "tax on extreme wealth in California," which would apply to "households with net worths of more than $50 million."[34] According to Lee's office, his proposal would be an estimated $21.6 billion annual tax increase.

Lee says that his proposal would be a "modest tax" on those who "pay a lower effective tax rate than the bottom 99%."[35]

Tax fairness, of course, is in the eye of the beholder – or, in this case, the eye of the liberal legislator looking for more money to spend on government programs.

LEFT COAST SURVIVOR'S BADGE

— ★★★ —

TAX FIGHTER

Not surprisingly, the state's income tax system is already very progressive. California's Legislative Analyst's Office notes that taxpayers whose returns exceed $1 million account for only 19.4 percent of the state's total adjusted gross income, yet paid 39.6 percent of income tax revenues generated.[36]

If enacted, a wealth tax would carry large administrative costs, as the state would have to hire a significant number of new tax bureaucrats to calculate the worth of the assets that would be taxed under the plan.[37]

The proposal would impose an excise tax on the "worldwide net worth" of an individual, meaning that a Californian would potentially be forced to pay state taxes on income earned outside the state.[43]

 As much as they might want to prevent citizens from leaving, California is not East Berlin."[44]
—Jon Coupal,
President, Howard Jarvis Taxpayers Association

The proposal is part of a "concerted effort" to enact wealth taxes across the country, noting that similar proposals have been introduced in Connecticut, Hawaii, Nevada, New York, Maryland, Illinois, and Washington state.[45]

Lee said of his proposal that, "we've been losing our lower and middle-income residents that are being priced out of this state because they can't afford the high cost of living."[46]

Of course, that's not the fault of wealthy taxpayers not paying enough in taxes.

The reason they're leaving is due to policies enacted over the years that have created in California one of America's highest cost-of-living burdens. Perhaps that should be the focus of Lee and his fellow Democratic Socialists – making life better for all Californians so they won't want to leave.

BEWARE THE NEW "FOOL'S GOLD"— BASIC INCOME

Visitors to the Left Coast looking to try their hand at making a fortune will surely want to visit the Sacramento Valley, where gold was discovered by James Marshall at his water-powered sawmill owned by John Sutter near Coloma in 1848.[47]

> "Basic income is fool's gold that does not even attempt to offer economic empowerment."[53]
> —Damon Dunn, former NFL player turned entrepreneur, author of the PRI book *Punting Poverty: Breaking the Chains of Welfare*

In the first four years after the discovery, $2 billion worth of gold was extracted from the area and the then-California territory's population grew 100 times over.[48]

Fortune seekers would be wise to be on the lookout for fool's gold, also known as pyrite, which deceived many prospectors into thinking they had struck it rich, only to learn later that they had found a mineral that was virtually worthless.[49]

In recent years, California has found a new form of fool's gold in basic income.

Then-Stockton Mayor Michael Tubbs – who was swept into office in 2016 with the support of Oprah Winfrey and others impressed by his inspirational personal story, but was defeated just four years later after a term spent chasing national media attention rather than solving the city's problems – proposed a basic income "experiment."[50]

The city – which once had to declare bankruptcy after going on a 15-year spending binge[51] – launched an initiative called the Stockton Economic Empowerment Demonstration. It was the first U.S. city to provide a guaranteed income. It provided several dozen Stockton families in the experiment with $500 a month, with no strings attached. The 18-month trial was funded by a nonprofit organization rather than taxpayers.[52]

A number of tech titans including Mark Zuckerberg, Elon Musk, and Marc Andreessen championed the initiative as a "simple and elegant solution" to economic disruption caused by artificial intelligence and other tech innovations.[54]

While Tubbs and program supporters touted a report commissioned by the Stockton Economic Empowerment Demonstration showing that the program was a success[55]—noting, for example, that "less than 1 percent of tracked purchases were for tobacco and alcohol"—this supposed success story is likely exaggerated as 40 percent of money on the prepaid debit cards was transferred to bank accounts or withdrawn as cash.[56]

Following Stockton's lead, the program caught on elsewhere in the state. Then-Oakland Mayor Libby Schaaf announced a privately funded $500 per month basic income program.[61] Then-Los Angeles Mayor Eric Garcetti announced a basic income program to provide $1,000 a month to 2,000 families – at a $24 million annual cost – paid for by taxpayer dollars.[62]

Meanwhile, Gov. Gavin Newsom proposed $35 million over five years to pay for universal basic income pilot programs statewide.[63]

THE REVERSE MIDAS TOUCH

Whether in California or around the world, basic income schemes have been an expensive failure.

- Finland set up a pilot basic income program in 2017, offering $685 per month to a selected group of 2,000 participants. The program was dropped in 2018 after "disappointing results."[57] The experiment did not "make them more likely to work" as "proponents had hoped."[58]

- The Canadian province of Ontario abandoned its universal basic income program after just one year, which was implemented at a projected cost of $150 million per year.[59] The new government determined "the program discouraged participants from finding work" and Social Services Minister Lisa MacLeod declared that, "it really is a disincentive to get people back on track."[60]

In his PRI book *Punting Poverty*, Damon Dunn, who grew up in extreme poverty in Texas and later became an NFL player turned successful entrepreneur, perhaps best sums up the movement to provide basic income:

> Offering my family $500 per month may have made us a little more comfortable in poverty, but my grandparents still would have died poor because the hurdles to get out would have been raised even higher.[64]

CHAPTER 9
Honest Pay for a Good Day's Work:
Minimum Wage Blues

Agri-tourism is growing in popularity in California with Left Coast visitors increasingly wanting to see firsthand the state's wineries, farms, dairies and ranches.[1]

That visitors are flocking to see California ag is not surprising. After all, the state has been called "America's food-producing powerhouse," ranked as the fifth-largest supplier of food and agricultural products in the world, generating 11.04 percent of all U.S. agricultural value despite having just 4 percent of the country's farms and ranches.[2]

Unfortunately, a tiny insect has been wreaking havoc on California agriculture since the 1970s – the infamous Mediterranean fruit fly, or medfly for short. These bugs can infest more than 250 different types of fruits and vegetables.[3]

The state has battled medflies since 1975. They reached outbreak levels between 1980 and 1982, prompting then-Gov. Jerry Brown to promote mass malathion spraying to eradicate their spread.[4] While they have been contained over the years, the state has experienced multiple infestations.

One study estimated that medflies in California result in roughly $875 million in annual direct costs, and an embargo on California-grown products due to medflies could impose an additional loss of $564 million – threatening 14,000 jobs.[5] If left unchecked, the impact on California agriculture could be catastrophic.

It's astonishing to think something as small as an insect could be so destructive to California.

Another seemingly small item has proved to be just as destructive to California's economy – the continual push by liberal politicians to increase the minimum wage.

California's minimum wage most recently increased to $16 per hour on January 1, 2024, due to rising inflation.[6] The law, enacted in 2015, raised the minimum wage incrementally to $15 by 2022, along with annual boosts accounting for inflation.[7]

MINIMUM WAGE, MAXIMUM DAMAGE

More than 40 cities across the state require higher minimum wage pay than the statewide $16 per hour:

- Oakland: $16.50 per hour
- Los Angeles: $16.78 per hour
- San Jose: $17.55 per hour
- San Francisco, Sunnyvale, Berkeley, Emeryville, Mountain View: Between $18 and $19 per hour
- West Hollywood: $19.08 per hour[8]

While a minimum wage increase might seem as small economically as an insect ("It's only a $2 per hour increase!"), the impact can be incredibly destructive for employers, jobs, and the cost of living.

A minimum wage increase could result in a decline in revenues of $9,000 per year for the average small business. While they may choose to live with these lost revenues, PRI senior fellow in business and economics Dr. Wayne Winegarden argues that this figure is "unsustainable for many small businesses."[9]

> " The minimum wage increase could drive many small businesses into bankruptcy. Rising bankruptcies and declining profitability worsens the incentives for entrepreneurship, a major driver of the economy and productivity."[10]
> —Dr. Wayne Winegarden
> PRI Senior Fellow in Business and Economics

Policies such as minimum wage increases also contribute to California's status as having one of the most unaffordable costs of living in the entire country. PRI research has found that the minimum wage, coupled with unaffordable taxes and other expensive regulatory burdens that drive up housing costs, add a 20 percent net income deficit when compared to other states.[11]

As will be discussed later in this chapter, the minimum wage for fast-food restaurant workers increased to $20 per hour on April 1, 2024. Additionally, other enacted state and local minimum wage proposals granted "hero pay" to certain workers during the COVID-19 pandemic and hiked wages for hospital workers.

Meanwhile, California voters will decide the fate of a November 2024 ballot measure to incrementally increase the minimum wage to $18 per hour.[12]

HOW MUCH WILL YOU PAY FOR A BIG MAC? MINIMUM WAGE INCREASE FOR RESTAURANT WORKERS

Workers at California fast-food restaurants became the highest paid in the nation on April 1, 2024, when a newly enacted state law went into effect boosting the hourly wage for workers at McDonald's or Starbucks to $20 while workers in nearly all other industries continued to make $16 per hour.[13] The law effects about 553,000 workers statewide.[14]

It later came to light that the legislative sausage-making behind the law was unseemly when Bloomberg News reported in February 2024 that Gov. Gavin Newsom allegedly pushed for a carve-out from the law for a donor who gave $100,000 to fight the 2021 recall effort against Newsom and then another $64,000 to the Newsom re-election campaign in 2022.[15] Newsom denies the accusation.

The donor owns several Panera franchises in the state.[16] It's still unclear what happened because those negotiating the final legislation were required to sign a non-disclosure agreement before entering into discussions, but the California Legislature's Republican leaders consider it "Paneragate" and a "crooked deal."[17]

The backroom dealing aside, there should be no surprise that restaurants from big chains to small mom-and-pop diners were forced to raise prices on their customers due to the minimum-wage increase.

"There isn't a quick-service restaurant owner in California who can easily shoulder an immediate 25% wage increase for all their employees," Mike Whatley, vice president of state affairs and grassroots advocacy for the National Restaurant Association, told CBS News after the law was implemented.[18]

Research has shown that is exactly how restaurants respond to minimum wage hikes – passing costs onto their customers.

HOW MUCH WILL YOUR FAVORITE HAMBURGER COST AFTER MINIMUM WAGE HIKE?

Left Coast visitors should plan to bring some extra money for meals on their next trip to California. After the state's $20-an-hour minimum wage for restaurant workers went into effect in the spring of 2024, popular restaurants announced the following price increases:

- Chipotle boosted prices by 3% in fall 2023 in advance of the minimum wage increase, but expects prices to go up another 5% to 9% to keep up with a 15% to 20% labor cost increase.[19]
- Starbucks won't say how much prices will rise and when across the company's California stores, but a Starbucks franchisee who owns 18 stores in the state raised prices between 5% and 7% in anticipation of the rate increase.[20]
- The CEO of Jack in the Box says menu prices will go up 6% to 8%.[21]
- The owner of 10 franchise restaurants in the San Francisco area anticipates that he will have to raise prices by roughly 10% in 2024.[22]

Economists have shown time and time again that higher minimum wages result in higher prices, what is termed "wage push inflation."[23]

An independent research report published in 2021 studied the impact of minimum wage increases on the prices of McDonald's Big Macs.[24] The researchers concluded that, in fact, Big Mac prices rise along with minimum wage increases.[25]

"The pay levels in McDonald's restaurants, the largest U.S. franchise chain, are powerfully affected by minimum wage legislation," the researchers concluded.[26]

Customers in California are, not surprisingly, not too happy about rising prices at their favorite fast-food restaurants.

" **There is no such thing as a free lunch."[27]**
—Nobel laureate
Milton Friedman

South Los Angeles resident Roshonda Baker told the *Los Angeles Times* that she was "angry about the looming price hikes" and said that she "can definitely see it taking an effect on families."[28] Baker lives in an area where nearly one-third of residents live below the poverty line.

Not only will Californians face inflated prices, fast-food workers now face two new threats from the wage increases — reduced hours and increased automation.

A July 2024 survey released by the Employment Policies Institute found that nine in 10 restaurant owners surveyed have cut their employees' working hours while 98 percent raised menu prices and 70 percent had reduced staff or consolidated positions.[29]

California made headlines a few years back with the introduction of Flippy, the world's first automated grill master at the Pasadena location of Caliburger.[30]

To be fair, Flippy was fired shortly after being introduced due to the overwhelming demand at the restaurant with eager customers lining up to have their hamburger flipped by a robot. However, he was soon reintroduced after a few tweaks. He was later joined by thousands of his cousins at fast food restaurants across the country, along with order-and-pay kiosks that are becoming the industry standard — displacing many human workers.[31]

It is estimated that 80 percent of today's work will ultimately be automated.[32] Fast food workers can thank California's latest minimum wage hike for accelerating that trend.

HONORING OUR HEROES WITH LAYOFFS?
"HERO PAY" FOR GROCERY WORKERS

During the COVID-19 pandemic, workers in so many fields risked their health and worked incredibly long hours to keep people healthy and fed and our economy functioning.

Grocery workers were an example of those who worked under unusually difficult circumstances during a trying time. Many grocery store companies opted to pay their workers "hero pay," or temporary hourly wage increases, to thank their loyal employees for their hard work.

As Winegarden notes, "offering a temporary pay increase to grocery workers. . .makes a lot of sense when grocers voluntarily provide this additional compensation to their employees."[33]

After all, he adds, "grocery workers are taking on additional health risks, suffering additional stresses, and must work in more difficult environments, which all warrant additional compensation."[34]

But what doesn't make sense is for government to mandate "hero pay" through legislation enacting temporary minimum-wage increases. But that's exactly what several local governments in California did during the pandemic.

The Los Angeles City Council in March 2021 enacted an ordinance requiring large grocery stores and pharmacies to pay a temporary $5 per hour wage increase for 120 days.[35] Los Angeles County passed a similar 120-day increase for retailers in the unincorporated parts of the county.[36] The city of Long Beach enacted a $4 per hour wage increase for 120 days in December 2020.[37]

> " Stores can pass on additional labor costs to the public through price increases. However, they may also reduce the hours of the impacted workers or decrease the number of employees that they hire."
> —Los Angeles County Supervisor Kathryn Barger[38]

As Winegarden notes, labor costs for grocery stores are 9.4 percent of total sales with an average profit margin of 2.2 percent.[39] A $4 or $5 minimum wage increase would be a roughly 20 percent increase in labor costs, effectively wiping out their profit margins.[40]

Los Angeles-area grocery stores, not surprisingly, responded to the ordinances by announcing closures. Grocery chain Kroger announced that it would close two Ralphs locations and one Food 4 Less store.[41]

"It's never our desire to close a store, but when you factor in the increased costs of operating during COVID-19, consistent financial losses at these three locations, and an extra pay mandate that will cost nearly $20 million over the next 120 days, it becomes impossible to operate these three stores," the company said in a statement.[42]

RAISE MINIMUM WAGE, CLOSE HOSPITALS – HEALTH CARE WORKER MINIMUM WAGE

California lawmakers found a new way to raise the minimum wage in 2023. They enacted and Gov. Newsom signed into law legislation (Senate Bill 525) to incrementally raise the minimum wage for health care workers to $25 per hour by 2026.[43] The state law followed a local ordinance enacted in the city of Inglewood in 2022.[44]

The new law's author, former labor union president and now Democratic Sen. Maria Elena Durazo, said "higher wages will help restore health care jobs to the status of a job in which a person can support a family."[45] While that might be true on paper, the impact of the $25 health care minimum wage could be lost jobs and hospital closures.

An analysis of the law's fiscal impact on the state issued after the measure was signed into law found that it would cost California taxpayers an estimated $4 billion per year.[46]

Another union giveaway ran headfirst into the fiscal realities of the State of California in June 2024, when the measure's implementation was delayed until Oct. 15, 2024—if revenues are sufficient—or Jan. 1, 2025 if not.[47]

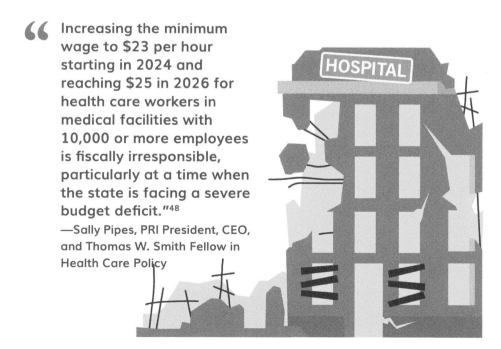

❝ Increasing the minimum wage to $23 per hour starting in 2024 and reaching $25 in 2026 for health care workers in medical facilities with 10,000 or more employees is fiscally irresponsible, particularly at a time when the state is facing a severe budget deficit."[48]
—Sally Pipes, PRI President, CEO, and Thomas W. Smith Fellow in Health Care Policy

Despite record public health care spending in California – health and human services spending accounts for 30 percent of the state budget, second to education – California hospitals are reimbursed for only 74 percent of the services provided through Medi-Cal, according to a California Hospital Association report.[49] More than half of California hospitals are losing money and one in five California hospitals are at risk of closure.[50]

A lawsuit against the Inglewood minimum-wage law filed by the California Hospital Association alleges the following impacts from the new law:

> Layoffs, reductions in premium pay rates, reductions in non-wage benefits, reductions in hours, and increased charges are consequences of an employer having less money to spend— which will necessarily be the case given the significant increase in spending on wages due to the minimum wage.[51]

CHAPTER 10
The Entrepreneur: An Endangered Species

Travelers to the Left Coast should bring their binoculars and cameras since there's always a small chance they'll be treated to a rare sighting of one of several endangered species that are still found in California's particularly harsh environment.

A species that has been dying particularly fast in recent years is the entrepreneur – the self-starting, independent force who makes a living as their own boss.

The lucky traveler might even come across one of the rarest species of all – the gig entrepreneur. Moving toward becoming extinct after policymakers forced them to become hired employees – ideally in the clutches of labor union bosses – gig entrepreneurs once thrived in California. But that was when the economic climate was better.

Gig entrepreneurs are creative and hard-working. They toil by the task for customers, friends and neighbors who need their services but can't take on full-time employees to do the work.

The peaceful gig entrepreneur is seeking nothing more than to earn extra money, help a business needing an extra set of hands or assist the elderly with chores around the house.

ENTREPRENEURS GOING THE WAY OF THE DODO BIRD

Since AB 5 was enacted in California, gig work in a long list of fields has been sharply declining. Affected occupations, to name just a few, include:

- Bartenders
- Bookkeepers
- Construction Workers
- Fishing Guides
- Interpreters
- Nurses
- Paralegals
- Pharmacists

California's politicians – particularly those who say they are fighting for the working class – are on the hunt and it's these species they are looking for. Now, they are bringing in reinforcements from Washington, D.C.

The Biden-Harris administration's Labor Department moved in January 2024 to eliminate gig work for millions of Americans. Where did he get such a callous idea? From his travels through California, of course, where cruelty is sport among more than a few policymakers.

How did things get so bad for the gig entrepreneur in California?

In 2019, the California Legislature passed, and Gov. Gavin Newsom signed, Assembly Bill 5, in effect outlawing gig work in California. It was a "rescue" that no one outside a few rideshare drivers and union agitators was asking for.[1]

And its harm began overnight. *Vox* fired more than 200 California freelance writers, ultimately retaining just 10 percent for part-time and full-time work, leaving more than 180 freelancers without their paying gigs. An entire staff of freelance barbers left their jobs at a Sacramento barbershop, because of the California Supreme Court ruling in the *Dynamex* case which gave AB 5 its, so to speak, wings.

"You can't hire and structure things the way (barbershops) have for decades," said Bottle & Barlow owner Anthony Giannotti. "They've just destroyed the pay structure for the barber and cosmetology industry."[2] Giannotti predicted that "a lot of shops" were going to be closing.

GOING, GOING GONE—EMPLOYMENT DROPS IN CALIFORNIA UNDER AB 5

While traveling in California, you may see a long line of people who are unable to perform gig work in the field of their choice going the other way, fleeing the state. According to a study from the Mercatus Center at George Mason University, since AB 5 was enacted:

SELF-EMPLOYMENT INCREASED BY **10.5%** ON AVERAGE FOR THE AFFECTED OCCUPATIONS	**OVERALL EMPLOYMENT IN CALIFORNIA DROPPED BY** **4.4** PERCENT	**HOPED-FOR GROWTH IN TRADITIONAL EMPLOYMENT DID NOT OCCUR**[3]

The foundation of AB 5 is built on a test that the Court used to determine who is and isn't eligible to work as an independent contractor. It was designed to be a trap from which there is no escape.

WHO GOT OFF SCOT FREE? A GUIDE TO GIG WORKERS YOU CAN STILL FIND IN CALIFORNIA

The backlash from AB 5 was so savage that subsequent legislation carved out exemptions for more than 100 employment categories. Those professionals who are among the fortunate who were permitted to slip the load of AB 5 include:

- Workers in the music and entertainment businesses
- Document translators
- Home inspectors
- Brokers
- Media professionals[4]

Other states, eager to show how much they too cared for independent contractors, have now followed the California "lead." By the time the pandemic had arrived, with all of its government-imposed shutdowns and the attendant economic devastation, four states had introduced copycat AB 5 legislation.[5] A number of cities have proposed "protections" for gig workers, as well.[6]

Washington was also inspired to help the downtrodden who are clearly unable to make good decisions on their own. Multiple versions of the Protecting the Right to Organize (PRO) Act, which includes a worker classification provision similar to that of AB 5, have been debated in the U.S. Senate since 2021. It remains a Biden-Harris administration top priority despite the White House's inability to enact the bill into law.[7]

The Biden-Harris administration even called up California's general in the war on independent contractors, Julie Su, the state's Labor and Workforce Development Agency secretary when AB 5 was enacted, for a national tour of duty. She now works at destroying freelancers' livelihoods from Washington, D.C., where she's the acting Labor secretary.[8]

She has a history of being an "aggressive enforcer" of AB 5.[9] While California's government labor boss, she threatened "investigations and audits" of voluntary, mutually beneficial working agreements. She was also eager to issue citations and assess wage and tax penalties.[10]

WARNING FOR CALIFORNIA TRAVELERS

Those hoping to earn a few extra dollars to buy souvenirs or pay for nice meals while in California, beware. Despite the state having a multi-billion dollar budget deficit, state enforcement of AB 5 is at the top of state's spending priorities. Starting shortly after its enactment, Gov. Newsom dedicated nearly $21 million in state funds for enforcement of AB 5 in the state budget.[11]

In the meantime, the second pen-and-phone administration of the 21st century jumped the constitutional process for making sausage and simply changed the rules, revising the Labor Department's "guidance on how to analyze who is an employee or independent contractor."[12] The change, its heart as black as the detested AB 5, went into effect in March 2024.

U.S. Rep. Kevin Kiley, R-California, who had seen the damage caused by AB 5 while serving in the California Assembly, introduced a Congressional Review Act resolution to overturn the Labor Department rule, which he called "a threat to the livelihood of millions of Americans," that "could destroy the independent contractor model as we know it."[13]

That was California's goal, to set fire to the independent contractor model and then, like the pyromaniac who derives great pleasure from just watching things burn, watch the flames spread across the country.

AB 5 IS A THIEF: STEALING OPPORTUNITIES FROM COMMUNITIES OF COLOR AND LOW-INCOME WORKERS

In testimony before the California advisory committee to the U.S. Commission on Civil Rights on the civil rights implications of AB 5, Wayne Winegarden, the Pacific Research Institute's senior fellow in business and economics, noted "that AB 5 will impose net negative impacts on the economy and reduce entrepreneurial opportunities, with a particularly negative impact on low-income communities and communities of color."[14] His testimony rested on three points:

- Entrepreneurship is an important pathway, particularly in communities of color, for climbing the economic ladder.

- The development of the gig economy has produced unprecedented options that empower individuals to engage in entrepreneurial ventures.

- AB 5 creates barriers that obstruct the gig economy and, consequently, reduce entrepreneurial sector vibrancy.

Without entrepreneurial opportunities, the wealth gap, between White, non-Hispanic households, Black, non-Hispanic households and Hispanic households will never close. The net worth of white, non-Hispanic households in 2019 was $189,100, nearly eight times higher than the $24,100 net worth of black households, and more than five times higher than the net worth of Hispanic households, which was $36,050.[15]

As it turns out, the Congressional Black Caucus dug into the numbers and found that being a business owner materially improves the financial conditions of African Americans. When they own businesses, their net worth is 12 times higher than the net worth of African American nonbusiness owners.[16]

Don't think that every minority "business owner" is a shopkeeper. In many cases, the business can be supplemental to a traditional job. Opportunities range from being a rideshare driver to handyman to caregiver to using gig economy platforms to engage in entrepreneurial ventures.

Minority-owned businesses also benefit from the gig economy by using independent contractors rather than hiring workers, whose costs to employers can be unaffordable due to burdensome business regulations.

As Winegarden pointed out, "a small business that employs five people already spends $80,000 a year in tax and regulatory compliance costs. To put these costs in perspective, eliminating these costs enables small businesses to give every employee a $16,000 raise without reducing the profits of the company."[17]

Would an administration that swears it's devoted to bringing prosperity to minorities and the poor block a key path out of financial hard times? Yes, that is exactly its plan.

ASSEMBLY BILL 5 ROBS WORKERS OF THEIR FREEDOM OF CHOICE

There was never a groundswell of workers begging lawmakers to save them from working as independent contractors.

In fact, most freelancers are happy with their work arrangements. U.S. Bureau of Labor Statistics data from 2017 clearly showed that 79 percent of independent contractors preferred gig jobs over traditional jobs, which don't provide the flexibility that's been created by the gig economy.[18]

Another survey found that 84 percent of freelancers "are living their preferred lifestyle" while only 54 percent of those working in traditional jobs say the same.[19] More than half, 56 percent, say they feel more secure than they would in traditional jobs, and 51 percent would not go back to traditional work for any amount of money.[20]

Why would they say these things? To start with, independent contractors are free to choose their hours, and the companies they work for. They can try new fields at any time, take advantage of the mobility that lets them avoid nasty bosses, and have the option to work only when it's necessary. And as Winegarden pointed out in his testimony, roughly three-quarters of gig workers have health insurance.

Gig jobs allow workers to pull down extra dollars for financial emergencies, to pay off that big Christmas bill, and build a down payment for a home or automobile purchase. Those options will no longer exist if an AB 5-style law becomes federal policy.

WHEN THE TRUCKS STOP ROLLING

Independent operators make up about 9 percent of all truckers in the United States. (There is an also estimated shortage of drivers of about 80,000.)[21]

California is home to about 70,000 independent truckers. Imagine if one day they stopped hauling their loads because their work was considered outside the law?[22]

We caught an ugly glimpse of what would happen when independent truckers shut down the Port of Oakland, the largest U.S. hub from which chilled meat products are shipped to other Pacific ports, in July 2022. Meat that couldn't be moved had to be frozen to avoid spoilage, and in doing so it lost its value in overseas markets, says Pam Lewison, a farmer and Pacific Research Institute fellow.[23]

Restrictions on independent truckers can "cause food shortages and increased food costs across the country by virtue of limiting access to food across the supply chain," she says.[24]

"For example, truck shipments in California represented more than $1 trillion in value, trailing only Texas in value of shipments trucked in 2017, the most recent year data is available. Among those valuable shipments, approximately $34 billion in food items were shipped by truck across the U.S."[25]

The worst might still be ahead.

In January 2024, Judge Roger Benitez of the U.S. District Court for the Southern District of California essentially told the state's independent truckers to park their rigs, denying "the California Trucking Association's (CTA) and Owner-Operator Independent Drivers Association's (OOIDA) latest request to enjoin" the application of AB 5, says Los Angeles litigation firm Eanet.[26]

Two months later, he "rejected arguments that the state's independent contractor law, AB5, should be barred from regulating California's trucking industry," according to Freight Waves.[27]

The truckers have since appealed to the Ninth Circuit U.S. Court of Appeals, also known as "being the appellate court most likely to be reversed by the U.S. Supreme Court," which is made up of jurists whose reading of the law is not unlike the corrupt thinking that churns out detritus from the California Capitol.[28]

CALIFORNIA FREELANCERS LIVING THE DREAM (OR THE NIGHTMARE)

- One survey found that 84 percent of freelancers nationwide "are living their preferred lifestyle" while only 54% of those working in traditional jobs say the same.[1]

- More than half, 56 percent, say they feel more secure than they would in traditional jobs, and 51 percent would not go back to traditional work for any amount of money.[2]

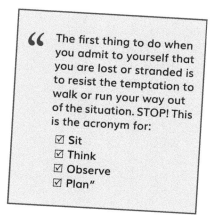

> **" The first thing to do when you admit to yourself that you are lost or stranded is to resist the temptation to walk or run your way out of the situation. STOP! This is the acronym for:**
> ☑ Sit
> ☑ Think
> ☑ Observe
> ☑ Plan"

CHAPTER 11
Dangers from Abroad and Within: How Not to Deal with a Pandemic

When confronted with a difficult, challenging or unfamiliar situation, stay calm. "Get control of yourself, avoid panic," J. Wayne Fears, an Eagle Scout who received survival training from both the U.S. Army and U.S. Air Force, wrote in *The Scouting Guide To Survival*.[1] Good advice. It's too bad California officials haven't read his book. When the coronavirus pandemic arrived in 2020, they panicked.

Gov. Gavin Newsom, local lawmakers and unelected public health officials around the state weren't lost or stranded in the wilderness when the novel coronavirus hit the U.S., but they veered off course almost immediately. They didn't sit, they spun themselves into a frenzy. They didn't think, they snapped. They didn't observe, they overreacted. They didn't plan, they were impulsive.

And they even violated the rules they expected everyone else to live by, most famously in the person of Newsom, who was caught at Napa Valley's Michelin three-star French Laundry restaurant celebrating the birthday of a political crony with a large, mask-free group.[2]

The nation's first stay-at-home order, "to protect the health and well-being of all Californians and to establish consistency across the state in order to slow the spread of COVID-19," was issued by Newsom on March 19, 2020.[3] "America's most populous state" ordered "residents to stay indoors," the *New York Times* said, calling it "the most drastic step of any state leader to slow the spread of the coronavirus."[4]

Eight days earlier, the governor banned mass gatherings (those in excess of 250 people) as well as social gatherings of more than 10 "individuals who are at higher risk for severe illness from COVID-19."[5] These restrictions were to continue until the end of March.

On March 13, the four largest school districts in the state, Los Angeles Unified, San Diego Unified, Fresno Unified and Long Beach Unified, announced they were closing their classrooms. "District officials," the *New York Times* reported, "(expected) the closures to last weeks."[6]

In early April, officials were "easing" what had "for months been some of the nation's most stringent lockdowns," said the *Times*.[7] Near the end of the month, a timeline for reopening in phases was taking shape.

Then minds changed. Newsom issued a statewide mask mandate in June,[8] then ordered businesses to close again in July.[9] In that same month he told schools there would be no in-person learning for 90 percent of California's students.[10]

Near the end of 2020, months after officials shut down the state, PRI president and CEO Sally Pipes warned "fellow Californians" that they should "get ready to stay home indefinitely" as "Gov. Gavin Newsom has suggested that the stay-at-home order he issued Dec. 3 will likely be extended well into January."[11]

The suffering from the lockdowns was widespread. Jobs were lost. Many closed businesses never reopened. Students fell behind and still haven't caught up. Families lost members they weren't allowed to see as their lives wound down. Missed doctor visits and health screenings caused increased illness and death. Mental health among Californians deteriorated. And they became hungry. The number of food insecure in the state increased by more than 2 million due to the pandemic.[12]

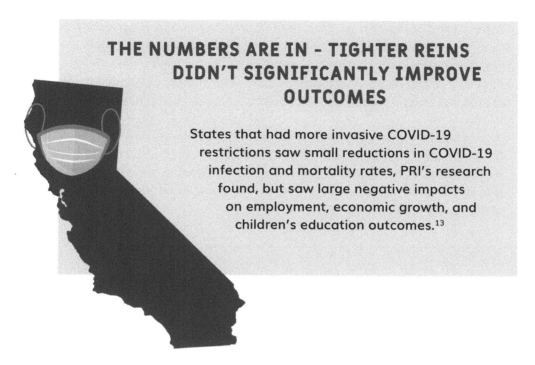

THE NUMBERS ARE IN - TIGHTER REINS DIDN'T SIGNIFICANTLY IMPROVE OUTCOMES

States that had more invasive COVID-19 restrictions saw small reductions in COVID-19 infection and mortality rates, PRI's research found, but saw large negative impacts on employment, economic growth, and children's education outcomes.[13]

The first wave of lockdown orders caused the unemployment rate to shoot up from 4.4 percent in February 2020 to 16.1 percent in April 2020. From that peak, it fell to 3.8 percent in August 2022 but was back up to 5.2 percent just before publication.[14]

In the short period of March to May 2020, there were more than two times as many job losses as there were during the 2008 Great Recession.[15]

Livelihoods were lost because of a jittery, overbearing government. In fact, 3 million jobs were wiped out, though most were eventually filled again.[16] But the negative effects lingered. "California's job growth was essentially cut in half by the coronavirus and the state's reaction to the pandemic," says the *Orange County Register*. It was the "largest job-growth drop" in the country.[17]

Businesses, which some policymakers and many among the coastal elite don't welcome in California anyway, struggled for years after the virus arrived. Many didn't make it. As early as November 2020, thousands had closed forever.[18] Roughly 7,500 small businesses were permanently shuttered in Los Angeles County alone.[19]

Owners tried to survive as best they could, even when they were told their power would be turned off and their business licenses yanked if they didn't surrender to government directives.[20] Some businesses courageously defied Newsom's orders, in particular multiple Orange County restaurants that in late 2020 stayed open for in-person dining.[21]

Gyms were in a category almost by themselves in refusing to comply with politicians' demands, with one showdown in San Luis Obispo County becoming "ugly." Owners ignored closure orders and members, fed up with the boot of the state on their necks, donated to funds that were used to pay off fines.[22]

HONEST MEN BECOME UNLAWFUL OPERATORS

"Ever since California went into lockdown to mitigate against the spread of COVID-19 last March, many of the state's 'non-essential' businesses have taken their chances operating underground to try to stay above water," Fox News reported in January 2021.[23]

Business operators and employees would meet customers in back alleys, turn off lights, draw curtains, and would make house calls when that was the best option available, hoping to come and go unseen by nosy neighbors.[24]

Students, locked out of their schools, were big losers, too. The UCLA Center for the Transformation of Schools says that "almost four years later, students have been severely impacted. Students' learning and academic growth as well as their social and emotional development have declined." Those from "low-income and communities of color" were "disproportionately affected" as the "radical shift to remote learning" "exacerbated existing educational disparities."[25]

Learning loss in California was so extensive that the state settled a lawsuit for a minimum of $2 billion. It was brought by parents who, according to *CalMatters*, said "that in many schools, remote learning was so inconsistent and ineffective that thousands of students – especially low-income, black and Latino students – were denied their right to an education."[26]

The way the students were treated caused a flight from public schools. PRI's Lance Izumi noted that from the 2019-20 school year to the 2020-21 school year, public school enrollment dropped 2.6 percent, a decline never before seen in California. Around 160,000 students left their neighborhood public schools.[27]

Again, Newsom was a violator of restrictions that were apparently meant for other people. He admitted in October 2020 that his children had returned to in-person learning at their private school even "as many schools across the state remain(ed) shuttered due to COVID-19 – including nearly all public schools in Sacramento County where the governor lives," *Politico* reported.[28]

Though officials said lockdown policies were intended to save lives, the unintended consequences led to an increase in non-COVID deaths over the pandemic's first year. A National Bureau of Economic Research report found that policies restricting movement and fearmongering by officials discouraged people from seeing their doctors. Patients missed regular health screenings. Drug and alcohol use rose, as did deaths caused by substance abuse.[29]

"It should be no surprise that a widespread disruption to patient circumstances would degrade health and even elevate mortality from chronic conditions," say the authors of "Non-Covid Excess Deaths, 2020-21: Collateral Damage of Policy Choices?"[30]

The effects were particularly severe in California, because officials set highly confining boundaries, maintained them for an extended period and kept the populace in a state of anxiety.

Closing the state also caused psychological problems.

"All the uncertainty and joblessness has also sparked a mental health crisis," Pipes wrote in late 2020. "By July, 44% of California adults had symptoms of[31] depression or anxiety disorders. In San Francisco, drug overdose deaths have actually exceeded those from the virus in 2020."[32]

It's not unreasonable to argue that the mental health fallout from the lockdowns has been more difficult on Californians than others. Other parts of the country have been shut down, but this state has been on a particularly short leash. No state has held captive more of its residents.[33]

At that time, about 33 million of the state's nearly 40 million residents had been told by Newsom to stay home. Anyone who did venture out was expected to comply with his 10 p.m. to 5 a.m. curfew.[34] With such rules in effect, how could anyone be expected to operate at peak mental health? No wonder that doctors were "seeing between eight to 10 (patients) a day that are expressing suicidal ideations" and others who were responding with anger to the conditions imposed by the government.[35]

California wasn't the only state to lock down. But few behaved and performed as poorly. It was obvious within a year of the arrival of the virus that California's policies were causing problems.[36]

The Committee to Unleash Prosperity gave the state an "F" in its 2022 report card on state responses to COVID-19. New Jersey, New York, Illinois and Washington, D.C., also earned "Fs" for their "high age-adjusted death rates" and "high unemployment and significant GDP losses." All "kept their schools shut down much longer than almost all other states."[37]

The Paragon Health Institute released a report in April 2023 that declared "Freedom Wins," as the states that enacted more open COVID policies "outperformed states with more restrictive COVID policies." There was "little, if any, health benefit from California's severe approach," and the state in fact "suffered far worse economic and education outcomes" than did Florida, which was often compared to California. It took an opposite approach than did the Golden State – and was criticized by Newsom.[38]

"The Florida approach proved to be better overall. The lockdown measures imposed in California and other (largely blue) states did little to improve health outcomes and led to significantly worse economic scores and overall COVID response scores than in Florida."[39]

The Council on Foreign Relations, an establishment organization made up of staffers more politically in line with California than Florida, placed California 36th – and Florida seventh overall – in its ranking of state COVID actions based on "health and economy and education, giving more weight to health." The state was 30th in health, 32nd in economy and education.[40] National Public Radio even acknowledged that Florida outperformed California.[41]

While a number of other governors decided within months that subjugating their residents was counterproductive – and wrong – Newsom didn't lift his declared state of emergency until February 2023, almost three years to the day that he began to issue unilateral orders.[42]

Government often abused its emergency powers and made decisions "not grounded in science, evidence, or logic."[43] At one point, Eric Garcetti, the then-mayor of Los Angeles, said "it's time to cancel everything."[44]

It was all theater with a dual purpose: to politically and socially cover backsides ("We were trying to protect people"), and to ride out the power trips as long as possible.

CHAPTER 12
Getting Good Grades: How Not to Let a Great Education System Fall Off A Cliff

Americans moving to the Left Coast to make a better life for their families often come to take advantage of what former Gov. Arnold Schwarzenegger called the "Golden Dream by the sea" in his inaugural address in 2003.

For families with children, there's no state that offers a better natural environment for learning than California. Traveling the state, students can experience oceans and mountains, beaches and forests. From its birth as a state during the Gold Rush era, the state has been a home of entrepreneurship, innovation, and creativity in every field from agriculture to bioscience.

Unfortunately, the state's public school system has been taken over by political activists who are determined to push what were once the nation's best K-12 schools and public colleges and universities off the peaks of Mount Whitney, the highest mountain in California and the Lower 48.

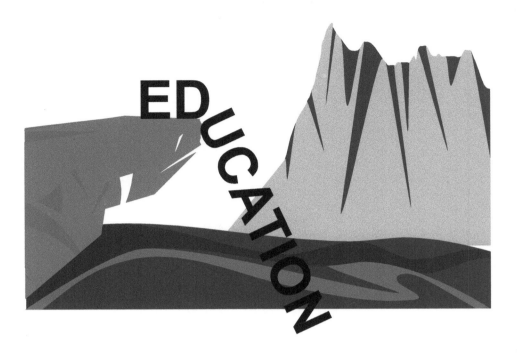

Parents who want their kids to learn the three Rs – reading, writing, and arithmetic – are having to navigate a school system today that promotes three different Rs – racism, redistribution, and revolution.

In this chapter, we'll explore how Left Coast parents are often left to fend for themselves in shielding their children from radical and divisive curriculum that isn't preparing students to meet the demands of the global workforce or succeed in life, nor training creative entrepreneurs – but is good for churning out eternal victims. You'll learn about efforts to inject politics into the teaching of math and reading, and a controversial new ethnic studies curriculum that encourages division rather than cohesion.

CALIFORNIA'S PUBLIC SCHOOLS FAIL TO HELP STUDENTS SURVIVE LEARNING WILDERNESS

One of the essential skills taught to Boy Scouts and one of the key merit badges earned by scouts is surviving in the wilderness.

As the *Scouting Guide to Survival* notes, "a survival crisis can confront anyone suddenly, without warning."[1]

"The keys (to survival)," the *Guide* advises, "are to learn that an emergency can befall you and then know what to do."[2]

LEFT COAST SURVIVOR'S BADGE

★★★

LEARNING WILDERNESS SURVIVAL

Every American was suddenly confronted with an emergency with the onslaught of the COVID-19 pandemic in March 2020.

But government officials and regular Americans alike clearly had not earned their wilderness survival badges. They didn't know what to do when a crisis threatened millions of lives.

On the Left Coast, no one was caught more unprepared than California public school officials and political leaders, including Gov. Gavin Newsom.

With government issuing mass shutdown orders, California's public schools closed to in-person instruction. For the next 18 months, most students suffered through "Zoom school," hybrid in-person and online learning, and other hastily arranged alternatives.

The impact on students was catastrophic and long-lasting.[3] A July 2021 McKinsey & Company study showed that students were left "on average five months behind in mathematics and four months behind in reading by the end of the school year."[4] A study by Harvard and Stanford Universities documented learning losses of a year and a half for students in some cities.[5]

Worse, 80 percent of parents surveyed in the McKinsey study had been worried about their child's mental health or social and emotional development since the beginning of the pandemic.[6]

As *Education Week* noted, schools during the pandemic "relaxed grading policies, canceled end-of-year assessments, or directed teachers not to fail students because of work not completed during shutdowns."[7]

 There is no such thing as learning loss. Our kids didn't lose anything. It's OK that our babies may not have learned all their times tables."[8]
—United Teachers of Los Angeles president
Cecily Myart-Cruz, 8/26/21

The flippant reaction of the head of the Los Angeles teachers' union about learning loss perhaps explains why California did not return to full in-person instruction until fall 2021 – longer than nearly any other state.[9]

Gov. Newsom and legislators responded to the crisis by throwing more money at the state's failing public schools – increasing K-12 and community college spending by 39 percent from 2019-20 to 2021-22.[10]

The money didn't help students struggling to stay afloat academically and mentally during the pandemic and the immediate aftermath.

CALIFORNIA STUDENTS NOT GIVEN EDUCATION SURVIVAL SKILLS DURING PANDEMIC

Despite throwing billions at public education, California's public school students were drowning during the global pandemic – and are barely treading water today.

MATH TEST SCORES

- Math – In 2019, 29% of California eighth graders scored at the proficient level on the National Assessment of Educational Progress exam, often referred to as the nation's report card. In 2022, that number fell to 23%.[11]

- Minority Students – Just 10% of black California eighth graders scored proficient on the math exam in 2019 versus an appallingly low 7% in 2022. Hispanic student proficiency fell from 15% in 2019 to 11% in 2022.[12]

The state recently settled a lawsuit filed on behalf of Oakland and Los Angeles students who suffered the most due to learning-loss. Gov. Newsom is proposing an additional $13 billion in education spending to address learning loss and promote student learning recovery.[13]

The attorney representing the Oakland and Los Angeles plaintiffs told the respected education publication *EdSource* that, "the urgent vision of this historic settlement is to use strategies that not only recoup academic losses but also erase the opportunity gaps exacerbated by the pandemic."[14]

The settlement would require the state for the first time to monitor student progress, collect data, and craft remediation plans targeted to the students' specific needs – focusing on outcomes and accountability for the first time.[15] As one expert witness in the case said, "Data collection was minimal to non-existent, and monitoring of the learning and community plans was superficial at best."[16]

Given the state's track record, it's no wonder that California public school enrollment fell by 271,000 from 2020 to 2022.[17] A February 2022 poll by the UC Berkeley Institute for Governmental Studies poll reported that just 35 percent of parents gave their local public schools an A or B grade – a drop of 20 percentage points from the 2011 survey.[18] Parents are voicing their displeasure with the performance of their child's school by voting with their feet.

PARENTS AND STUDENTS NEED HELP TO FEND OFF CHARTER SCHOOL PREDATORS

In *The Scouting Guide to Survival*, future Boy Scouts are cautioned that "anyone going into wilderness areas should be aware of the potential dangers that exist," primarily from snakes, bears, and mountain lions one might encounter in the wild.[19]

If confronted by a mountain lion, Scouts are advised to "seem as large as possible. . .make noise, yell, shout. . .(and) act defiant, not afraid."[20]

It's also wise advice for Left Coast parents who face a different kind of danger in the wilds of California schools – teachers' unions and defenders of the education status quo who prey on charter schools and want to trap every student in a failing traditional public school.

 Charter schools 'are a drain on many of our public schools.'"[21]
—Eric Heins, Then-President, California Teachers Association, May 22, 2019

Charter schools are publicly funded schools that are independent of school districts with greater autonomy to innovate.[22] They often receive far fewer taxpayer dollars and non-public funding than conventional public schools.[23]

Data show that students attending California's charter schools – especially Latino and African Americans – routinely outperform students attending traditional public schools.[24]

Students attending charters in Los Angeles and Oakland rated higher on state math and English exams across every demographic than students attending traditional public schools.[25]

They're also doing a better job of getting into college. The California Charter School Association notes that "charter schools had higher rates of UC/CSU enrollment with all subgroups" than regular public schools in 2018, and were "especially successful at getting black, Latin(o), and low-income students into these universities."[26]

> " Recent successes by opponents would trap students in failing schools – and prevent their escape to alternatives that will better prepare them for the future."[27]
> —Lance Izumi, Senior Director, PRI's Center for Education

California was once known as a state with strong and innovative laws promoting the creation and expansion of charter schools. But much like the changing of the winds that caused Mary Poppins to leave town, political winds in the state changed from pro-charter Gov. Jerry Brown to his successor Gavin Newsom, who is an opponent of charter growth.[28] Now charter parents and students are under attack.

In recent years, teachers' unions in Oakland, Los Angeles and elsewhere have called strikes and used contract negotiations to push for new charter school moratoriums and restrictions on charter school flexibility, such as expanding charter school teacher unionization.[29]

A primary line of attack surrounds charter school finances. Teachers' unions claim that charters "drain" funding away from regular public schools.[30] Gov. Newsom signed legislation in 2019 (Assembly Bill 1505) that gave hostile school districts loopholes to deny charter school petitions and renewals, claiming charters adversely affect districts on fiscal grounds.[31] This is a false claim, given that charters typically receive less money than regular schools. Several recent studies have found that charters have little impact on the financial distress of school districts.[32]

TEACHERS' UNIONS STARVE THEIR PREY— CHARTER SCHOOLS

A University of Arkansas study gave Los Angeles and Oakland school districts an "F" grade for overwhelming funding gaps that favor traditional public schools over charter schools.

- There was a $5,226 or 27% funding gap between regular public schools and charter schools in Los Angeles. In Oakland, the gap was $7,103 or nearly 34%.
- In Los Angeles, 77% of charter school students come from low-income households or are non-English-fluent or special education students.[33]

ONE PLUS ONE EQUALS FOUR? IT MIGHT UNDER CALIFORNIA'S WOKE MATH PROPOSAL

Girl Scouts can earn merit badges for learning about math while exploring nature. Some of the things they will learn to earn a math merit badge include measurement, sorting, and estimating.[34]

There are other badges offered that require good math skills, such as "Coding for Good," "Cookie Entrepreneurship," "STEM Career Exploration," "Space Science Explorer," robotics, and mechanical engineering, to name just a few.[35]

Left Coast parents who want their kids to learn math and science would be advised to avoid public schools and instead homeschool. The reason? Newly adopted state math curriculum and ineffective state reading curriculum prioritizes "environmental and social justice" and "social inequities" over preparing students with essential skills for the job market.

California recently adopted a new math curriculum framework, which guides teaching in the classroom. Instead of focusing on how to best teach students algebra, calculus, or geometry, state officials are more interested in teaching politics in math class.

PREPARING STUDENTS FOR THE SOCIAL JUSTICE SCOUT BADGE

California's controversial new woke math curriculum sets social justice issues as the core priority of teaching math, not how to add or do an algebra equation. Here are the state's official new math education priorities:

- Lessons are based on the concept of "equity."
- Teaching math is supposed to promote "social justice."
- Teachers are encouraged to promote "sociopolitical consciousness" among students.
- Math classes push a "justice-oriented perspective" at all grade levels.[36]

LEFT COAST SURVIVOR'S BADGE

—★★★—

SOCIAL JUSTICE

What does equity in math education look like? As PRI's Lance Izumi notes, "while equality means giving students the equal opportunity to succeed based on their own talents and hard work, equity means the same results for all students, regardless of their talent or their individual effort."[37]

An example of math equity is pushing all students to take algebra in the ninth grade – even though most took algebra in the eighth grade. This would make it virtually impossible for students to complete calculus by the 12th grade – a requirement for many colleges.

"The State Board of Education would rather homogenize all students into their equity box so that all students receive the same dumbed-down math education," says Izumi.[38] He laments that fewer students will be able to major in STEM fields and fewer graduates will be qualified to work in high-tech and STEM fields.[39] Trapping more students on the lower rungs of the economic ladder would seem to be the opposite of addressing inequality.

Meanwhile, a staggering 69 percent of California fourth graders fell short of reading proficiency on the National Assessment of Educational Progress test.[40]

A study from the National Council on Teacher Quality noted that, "more than 90% of all students could become proficient readers if they were taught by teachers employing scientifically based reading instruction."[41]

Unfortunately, California students are widely taught using ineffective reading instruction methods. Many are taught using a flawed instructional approach called "balanced literacy," which downplays the significance of teaching phonics in favor of contextual and meaning-based instruction.[42]

> In a 'balanced literacy' classroom, a child might see a picture of a horse and the word 'horse' below it in a book, but they could incorrectly guess that the word is 'pony' instead of 'horse' and still be considered correct."[43]
> —Megan Bacigalupi, California parent

As the NCTQ notes, 72 percent of early-grade teachers surveyed in the study "admit to using literacy instructional methods that have been debunked by cognitive scientists many years ago."[44]

CALIFORNIA'S MOST TREACHEROUS GAP —
THE PERFORMANCE GAP

Left Coast visitors looking to experience all the beauty California has to offer will surely be drawn to the Sierra Nevada mountains and Emigrant Gap.

Located to the west of Donner Pass, Emigrant Gap earned its legacy, according to California State Parks, as the spot in the spring of 1845 where the first covered wagons were able to navigate through the seemingly impassable Sierra Nevada mountains.[45] As the marker at 5,190 feet denotes, once covered wagons reached Emigrant Gap, they "were lowered by ropes to the floor of Bear Valley" in what was a very "hazardous portion" of the trail.[46]

California has another hazardous gap — and it might be even more treacherous than what the first settlers experienced in the Sierras — the state's persistent performance gap.

JUST HOW STEEP IS CALIFORNIA'S
PERFORMANCE GAP?

The most recent California state test scores underscore how treacherous California's performance gap has become.

- Two-thirds of students failed to meet or exceed grade-level standards in math in 2022-23.

- More than half of students failed to meet or exceed grade-level standards in reading.[47]

California state education officials cheered the abysmal performances of its students on the annual exams by bragging that the state is showing "promising gains in student mathematics" and "consistent scores" in English language arts.[48] Izumi said the department's spin was equivalent to a headline reading, "Not Everyone Died in Massive Train Wreck, Say Railroad Officials."[49]

He argues that if the state continued the trend of a tiny 1.2-percent increase in students scoring at grade level, which the department press release characterized as "particularly promising," it would take more than 50 years for all California students to reach grade level in math.[50]

Gov. Newsom also touts the state's figures by noting how much money the state has thrown at the problem.

"That's why we've made record investments in education, created a new pre-K grade, implemented universal free meals, expanded before and after school programs, bolstered mental health, and more," he said.[51]

Though there's little to show for it. California's achievement gap problem was vividly illustrated in testimony in May 2020 from then-University of California (UC) system president Janet Napolitano.

"The biggest contributor to underrepresentation at UC," she said, "is that students do not fulfill A-G subject requirements for admissions."[52]

A UC Academic Senate task force found that there was "a 22-percentage point gap between the share of [underrepresented minorities] in the grade 12 class and the pool of California resident students admitted by UC." According to the California Department of Education, in 2017-18, 43 percent of Hispanic students and less than 40 percent of African-American students met the basic UC admission requirements.[53]

One way to overcome the achievement gap is to break students – especially those living in poor and minority communities – out of failing public schools and enroll them instead in charter schools that have shown themselves to be more successful in preparing every student for a bright future.[54]

A resolution enacted by the NAACP chapter in San Diego noted that the 10 school districts with the highest enrollment of African-American students, "have an average African-American achievement gap of 14.5 percent in [English language arts] and 15.2 percent in math when compared to the performance of all students."[55]

However, "African-American students enrolled in public charter schools achieve academic outcomes exceeding their peers in district-run schools."[56]

Indeed, a 2015 Stanford University study found that, "black students in poverty [in charter schools] receive the equivalent of 59 days of additional learning in math and 44 days of additional learning in reading compared to their peers in [traditional public schools]."[57]

Tell that to California's teacher unions, which routinely prey upon charter schools and work to keep all students confined to failing traditional public schools.

ETHNIC STUDIES OR INDOCTRINATION? CALIFORNIA STUDENTS STRUGGLE UNDER CONTROVERSIAL NEW LAW

One of the main attractions for Left Coast visitors in California is its tapestry of countless backgrounds woven together into one. Nowhere in the world can travelers immerse themselves in such rich cultural diversity.

Travelers in San Francisco, for example, can walk through the streets of Chinatown and enjoy delicious Far East delicacies for lunch, then go on a short walk to the Italian community of North Beach and enjoy dinner at Fior d'Italia, which is America's oldest Italian restaurant.[58]

Students at California's public schools literally learn in a melting pot. Every day, school systems serve students speaking 108 different languages.[59] Students have the opportunity to study their fellow classmates' language and culture – and learn to build a sense of community despite coming from different backgrounds and points of view.

Unfortunately, the state's controversial new ethnic studies curriculum threatens to disrupt this harmony and inject politics, racism, and religious discrimination into the classroom.

In 2021, Gov. Newsom signed legislation (Assembly Bill 101) requiring every state high school student to take an ethnic studies course in order to graduate.[60]

 California parents are not being told the truth about a potentially significant change in the education of their children."[61]
—UCLA Professor Richard Sandler and University of Pennsylvania Professor Abraham Wyner

As Izumi wrote of the new ethnic studies requirement, "despite window-dressing language meant to reassure the public that these courses do not promote bias or bigotry, the reality is that the law opens the floodgates to the political indoctrination of children."[62]

According to the text of the law, school districts can satisfy this requirement through various avenues, including "a locally developed ethnic studies course approved by the governing board of the school district or the governing board of the charter school."[63]

One example of how troubling the curriculum can be is the program adopted by the Salinas Unified School District, which is based on the radical "liberated ethnic studies" concept – a 1960s discipline that combines Leninism, Marxism, and Maoism with antisemitism and emphasizes an oppressor-victim worldview.[64]

Outlining plans for ninth and tenth grade ethnic studies curriculum, district officials say that "students will build complex and nuanced understandings of power, privilege, oppression, and resistance" while critiquing "color-blindness," "meritocracy," and "claims of neutrality and complete objectivity."[65]

One lesson in particular the school district wants students to learn is that "we can decolonize our minds, regenerate our roots, critique oppression, and take action for social justice in education, community and world, daily."[66] Similar curriculum, unfortunately, has been adopted by other districts around the state.

The initially proposed state ethnic studies curriculum – termed the "most controversial curriculum that has ever come out in the state of California" – had to be revised after receiving significant criticism.[67] More than 70,000 public comments were received by the board on the draft curriculum.

Fortunately, provisions were included in state law to ensure that ethnic studies courses are "appropriate for use" with students of all races, religions, and backgrounds and does not "reflect or promote" bias, bigotry or discrimination within a protected group, and local ethnic studies plans must be presented at a public hearing before approval.[68]

Despite these protections, the type of curriculum being adopted in Salinas has many wondering if radical ethnic studies curriculum will be the exception or the norm in California's public schools in the years ahead.

CHAPTER 13
Sound Body, Sound Mind

From its origins, travelers have flocked to the Left Coast seeking "the cure."

Many were told that the "pure Western air would make them strong and well again."[1]

Writer Charles Willard, who had been diagnosed with tuberculosis, arrived in California in 1886 seeking to improve his health. Thousands of other Americans traveled west during this time looking for a warmer climate to facilitate better health.[2]

"Although I came to Los Angeles a physical wreck – pale, haggard and debilitated – my health has been restored," publisher W.C. Patterson wrote. "The 'glorious climate' (which is all that has been claimed for it, and more) enables me to enjoy life better and appreciate life more."[3]

He later started a journal called *The Land of Sunshine*, which was filled with "residents' testimonials to the healing powers of the California climate."[4]

Current travelers seeking California's healing powers will be surprised to find the opposite. Meddling lawmakers believe that they have "the cure." State government in recent years has embarked upon a push to provide massive new government health care programs that would give any taxpayer "the vapors."

Undertaking initiatives ranging from forcing every Californian into a new government-run health care system that would outlaw private insurance to creating its own California "drug label," the state is also issuing health care insurance to migrants who are not here legally. The cost and problems these efforts would bring the state will send many to their sickbeds.[5]

These lavish initiatives have been projected to cost double the state budget, require tens of millions in new taxes, and lead to reductions in the quality and availability of care. As is usually the case, lawmakers who brag they're launching something that is supposedly "free" are going to send the bill to taxpayers.

They've also tied knots in the delivery of health care that even the best scout would have trouble unraveling. A statewide health policy survey funded by the California Health Care Foundation determined that in addition to rising health care costs, "strains on our mental health system, persistent provider shortages, and increasing wait times for care[6] in many communities" are serious concerns among California adults. One in five hospitals is at risk of closure, and more than half lose money every day.[7]

ANOTHER MONEY-LOSING GOVERNMENT PROGRAM — CALIFORNIA DRUG LABEL

As part of his agenda to create government-run health care in California. Gov. Gavin Newsom has put the state in the drug-making business.

First as an executive order, and later enacted into law by the Legislature, the CalRx label would have the state contract with generic pharmaceutical manufacturers to make drugs to sell to Californians, presumably at a lower cost than what's on the market today.[8]

For its first effort, the state has launched a biosimilar insulin initiative, spending $100 million funding the project and building a California manufacturing facility, with the intent of distributing it to patients at a cost of no more than $30 per 10mL vial.[9]

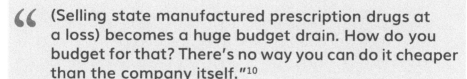

> " (Selling state manufactured prescription drugs at a loss) becomes a huge budget drain. How do you budget for that? There's no way you can do it cheaper than the company itself."[10]
> —Dr. Wayne Winegarden,
> Director of PRI's Center for Medical Economics and Innovation

As PRI's Dr. Wayne Winegarden notes, "generic drugs are already quite affordable (with) ninety-five percent of prescriptions for generic drugs costing $25 or less. . .(and) accounting for 9 in 10 prescriptions filled."[11]

Given the affordability of generics today, Newsom's plan would have the state government health care program do what Sacramento does best – lose money.

"If Newsom's new drugmaker is going to undercut existing generic prices," Winegarden argues, "it will have to sell its wares at loss-inducing prices. . .(which will be) compounded by the additional costs the state will incur monitoring its new drug retailing entity."[12]

"The taxpayers of California will be forced to cover these losses," he says.[13]

TRAVELER ALERT — TAKE CARE OF YOURSELF

Don't forget to pack plenty of your prescription medications when traveling to California. A California drug label coupled with drug price controls and government-run health care will mean patients will lose access to life-saving medications and will have to pay far more for drugs in the future.

Those pushing California's drug label ignore the fact that prescription drug prices are not driving up overall U.S. health care costs and generics save the system $293 billion annually.[14] Due to the broken drug supply chain, patients overpay for prescriptions by as much as $2.1 billion, according to one study.[15] The problem is not corporate greed, but a drug-pricing system that incentivizes higher out-of-pocket costs.

Instead of creating new government programs, California should reform the complex drug-pricing system, increase transparency, and put an end to pharmacy benefit managers (or PBMs) pocketing discounts instead of patients, to lower drug prices and health care costs.[16] Price controls and regulations, however, will only exacerbate America's health care affordability problems.[17]

The irony is that all those who come to California seeking better health may have to travel elsewhere as life-saving drugs may not be available or affordable before you know it.

WHEN SOMETHING FREE REALLY ISN'T: THE PUSH FOR SINGLE-PAYER HEALTH CARE

As the old adage goes, something that is free usually isn't.

This is especially true with the push by Gov. Newsom and liberal California politicians to enact a government-run health care scheme.

The latest incarnation of single-payer health care legislation (Assembly Bill 2200) would ban private health insurance and force all state residents into CalCare, a Sacramento-centric plan.[18]

How to Earn a Merit Badge for Single-Payer

Survivalists seeking to earn a merit badge for first aid[19] will have plenty of opportunities to earn one in California if the state enters a government-run health care system, destroying the provision of medical care as we know it. Here are a few ways your first aid skills can help Californians needing treatment if forced to live under single-payer health care:

- Prepare first aid kits. This might be the only way to treat Californians in distress, as there will be long wait times to see a doctor.
- Learn how to triage the ill and the hurting, as there will be fewer specialists in the state and longer wait times to see those who remain.
- Teach others how to perform first aid. Many doctors and nurses will surely leave the profession rather than being forced to take low reimbursement rates or unionized wages.

Based on experiences from around the world in single-payer health systems, what's in store for Californians could be disastrous.

- The median wait in Canada for specialist treatment following referral by a general practitioner is more than six months.[20]

- A Canadian in need of a hip replacement traveled to a clinic where the prohibition on private care doesn't apply — and paid $23,500 out of pocket, waiting just two months. He would have waited nine to 12 times as long had he used his government health coverage.[21]

- Nearly 7.6 million people in England were on waiting lists to see a doctor as of January 2024.[22]

- In the UK, it routinely takes more than 90 minutes for ambulances to respond to serious conditions including heart attacks and strokes.[23]

Concerned that CalCare would slash physician reimbursement rates to lower costs, Democratic Assemblywoman Akilah Weber, a physician, said during the Assembly Health Committee Hearing on AB 2200, "We already have a provider shortage, and if we don't do this correctly, we'll just worsen that."[24] Under the current system, state Medicaid programs underpay doctors by around 30 percent and hospitals by 22 percent.[25]

> " As with all 'free' goods, CalCare would also incentivize patients to overuse healthcare. Faced with surging patient demand and declining numbers of providers, the state will inevitably impose strict access restrictions that will result in patients having less access to innovative therapies, longer wait times for procedures, and even restrictions on the types of procedures they can receive. In short, patients will receive worse healthcare."[26]
>
> —Dr. Wayne Winegarden, Director of PRI's Center for Medical Economics and Innovation

Cost estimates of prior versions of California single-payer health care legislation pegged the price at roughly $400 billion, significantly more than the state budget.

A similar previous version of the bill was proposed to be funded with a 2.3 percent gross receipts tax on business revenues of more than $2 million, a 1.25 percent tax on California-based employees in companies with 50 or more people, and a series of progressively higher marginal tax rates on higher income families.[27] Another analysis of a prior single-payer bill projected taxes would have to increase $12,250 per household to pay for it.[28]

A Pacific Research Institute analysis for its Spending Watch project found that establishing the CalCare system in California would lead to:

 2.8 PERCENT LESS ECONOMIC GROWTH

 333,000 FEWER JOBS

 $1,200 SMALLER AVERAGE INCOMES

 AN ADDITIONAL 345,000 PEOPLE LEAVING THE STATE[29]

Winegarden, the author of the analysis, commented that, "past experiences demonstrate that state-run single payer healthcare systems are less efficient (and) if adopted in California, the consequences would be reduced healthcare quality, rationed care, and weakened economic prosperity."[30]

Assembly Speaker Robert Rivas says of the proposal that, "We need to see how this is funded," adding that "it's a tough, tough sell, especially in a budget climate that we are experiencing now."[31] Not surprisingly, AB 2200 was shelved in May 2024.

It will also be a tough sell with the public, which doesn't want to pay massive new taxes. People don't want to lose their doctors, either. Polling from the respected Public Policy Institute of California found that support for single payer dropped from 65 percent to 42 percent when voters learned they'd have to pay new taxes to fund it.[32]

"YOU GET FREE HEALTH CARE, YOU GET FREE HEALTH CARE!": MEDI-CAL FOR ILLEGAL IMMIGRANTS

Throughout its 25 years on the air, women were known to stand in line for hours and hours or wait months for their chance to get tickets to the *Oprah Winfrey Show.*

Why was there such demand for tickets for a daytime talk show?

The former "queen of daytime talk" was known to give away great stuff – and lots of it – to her audiences. Lucky attendees came home with gifts ranging from free Pontiacs to trips to Australia and Tina Turner concert tickets.

Thanks to the legislature and Gov. Newsom, California is now the *Oprah Winfrey Show* of free health care.

On January 1, 2024, California became the first state in the union to offer taxpayer-funded health care to all illegal immigrants.[33] Every adult, regardless of their age or legal status, can now apply for Medi-Cal, the state's Medicaid program.[34]

Over the years, California has been making more and more illegal immigrants eligible for taxpayer-funded health care, starting with children in 2016, then young adults up to age 26 and seniors over 50,[35] and now the 700,000 illegal immigrants between ages 26 and 49.[36]

> " The total annual cost of providing Medi-Cal to all illegal immigrants is $4 billion. And that doesn't consider the potential cost of undocumented people from other states coming to California to claim this new state-funded benefit."[37]
> —Sally C. Pipes, PRI President, CEO, and Thomas W. Smith Fellow in Health Care Policy

The cost for providing free health care to illegal immigrants is by no means free. According to estimates:

- Providing Medi-Cal to illegal immigrants between ages 26 and 49 will cost $2.3 billion a year.
- Medi-Cal for children and teens who are undocumented costs more than $360 million a year.
- It costs $260 million to provide Medi-Cal to undocumented who are aged 19 to 26.[38]

As PRI's Sally Pipes told *CalMatters* about the state's efforts to expand Medi-Cal to the undocumented, "It's not fair to those who are taxpayers and those who are middle- and lower-income and have a lot of stress in paying for healthcare. Why would they need to pay more to subsidize these people?"[39]

CHAPTER 14
The Price is Wrong

Left Coast visitors flock to Southern California to take in the sights and sounds of Hollywood, the global capital of the entertainment industry.

One of the most fun experiences to have when visiting Hollywood is to get tickets – which are typically free – to see a live taping of one of the many television shows that film on the area's numerous studio lots. Perhaps the most popular – and most fun – to attend is the popular game show, *The Price is Right*.

Revived in 1972 at the iconic CBS Television City, *The Price is Right* is the longest-running game show in television history.[1] Audience members whose names are called are invited to "come on down" to guess the price of an item up for bid, and hopefully win thousands of dollars in cash and prizes. More than 2 million people have attended tapings of *The Price is Right*, with more than 68,000 called up as contestants.[2]

When it comes to one very controversial proposal being pushed in California, a new game show could be launched – *The Price is Wrong*.

THE PRICE IS WRONG ON CALIFORNIA'S REPARATIONS PLAN

If proponents of the plan produced by the California Reparations Commission have their way, and $1.4 million reparations payouts are authorized to the estimated 2 million people who would be eligible, the out-of-pocket costs paid by Californians and the impact on the economy would be catastrophic:

$2.8	**TRILLION TOTAL COST**
54%	**INCREASE IN MARGINAL STATE INCOME TAX RATE AND SALES TAX BURDEN**
5.69%	**LOWER HOUSEHOLD INCOME OVER FIVE YEARS**
1.84	**MILLION MORE PEOPLE LEAVING THE STATE**
11% SMALLER	**ECONOMY OVER FIVE YEARS (COMPARED TO BASELINE)**
4.9%	**FEWER JOBS OVER FIVE YEARS (COMPARED TO BASELINE)[3]**

In June 2023, the nine members of the state reparations task force released their 1,000-page report detailing the commission's recommendations for paying reparations to legacy descendants of slaves in the United States.[4] Gov. Gavin Newsom signed legislation in 2020 creating the task force and commissioning its work, even though California was a free state during the Civil War.[5]

Though much of discussion surrounding the commission's report centered on paying cash reparations to Californians who are determined to be eligible – through the creation of a state "Freedman's Affairs Agency" – commissioners and legislators who support reparations shy away from the discussion of cash payments and costs for good reason.[6] Reparations, if implemented, would bankrupt the state and California taxpayers who would have to pay them alike.

It is estimated that about 80 percent of California's African-American residents would be eligible for reparations, or nearly 2 million people. The California Reparations Report breaks down the proposed reparations per eligible recipient this way:

- $953,330 for health harms
- $115,248 for "mass incarceration and over-policing"
- $235,620 for housing discrimination
- $77,000 for "devaluation of businesses"
- An unknown amount – likely to be significant – for "unjust property takings"[7]

Altogether, this adds up to potential reparations payments of at least $1.4 million per eligible recipient.[8] PRI's Dr. Wayne Winegarden, in analyzing the fiscal effects of the task force's recommendations, estimates the total cost at $2.8 trillion, which would sock taxpayers with huge new tax bills and result in the destruction of the state's economy.[9]

In 2024, members of the California Legislative Black Caucus introduced more than a dozen bills to begin implementing the task forces' recommendations.[10] Kamilah Moore, who chaired the reparations task force, told *CalMatters* that the bills create a "solid foundation for eventually a direct cash payments bill, maybe in the next legislative session."[11]

REPARATIONS OR WEALTH REDISTRIBUTION?

While the California Reparations Report focuses on cash payments to address the legacy of slavery, some reparations supporters apparently have a different goal in mind – redistribution of wealth.

- Reparations proponent Asm. Reggie Jones-Sawyer (D-Los Angeles) says the initial reparations legislative package introduced in 2024 will "have a significant impact on moving forward with closing the wealth gap."[12]
- State Sen. Steven Bradford, Gardena Democrat, perhaps the leading reparations proponent in California and a task force member, said "there's not enough money in the state's budget or in the national budget" to make slavery descendants whole.[13] He told *CalMatters* that "if he had to start somewhere, though, he would start with the wealth gap between average African-Americans and whites, pegged at around $370,000."[14]

"The biggest fight," San Diego County supervisor and commission task force member Monica Montgomery Steppe said at a commission hearing, "is implementation of all these recommendations."[15]

On this point, the vast majority of Californians have a clear message for reparations proponents – cash payments in excess of $1 million are a non-starter.

By a margin of 59-28, California voters oppose making cash reparations payments, according to a September 2023 UC Berkeley IGS poll.[16] Most of those opposed – 44 percent – said they were strongly opposed, as were Latino and Asian-American voters. Democrats were equally divided and just 35 percent of voters who call themselves "somewhat liberal" supported cash reparations.[17]

The current California reparations plan may be just the beginning.

> **"The initial down payment is the beginning of a process of addressing historical injustices; not the end of it."[18]**
> —California Task Force to Study and Develop Reparation Proposals for African Americans

In addition to the California plan, cities around the state and country have been forming their own reparations task forces to consider additional local payments on top of whatever the states authorize.

San Francisco established its own reparations advisory committee, recommending that African-American city residents who qualify receive a whopping lump sum of $5 million.[19] Among the more than 100 recommendations from the San Francisco committee are the elimination of credit-card debt, car and student loans, the ability to buy homes for $1, and guaranteed basic income of $97,000 per year for those eligible (adjusted for inflation).[20] An analysis of the plan by the Hoover Institution's Dr. Lee Ohanian estimates that it would cost non-black families an estimated $600,000 each.[21]

In the aftermath of the George Floyd incident, a group of mayors led by then-Los Angeles Mayor Eric Garcetti formed "Mayors Organized for Reparations and Equity" to push their own municipal reparations plans.[22] Additionally, another group of mayors, including Sacramento's Darrell Steinberg, are pushing for basic income payments, which they view as a form of reparations.

Meanwhile, California taxpayers are holding on to their wallets in anticipation of being stuck with a huge reparations bill.

CHAPTER 15
Home Sweet Home

When traveling to California, more and more Left Coast visitors are enjoying the comfort of renting a spare room – or even an entire house – for the length of their stay rather than paying for a hotel room for a short trip or buying a place for repeat visits.

Online marketplaces for short- and longer-term rentals such as Airbnb make booking a rental in California as easy as a click of a button.

Airbnb is another uniquely California company that began when two roommates in San Francisco came up with the idea of putting an air mattress in their living room and turning it into a bed and breakfast.[1]

Airbed & Breakfast, as it was initially known, put together a website targeting travelers who were unable to book a hotel room.[2] It created an industry revolution that grew to become a major international travel force, generating $9.9 billion in revenue in fiscal year 2023.[3]

Left Coast visitors coming to California would be advised to book their accommodations as far in advance as possible, as the state is facing a government-created housing crunch.

HARD TO COME BY FOR LEFT COAST VISITORS

Left Coast tourists are advised to bring their own shelter when traveling to California, given the state's ongoing housing crunch that shows little sign of abatement. Suggestions include packing a tent to pitch in one of the state's many beautiful beaches or parks, or driving an RV and staying at one of the nearly three dozen KOA Campgrounds in the state.[8]

California has had a housing shortage for about as far back as most people can remember. Hasn't it always been that way? Well, no. At one time homes were affordable in California even as the population grew. Building homes to keep up with the demand did not require miracles. Nothing ever stays the same, though.

"Beginning in about 1970," says the nonpartisan Legislative Analyst's Office, "the gap between California's home prices and those in the rest country started to widen."[4]

In the years from 1970 to 1980, California home prices soared from 30 percent "above U.S. levels to more than 80 percent higher," says the LAO, a trend that has not abated.[5] In April 2024, the median price for an existing single-family house reached $904,000 in California, an all-time high.[6] The U.S. median price for an existing single-family house in the same same month was less than half of that – $412,100.[7]

To afford a median-priced single-family home in Southern California requires a household income of nearly $201,000.[9] The coastal elites can easily afford it. Everyone else struggles, or lives in lesser housing.

So what happened in 1970 to set off the price explosion? The California Environmental Quality Act became law. It is the single greatest impediment to new home construction, adding more than $1 million to the cost of completing a housing development and causing unnecessary delays as government reviews are dragged out and cases are tied up in the courts. In some instances, entire projects have been shut down.[10]

There are other barriers, some of them related to CEQA, others simply hindrances in their own right. There are the NIMBYs, those who say "not in my backyard" to new housing – and often use CEQA as a legal bludgeon to ensure that nothing is built near their backyards. Rent control laws depress housing availability, while eviction moratoriums have similar effects.

THE CALIFORNIA ENVIRONMENTAL QUALITY ACT: AN OBSTACLE TO BUILDING NEW HOUSING

Passed as a means to protect the environment, CEQA has become a gauntlet that adds costs to, delays, and in some cases halts critical California projects. We're talking schools, infrastructure, homeless shelters – and housing.

"CEQA has been front-and-center in an emerging national conversation about the negative consequences of hyper-regulation and related threats of litigation and, especially, its regressive effects on low-income and minority communities," say Chris Carr, Navi Dhillon, and Lucas Grunbaum, who each rank among the state's top land use attorneys and who are the authors of the PRI study *The CEQA Gauntlet*.[11]

The law has grown faster than the Los Angeles phone book. It initially consisted of 13 separate code sections, but over the course of a little more than a half century, it has expanded to more than 190 code sections and 250 implementing regulations. It has 14 appendices.[12] The CEQA process has six steps: preliminary review, the initial study process, preparation of the CEQA document, the public review period, project approval, then litigation, in which anyone is allowed to file a lawsuit to stop whatever is being built.[13]

Litigants are mostly environmental groups that are opposed to progress and competitors that want to handcuff their rivals. Labor unions are also frequent petitioners as are "'bounty hunter' lawyers seeking quick cash settlements, even if they have no real client," says environmental lawyer Jennifer Hernandez.[14]

Consequently, housing affordability falls. In one particular "horror story," a planned 495-unit apartment complex in downtown San Francisco was scuttled. The development would have included 4,000 square feet of retail space and "a mixture of housing – 192 studios, 149 one-bedrooms, 96 two-bedrooms, and 50 three-bedrooms – 28 of which would be designated affordable, with another 45 affordable units to be built off-site."[15]

"The project appeared to be the perfect fit for a city in the midst of a severe housing shortage and affordability crisis," say *The CEQA Gauntlet* authors.[16]

Yet it was rejected.

The authors suggest remedies that would take some of the sting out of the law:

- Streamlining the CEQA review process to reduce time and unnecessary costs.
- Adopting reforms to the CEQA litigation process to preserve meritorious suits, crack down on frivolous or unnecessary actions, and improve efficiency.
- Increasing public transparency requirements so we know who is paying for CEQA lawsuits.[17]

Or lawmakers could just repeal CEQA and start anew with legislation that both protects the environment and allows developers to build the homes that they are no doubt itching to build, given the demand. The two goals are not mutually exclusive.

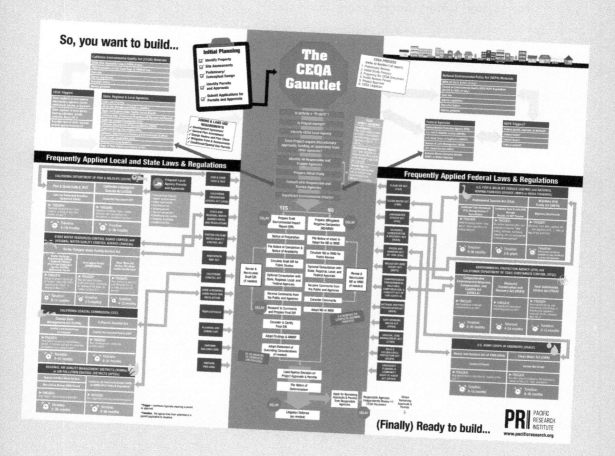

NIMBYISM — NO NEW HOUSING IN MY BACKYARD

It's quite clear that some people don't like growth and will do whatever they are able to stop it. The "not in my backyard" approach "provides an easy litigation path to almost anyone who wants to block a development project," says Loren Kaye in the Hoover Institution quarterly *Eureka*.[18]

The Legislative Analyst's Office says NIMBYs employ not only CEQA but local land-use policies to bar construction. This "opposition to new housing appears to be heightened on the California coast" — where the elites are thick. Their hesitancy toward "new housing can lead residents to pressure local officials to use their land-use authority to slow or block new development or may result in residents directly intervening in land use decisions via the initiative and referendum process. Compared with the rest of the country, these types of activities appear to occur more often in California's coastal communities, suggesting that community opposition to housing is heightened in these areas."[19]

NIMBYs are active in inland California, as well. Communities all over "have successfully prevented countless new development projects."[20] Much of the NIMBY opposition is directed at infill housing, and while that doesn't affect the state's housing stock, inland NIMBYs still target new development, and that is an impediment to critically needed increases in the housing supply.[21]

Related to the NIMBYs are the BANANAs, who stand on the canon of "building absolutely nothing anywhere near anyone" (or "anything"). They fight their battles with news releases, op-eds, letters to the editor, town hall meetings and social media posts. They solicit elected officials' support, testify at public hearings, call in to radio talk shows and hold petition drives.[22] They are also more extreme than their NIMBY cousins.[23]

RENT CONTROL – WHEN GOVERNMENTS PLACE CEILINGS ON PRICES, SHORTAGES RESULT

It's become a bit cliche to quote Swede Assar Lindbeck when discussing rent control. But the socialist economist's observation – "rent control appears to be the most efficient technique presently known to destroy a city – except for bombing" – nevertheless resonates, no matter how many times it's repeated.[24]

Rent control laws have a direct effect on housing. When governments place ceilings on prices, shortages result. This is just as true with housing as it is with widgets. The incentive to produce more is deadened by the artificial limits. What rational developer would build rental units if those units could not be leased at market value? That's no way to increase the housing stock.

It's no way to help renters, either. Landlords who own rent-controlled property are often better off selling their units, which can then be converted to other uses, or leaving their units unoccupied. One study showed that in San Francisco, rent control policies were responsible for a 15 percent reduction in the rental housing supply, and a 5.1 percent increase in rent costs city-wide.[25]

It has happened there before. "Following a 1994 rent-control expansion in San Francisco," according to Cato Institute scholars. "Research found that landlords converted rental properties to owner-occupied apartments and condos better suited to higher-income families to avoid being subject to the regulation."[26]

A decade of strict rent control in Berkeley, from 1980 to 1990, reduced rental units by about 3,300, a decline of almost 12 percent.[27]

STAYING BEHIND

"When Berkeley officials first voted in rent controls in the late 1970s, a large number of University of California-Berkeley students simply stayed in their apartments long after graduation, creating a massive shortage of housing for new students, who then had to look for housing in nearby cities like Oakland."[28]
—William Anderson

Rent control can also ruin a neighborhood one property at a time. Again, incentives and disincentives are at work. If landlords are by law unable to make a profit, their willingness, as well as their financial abilities, to make improvements and even basic repairs is diminished.

NOT FOR RENT

RESIDENTIAL SOLAR MANDATE – ADDING TO THE NATION'S HIGHEST HOME COSTS

The rule in California since January 2020 has been that all new single-family homes and multifamily housing from one to three stories must have solar power. Cost estimates vary. But one online resource reckons the mandate adds about $9,500 to the construction cost of a new home.[29]

When the rule came out, Meritage Homes, which builds in California and elsewhere, figured that forcing contractors to outfit new single-family homes with rooftop solar panels was going to increase the cost of each unit by $14,000 to $16,000.[30] Greenlancer, "founded to accelerate the adoption of renewable energy," is of course more optimistic, suggesting the added cost will be more like $8,400.[31]

Whatever the cost, most likely to be heavy, says PRI's Wayne Winegarden, the mandate will have little impact on greenhouse gas emissions and will worsen "the homelessness crisis by making it more difficult for the current homeless to obtain an affordable place to live."[32]

Though the mandate is relatively new, landfills are already stacking up used rooftop solar panels, and it seems that this caught policymakers by surprise. In July 2022, the *Los Angeles Times* reported the state "had no comprehensive plan to dispose of them," which is a grave oversight.[33]

Solar panels are made from "components that contain toxic heavy metals such as selenium and cadmium can contaminate groundwater,"[34] said the *Times*. Those metals happen to be "a potent source of hazardous waste," which means "that eco-virtue mightn't necessarily be its own reward," say the Hazardous Waste Experts.[35]

According to Environmental Progress, a Bay Area organization founded by author Michael Shellenberger, "solar panels create 300 times more toxic waste per unit of energy than do nuclear power plants."[36]

A solar panel "recycling industry is taking shape," writes the Associated Press, as a "tsunami" of solar waste piles up.[37] Even so, nine out of 10 retired panels are still ending up in "landfills or sitting in storage, waiting for better solutions to become available," says the Bay Area News Group, and it's not clear if the process can be "scaled up for the flood of panels to come."[38] By 2030, that "flood" could reach 1 million tons a year.[39]

EVICTION MORATORIUMS
THE RETURN OF "SQUATTER'S RIGHTS"?

Is California a delinquent tenant's paradise?[40] Seems so.

Los Angeles changed its municipal code in March 2023 to give tenants "permanent protections against eviction and burdensome rent increases." At roughly the same time, Los Angeles County extended its eviction moratorium, from the originally scheduled date of Jan. 31 to the end of March.[41]

Both COVID-related "protections" have expired. (It took the city until Feb. 1, 2024, to tell renters that they "must pay their full current monthly rent to avoid eviction for non-payment of rent.)[42] San Francisco's has expired, as well, on Aug. 29, 2023.[43] The statewide moratorium was over by the middle of 2022.[44]

But that doesn't mean that the policies won't return. In fact, the San Diego County Board of Supervisors held a meeting in January 2024, in which "special prohibitions against eviction and rent increases in 11 urban ZIP codes" where a recent flash flood had done the most damage were approved, the *San Diego Union-Tribune* reported. "Termed an 'urgency ordinance,'" it prohibited "residential evictions without just cause."[45]

The effects of eviction moratoriums are not unlike those of rent control. The incentive to build is quashed, and landlords have plenty of reason to take their properties off the rental market.

GIVING UP

" Landlords and developers are not happy that tenant protections are in fashion. Two surveys of landlords, from Harvard University and the University of California, Berkeley, suggest that financial hardship during the pandemic has led landlords to consider leaving the rental market altogether, potentially limiting the supply of units and pushing up rents further."[46]

—*The Economist*

If they do keep their properties, their reasons to maintain and repair them disappear. And landlords could be in trouble themselves. If they're not getting paid, some won't be able to pay their mortgages.

CHAPTER 16
Gimme Shelter: Homelessness in California

Once a haven of endless possibilities, California has become a land where, for many, living is little more than a matter of survival. Even more so for the nearly 200,000 homeless people who inhabit the state.

The homeless aren't Boy Scouts and Girl Scouts who have learned how to survive in difficult conditions, when there's no roof overhead or walls to keep out the elements, the predators and the pests (though almost 12,000 are veterans.[1]) They are the mentally ill (about two-thirds) and the addicted (again, about two-thirds)[2], which means many are suffering from both maladies. They are also disabled, or are otherwise in poor health. A few have lost their jobs and fallen on the hardest of times. Some of the homeless live in their vehicles, others in shelters, more than a few sleep on buses and trains. Far too many spend their nights and days on the sidewalks and other public spaces.

Nearly two-thirds are temporarily homeless but 36 percent are chronically homeless.[3]

Whatever the breakdown is at any given time, the painful fact is there are too many homeless persons in California. At last count, taken in January 2023, there were, officially, 181,399 unhoused Californians[4], which is likely a low-ball figure. "Experts agree the real number is higher than the count," says *CalMatters*.[5]

Even using the lower count means that 28 percent of the entire country's homeless population is found in California,[6] which after its "population drain"—its "hemorrhaging (of) residents to neighboring states like Texas, Arizona, and Nevada"—has only 11.7 percent of the overall domestic population.[7] Given that the 2023 count was, according to *CalMatters*, "up nearly 40% from five years ago,"[8] there's a transformation taking place in which the homeless are becoming a larger and larger portion of the state's total residents.

California also has the highest percentage (49 percent nationally) and highest overall number (123,423) of unsheltered homeless. The big cities are performing miserably. In San Jose, 75 percent of the homeless are unsheltered, in Los Angeles, the portion is 73 percent. Oakland (73 percent), Long Beach (72 percent) and Sacramento (72 percent) are all over 70 percent.[9]

Officials have tried. But they've rarely enacted or even discussed policies that work. They've spent tens of billions and will continue to spend but the problem just grows worse.

CALIFORNIA HAS THE HIGHEST PERCENTAGE (49 PERCENT NATIONALLY) AND HIGHEST OVERALL NUMBER (123,423) OF UNSHELTERED HOMELESS.

LEFT COAST VISITOR ALERT —
WATCH WHERE YOU STEP IN SAN FRANCISCO

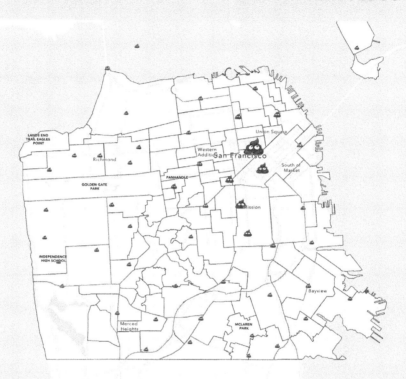

Left Coast visitors to San Francisco must remember to look down when walking down virtually any street in the city. There are thousands and thousands of incidents of human waste found on city sidewalks reported every year. Open the Books documented 270,000 incidents of human feces reported to city officials for cleanup between 2011 and 2023.[10] Florida Gov. Ron DeSantis even held up the map during his November 2023 debate with Gov. Gavin Newsom. As the map shows, you are not spared the problem in any part of the city.

HOUSING FIRST, RESULTS LAST

The California attitude, and official course of action, toward homelessness is "housing first." The California Department of Housing and Community Development describes it as a means "to serving people experiencing homelessness that recognizes a homeless person must first be able to access a decent, safe place to live, that does not limit length of stay (permanent housing), before stabilizing, improving health, reducing harmful behaviors, or increasing income."[11]

Housing first is a rigid, one-size-fits-all policy that is not open to the innovation that's needed to resolve homelessness. As a theory, housing first sounds reasonable. In reality, it is "housing and nothing else," since the mental illness and addiction that have forced many onto the streets and keeps them there are not addressed as they should be.

PRI's Emily Humpal has explained that even though "government policy and programs are largely focused on money, resources and more shelter," recipients of the "assistance usually end up back on the street or recycled through these programs numerous times." The revolving door doesn't continue to spin due to "a lack of programs, resources or housing, but the trauma or mental health conditions of those who experience homelessness from their past before they moved to the streets."[12]

The story is much the same with the addicted.

PROJECT ROOMKEY/HOMEKEY: DOING THE SAME THING OVER AND OVER AND EXPECTING A DIFFERENT RESULT

Officials' fixation on housing first was especially visible in April 2020, when Gov. Gavin Newsom announced the launch of Project Roomkey to help the homeless during the COVID-19 pandemic. Citing a public health emergency, the state vowed to place as many as 15,000 homeless individuals in hotels and motels that had been abandoned due to lockdown orders.[13]

Roomkey eventually became Project Homekey later in 2020. It was created by Assembly Bill 83, which directed state and federal emergency funds to be used to buy hotels and motels, renovate them, and "convert them into permanent, long-term housing for people experiencing homelessness."[14]

The programs never lived up to the promises made by officials. The homeless population grew by 20,000 over the three years since the programs were kicked off, from 161,548 in January 2020[15] to the present 181,399.

WHAT CAN OTHER STATES DO TO AVOID BECOMING THE NEXT CALIFORNIA

Instead of emulating California by throwing billions at ineffective government programs such as the Project Homekey strategy, other states would be wise to learn from California's mistakes and:

- Focus on programs that directly address addiction and mental health treatment;
- Better leverage public resources to connect homeless with resources and private nonprofits;
- Eliminate encampments by directing the homeless to public and private organizations offering temporary housing, rather than expensive permanent housing;
- Enforce laws against retail theft to discourage funding sources that fuel destructive habits and more homelessness; and
- Reform zoning laws and other impediments to increase housing supply and affordability.

Here are some additional relevant facts:

- An investigation by the *San Francisco Chronicle* found the city "spends millions of dollars to shelter its most vulnerable residents in dilapidated hotels," and "with little oversight or support, the results are disastrous."[16]
- Newsom said in his 2022 State of the State speech that Homekey had moved 58,000 people off the streets. However, federal data shows the number of sheltered homeless grew by 3,541 in 2021.[17]
- The so-called affordable housing projects built with Project Homekey funds cost upward of $1 million per unit.[18]
- The nonpartisan California State Auditor's office found in a 2024 statewide audit that the state agency tasked with overseeing homelessness programs has analyzed no homeless spending past 2021, and the cities of San Jose and San Diego failed to account for their spending, and measure in any meaningful way whether their programs are effective.[19]

WHY CALIFORNIA?

We've seen deniers say that California is a magnet for the homeless because of its climate. Whoever has said that never understood that when Mark Twain (according to legend) said the coldest winter he ever spent was a summer in San Francisco he was exaggerating only a bit. Nor have they noticed the homeless numbers in Florida.

The facts say that California has been a sanctuary state for the homeless.

> To be homeless in San Diego is actually not that hard, because usually we're low income, and when you're low income you get free phones, free food, free clothing. I think we're spoiled, the homeless and the underprivileged, I think we're spoiled to be honest with you. My sister is like 'where do I sign up?'"[20]
> —Mary, San Diego homeless woman

"We have moved as a city from a position of compassion to enabling (unacceptable) street behavior, and as mayor I don't stand for that," said Mark Farrell when he was San Francisco mayor.[21]

Farrell made those remarks in 2018 a few months before voters passed Proposition C, which imposes a tax on businesses in the city and county to raise as much as $300 million a year to "help homeless people secure permanent housing," for "construction, rehabilitation, acquisition, and operation of permanent housing with supportive services," and for "programs serving people who have recently become homeless or are at risk of becoming homeless."[22]

We said at the time "that, rather than reducing the number of homeless in San Francisco and helping those who remain on the streets, what is being called the biggest tax hike in city history will only increase their numbers and do little to nothing to improve their plight."[23]

While there was some improvement, with numbers falling from 2019 to 2022[24], there has been a reversal. The city counted 8,328 unhoused in 2023[25], more than in 2017, the year before Proposition C, and 2019, the year after. This happened even "after a jump in funding from $284 million in the 2018-19 fiscal year to $676 million in 2022-23," says the *San Francisco Chronicle*.[26]

In the wake of the June 2024 *Grants Pass* decision by the U.S. Supreme Court removing key legal hurdles, state and local officials have finally begun to crack down on outdoor camping.

CALIFORNIA'S POLICIES ARE FAILING WITH RESPECT TO ALL THE RISK FACTORS

The policy environment creates economic obstacles that push people into homelessness and make it much more difficult for homeless people to find stable housing. Policies also misalign incentives, which inadvertently promote more unsheltered homeless. The same policies incentivizing homelessness also limit the state's ability to sustainably address the crisis.[27]

Newsom was criticized by an investigative reporter for pledging "to house and feed the world's homeless population" while he was making "a whirlwind 'Comeback California' tour" designed "to stave off" the September 2021 "recall by angry voters."[28]

The state's Housing First blueprint is another troublesome policy. It's hard to turn down a free bed. This makes Los Angeles – all of California, really – "a magnet for the indigent from across America, from sea to sea," says Edward Ring of the California Policy Center.[29]

HOMEOWNERS INSURANCE CRISIS — MAKING IT HARDER, MORE EXPENSIVE TO BUILD AFFORDABLE HOUSING

California's home insurance market is deeply troubled. A former insurance commissioner said it's "in chaos."[30] Insurance Commissioner Ricardo Lara calls it "a real crisis."[31] Using more colorful language, the president of a Los Angeles agency told *The San Francisco Standard* that "if there's a major event" before the market is fixed, "we are in deep doo-doo."[32]

While it's more likely that the crisis will simply accelerate the exodus of people from California and discourage homebuilding, it's not out of the question that it will increase homelessness as it pushes the cost of owning a home to new heights.

Jim Vargas, president and chief executive of Father Joe's Villages, a homeless services charity in San Diego, told the *New York Times* that the organization's rising property insurance premiums could "derail not only our plans as a homeless services provider and developer from constructing additional buildings, but it could derail, frankly, the plans for housing in general to be developed in this state."[33]

The muddle that had grown over time became even messier when State Farm announced in March 2024 that beginning in a little more than three months, the company would, on a "rolling basis," decline to renew "approximately 30,000 homeowners, rental dwelling, and other property insurance policies." It would also "withdraw from offering commercial apartment policies with the non-renewal of all of those approximately 42,000 policies."[34]

Those fortunate enough to keep their State Farm policies were hit with 20 percent rate increases.[35]

The company has policyholders in all 50 states, but it's California that seems to be dominating its business decisions. Almost a year earlier, citing "historic increases in construction costs outpacing inflation, rapidly growing catastrophe exposure, and a challenging reinsurance market," State Farm said that it was done with offering new policies to "all business and personal lines property and casualty insurance" in the state.[36]

Allstate has also said it was quitting. "New homeowners, condo and commercial insurance policies" are on pause as "the cost to insure new home customers in California is far higher than the price they would pay for policies due to wildfires, higher costs for repairing homes, and higher reinsurance premiums."[37]

Farmers Insurance has soured on California, as well, with affiliates dropping 100,000 customers[38] across the state, including those who insured their autos through the company.

Over the longer term, seven of the top 12 insurance companies that had been doing business in California "have either stopped writing new policies or restricted them," *E&E News* reported.[39]

And it's not just California's problem anymore. The "deep doo-doo" seeped onto the Nevada side of Lake Tahoe, where, reports the *San Francisco Chronicle*, "increasing numbers of homeowners are facing insurance nonrenewals and soaring premiums — and few if any insurers willing to write new policies."[40]

The companies cite the risks associated with wildfires (which California has done little to prevent) and steep rebuilding costs. Further complicating matters is the state government's control over the market. The meddling makes it difficult for insurers to raise their rates to offset their exposure. For years, insurers that "do business in California have been forced to sell insurance at below-market rates, guaranteeing they will lose money," says Jerry Theodorou of the R Street Institute.[41]

Policymakers, who never sit idle in California — though the state would be better off if they were less energetic — are scrambling for solutions. Lara has introduced a "Sustainable Insurance Strategy,"[42] which the *Los Angeles Times* characterizes as "the biggest overhaul of industry regulations" since 1988's Proposition 103 "gave an elected insurance commissioner the authority to review and reject requests for rate hikes by insurers."[43]

Under this plan, carriers could pass on to their policyholders the cost of the reinsurance they buy to protect themselves. They could also "use computer models that project future claims risks" when they request rate hikes rather than rely on the historical data they've been tied to.

Another effort would tighten the timeline of the Insurance Department's review process in response "to insurer rate-review requests."[44]

Meanwhile, insurers flee the state, and with each loss, competition, which pressures prices downward, fades. Will the market ever reach the point to where there is *no market* and the insurer of last resort, the government-created, "already overstressed,"[45] "barebones coverage"[46] Fair Access to Insurance Requirements Plan, is the sole option?

If so, that would be a catastrophe in itself.

CONCLUSION
Stopping the Great Escape

Survival oftentimes requires escape. We've been seeing this in California for some time, with businesses fleeing steep taxes, smothering regulation and the dizzying price of real estate. Residents are fed up with their own tax burdens, the high cost of living, the deterioration of once-golden opportunity and a number of other stresses that have driven low the quality of life.

The great business exodus from California has been ongoing for more than a decade. Thousands of companies have relocated their headquarters elsewhere or simply left the state entirely. From 2008 through 2016, as many as 13,000 fled.[1]

"The hostility that California legislators — and their colleagues in regulatory agencies — show toward business enterprises is hardly imaginary," says relocation specialist Joseph Vranich. When he made that statement, more than five years before this book was published, he also said that for roughly "40 years California has been viewed as a state in which it is difficult to do business."[2]

Companies that leave save 20 percent to 35 percent a year in operating costs, according to Vranich.[3] What owner or business executive wouldn't choose that option?

EXIT SURVEY –
WHAT COMPANIES THAT LEFT CALIFORNIA ARE
SAYING ABOUT THEIR RELOCATIONS

A PRI survey of 200 technology, manufacturing, clean tech, and energy industry executives in regard to the state's business climate produced some interesting, telling and not terribly surprising comments. One said the state "is a tough spot because of all the regulations and red tape. There are so many fees associated with having a business in California for which we didn't get anything in return."[4]

Another said, "every single thing you can imagine" made California unattractive for business expansion or location – "the red tape and bureaucracy."[5]

Yet another suggested that "less legislation that is negative to business owners, less environmental restriction" would help attract business, and recommended that California "convert to a right-to-work state."[6]

Residents have been escaping for about as long as businesses have been, but the losses didn't get a great deal of attention until much later, not until the losses became a net negative. It happened in 2020, when, for the first time in its history, going all the way back to its 1850 admission into the union, California lost more people than it gained. It happened again in 2021. And in 2022.

There was a reversal in 2023, due to "a rebound in legal immigration and drop in COVID-19 deaths (which) fueled the increase of 67,000, or 0.2 percent," according to *Politico*. Even so, "California still lost more residents to other states than it gained from them — as has been the case for two decades."[7]

The shrinking population led to the state losing a seat in Congress – also an all-time first.

It was no coincidence that the losses began during the first year of the pandemic. California was one of the most locked-down states in the country and people raced for states where liberty still meant something.

Our own research during the first year of the pandemic found that people were fleeing the many harmful policy choices that have increased economic and quality-of-life concerns. So many Californians of every age group and income level had no choice but to pursue job opportunities across the state line.[8]

BUSINESS FLIGHT

Equity fund manager Grant Cardone left California in 2012 when the top state income tax rate was increased from 10 percent to 13.3 percent.[9]

"After living there 25 years, we sold our home and real estate holdings and looked for a friendlier business environment," Cardone wrote in an X post.[10]

Cardone had owned multiple businesses in California. With the move, he and his wife invested their tax savings in a consulting business in their new home state of Florida. That business "has grown from six employees to 1,000, revenue increased from $10 million to $650 million," says financial news outlet Benzinga, and it occupies "about 500,000 square feet of office space valued at $5 billion that generates $75 million in property taxes every year."[11]

Cardone estimates that California has lost $1 billion in tax revenue it would have brought in had he not left.[12] He writes:

> My story demonstrates how lower state taxes and favorable economic policies can stimulate business growth, boost employment and contribute significantly to the local and national economy. Advocating for more competitive tax policies and tax intelligence can lead to similar success stories, benefiting businesses, communities and the national economy alike.[13]

The top income tax rate is now 14.4 percent[14] (and the rate for the middle class is 10.4 percent, up from 9.3 percent[15]), even less hospitable to entrepreneurs and company executives than it was when Cardone left.

TAX

A WHO'S WHO OF WHO'S LEAVING

Prominent companies that have left California or moved their headquarters or in some way made a significant divestment from the state include: Toyota Motors North America, Carl's Jr., Jacobs Engineering Group, Nissan North America, Nestle, Jamba Juice and Occidental Petroleum.[16] Hewlett-Packard, whose founding is recognized as the birth of Silicon Valley; Tesla; SpaceX; Charles Schwab, which was started in San Francisco more than a half century ago; and Oracle are also among the many high-profile companies that have found more welcoming conditions elsewhere.[17]

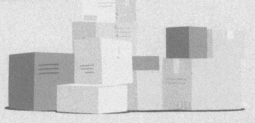

With its 2024 ranking, *Chief Executive* magazine named California the worst state in which to do business.[18] This has become a tradition. It was the 19th straight year that the state was at the bottom of the magazine's rankings, which are based on a survey of more than 650 CEOs.

After more than a decade of merely observing and recording his findings, in 2019, Vranich, for the first time, began actively recommending companies leave the state. He also started telling "companies thinking of moving to California" to "consider doing a U-turn" and reboot in "business-friendly states."[19] And he himself took his own advice, moving to Pennsylvania in 2018.[20]

In a 2022 follow-up to his first report, Vranich, working with UCLA economics professor and Hoover Institution senior fellow Lee Ohanian, found "that an additional "352 companies moved their headquarters to other states just in the period from January 1, 2018, through December 31, 2021."[21]

In the second year of the pandemic, the churn was particularly acute.

"Every month in 2021, twice as many companies relocated their head-quarters as in the prior year," said Vranich and Ohanian. "The monthly average for 2021 also significantly exceeds the monthly averages for 2018 and 2019. California lost both very large companies, including eleven Fortune 1,000 companies between 2018-21, and small, rapidly growing companies with the potential to become transformational. From this perspective, California is not only losing current leading businesses, but potential future leading businesses as well."[22]

The authors admit their numbers could have been a bit off. But not in a way that would favor California. They believe their count "is almost certainly biased downward significantly because relatively small business relocations are difficult to detect."[23]

> **California's Regulatory Environment is the most costly, complex, and uncertain in the nation. No other state comes close to California on these dimensions."[24]**
> —California Business Roundtable

The top five states for relocation by former California businesses—Texas, Tennessee, Nevada, Florida and Arizona—all have lower tax and regulatory burdens.[25]

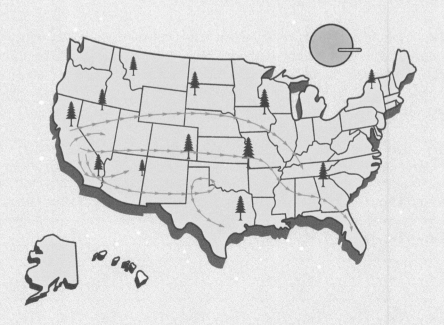

RESIDENTIAL MIGRATION

Of those five, only Arizona has a state income tax.[26] While it is the no. 2 destination for fleeing California residents, three of the top five, Texas, Florida and Nevada, don't tax their residents' incomes.[27]

While shedding the weight of a state income tax improves family and personal finances, it's not the sole reason to leave California. People ditch the state because they can better afford to live elsewhere.

The "California premium" is the price paid for living in a state in which public policy drives up the cost of living. PRI research indicates that, when compared to the rest of the U.S., median income households in California earn 13.7 percent more than the rest of the country. However, when state and local taxes and mortgage costs are factored in, California's income premium turns into a 19.6 percent net income deficit.[28]

But this is only part of the story. The California premium is further elevated by extreme costs for energy, groceries, gasoline, and health care, none of which were added to PRI's calculations.[29]

The state's increasingly detrimental policy environment creates numerous obstacles that reduce people's quality of life and inhibits their ability to prosper, which they can overcome by relocating. Reversing these trends requires a policy overhaul. The quicker we start, the sooner we can reinvigorate the California dream.[30]

The refugees racing away from the state cut across the demographic board. The only age group that has consistently migrated into California is the under-26 cohort. Those 35 and older consistently migrated away between 2012 and 2018, that final year arriving just before the state began to lose more residents than it gained.[31]

The flight was also found across all income groups. Low- and lower-middle-income taxpayers were the largest group, suggesting a sensitivity to higher costs of living and declining economic opportunity. But the well-off have left, as well, with upper- and upper-middle income earners' exit causing an unprecedented amount of income and tax revenue to leave the state.[32]

CALIFORNIA'S MOST COMPETITIVE INDUSTRY — MOVING VANS

Many of the 39 million who remain are jealous of those who have gotten away. A 2023 poll found that "swaths of residents are," according to the *Los Angeles Times*, "considering packing up and leaving. Many also believe that the state is headed in the wrong direction, and are anxious about the direction of the economy and their ability to pay their bills. ... More than 40 percent of residents say they're contemplating moving out of California, with nearly half of them saying they're considering that 'very seriously.'"[33]

The precipitous decline in people's overall quality of life is another factor that has been at work. California has some of the worst traffic in the country, yet it has put drivers on a road diet, which only makes conditions worse.[34]

Meanwhile, rising crime rates are making Californians feel less safe.[35]

Then there is the homelessness problem afflicting California that has reached crisis levels. The state continually throws billions of dollars annually at the problem, relying on an expensive yet ineffective "Housing First" approach.

When the cumulative reality of all these problems set in, living in California for many has become simply unsustainable. The best way for many to survive is to escape.

California has been called the de-facto think tank of the Biden-Harris administration by the *Los Angeles Times* for good reason.[36] The destructive laws, regulations and programs that we've shared in this book are spreading like one of the state's policy-fueled wildfires to Congress, other state capitols and city halls across the country.

That's why Kamala Harris is not exaggerating when she boasted in a speech in Sacramento to Democratic state legislators in January 2024, "I (say), maybe with a bit of bravado . . . what I think we all say: So goes California, goes the nation."[37]

Upon finishing this guide, readers might naturally ask, "How can free market ideas better address these policy challenges?" There's simply not enough room in these pages to produce a detailed free market policy agenda for countering progressive ambitions when they come to your community. However, by visiting leftcoastsurvivorsguide.com, you'll find a rich storehouse of facts, figures and analysis on all of the issues discussed here.

PRI scholars have produced dozens of detailed, proven market-based policy solutions on topics ranging from energy to health care. These are actionable proposals that you can replicate in your community and have the potential to garner bipartisan support and forge non-traditional coalitions around free-market ideas. By regularly reading PRI's daily "Right by the Bay" blog and listening to the weekly "Next Round" podcast, you can stay up to date with the newest Left Coast ideologies that will surely come after this book's publication.

It is our hope that readers in and out of the state will learn from California's mistakes and ferociously ring the alarm bells whenever and wherever poor public policies are proposed. It was our goal to compile the facts and provide the analysis that will give readers the intellectual arsenal they need when their community leaders want to make the "California turn." That way they won't have to later say, "we've been there, done that, and it didn't work!"

ENDNOTES

FOREWORD

1   Seybold, Matt. "The Apocryphal Twain: 'America Is Built on a Tilt and Everything Loose Slides to California.' (plus Things Mark Twain Really Said about California!)." Center for Mark Twain Studies, April 5, 2021. https://marktwainstudies.com/the-apocryphal-twain-america-is-built-on-a-tilt-and-everything-loose-slides-to-california-plus-things-mark-twain-really-said-about-california/.

2   Library, California State. "Arnold Schwarzenegger." Governors of California - Arnold Schwarzenegger. First Inaugural Address. Accessed June 21, 2024. https://governors.library.ca.gov/addresses/38-schwarzenegger01.html.

3   Ibid.

4   Beam, Adam. "California's Population Grew in 2023, Halting 3 Years of Decline, State Estimates." Associated Press, April 30, 2024. https://apnews.com/article/california-population-growth-pandemic-decline-0d2bfc2c0a4ced0c3c2ad934207818bc.

5   Harris, Kamala. "Remarks by Vice President Harris at the California State Legislature Democratic Caucus Reception," January 25, 2024. https://www.whitehouse.gov/briefing-room/speeches-remarks/2024/01/25/remarks-by-vice-president-harris-at-the-california-state-legislature-democratic-caucus-reception-sacramento-ca/

6   Halper, Evan. "Make America California Again? That's Biden's Plan." *Los Angeles Times*, January 17, 2021. https://www.latimes.com/politics/story/2021-01-17/make-america-california-again-how-biden-will-try.

7   Dewey, Caitlin. "States and Cities Eye Stronger Protections for Gig Economy Workers." *Stateline*, September 19, 2023. https://stateline.org/2023/09/19/states-and-cities-eye-stronger-protections-for-gig-economy-workers/ and Kingston, John. "15 States Jump into California's Ongoing AB5 Legal Battle ." Freight Waves, May 11, 2023. https://www.freightwaves.com/news/fifteen-states-jump-into-californias-ongoing-ab5-legal-battle.

8   Wiessner, Daniel. "Biden Administration Issues Rule That Could Curb 'gig' Work, Contracting." Reuters, January 9, 2024. https://www.reuters.com/world/us/biden-administration-issues-rule-that-could-curb-gig-work-contracting-2024-01-09/.

CHAPTER 1

1   Lofstrom, Magnus. "Testimony: Crime Data on Retail Theft and Robberies in California ." Public Policy Institute of California, January 4, 2024. https://www.ppic.org/blog/testimony-crime-data-on-retail-theft-and-robberies-in-california/.

2   Ibid.

3   Herlihy, Brianna. "California Crime Reform Gets 'unheard of' Support from Das, Small Businesses, Progressive Mayors." Fox News, April 28, 2024. https://www.foxnews.com/politics/california-crime-reform-gets-unheard-support-das-small-businesses-progressive-mayors.

4   Knopf, Keith. "Challenges and Opportunities of Doing Business in California." *Pacific Research Institute 2023 California Ideas in Action Conference*. Speech presented at the Pacific Research Institute 2023 California Ideas in Action Conference, February 15, 2023. https://www.youtube.com/watch?v=rCA7kROKbbk.

5   Smith, Steven. Issue brief. *Paradise Lost: Crime in the Golden State 2011-2021*. Pacific Research Institute, February 2023. https://www.pacificresearch.org/wp-content/uploads/2023/02/ParadiseLost_CrimeStudy2022_Final_Web.pdf.

6   Lofstrom, Magnus, and Brandon Martin. Issue brief. *Crime Trends in California* . Public Policy Institute of California, October 2023. https://www.ppic.org/publication/crime-trends-in-california/.

7   California Department of Justice, California Justice Information Services Division, Justice Data and Investigative Services Bureau, Criminal Justice Statistics Center, Crime in California 2023 § (2024). https://data-openjustice.doj.ca.gov/sites/default/files/2024-07/Crime%20In%20CA%202023f.pdf.

8   "25 Most Dangerous Places in the U.S. in 2023-2024." U.S. News and World Report, May 16, 2023. https://realestate.usnews.com/places/rankings/most-dangerous-places.

9   Smith, Steven. "Why Is California Experiencing More Crime Victimization?" *Right by the Bay*, Pacific Research Institute, May 16, 2023. https://www.pacificresearch.org/why-is-california-experiencing-more-crime-victimization/

10 Judicial Council of California Justice Services Staff, and Judge (Ret.) Richard Couzens. Prop. 47 Frequently Asked Questions, November 2016. https://www.courts.ca.gov/documents/Prop47FAQs.pdf.

11 Tyko, Kelly, and Nathan Bomey. "Target Closing 9 Stores Due to 'Theft and Organized Retail Crime.'" *Axios*, September 26, 2023. https://www.axios.com/2023/09/26/target-stores-closing-list-2023-theft-crime.

12 Barmann, Jay. "CVS Now Closing Lower Haight Store; Nearly Half of SF's CVS Stores Disappear." *SFist*, December 6, 2023. https://sfist.com/2023/12/06/cvs-now-closing-lower-haight-store-nearly-half-of-sfs-cvs-stores-disappear/.

13 Smith, Steven. Issue brief. *Paradise Lost: Crime in the Golden State 2011-2021*. Pacific Research Institute, February 2023. https://www.pacificresearch.org/wp-content/uploads/2023/02/ParadiseLost_CrimeStudy2022_Final_Web.pdf.

14   Winton, Richard, and Christopher Goffard. "A New Breed of Brazen Takeover Robbers Hitting California Luxury Retailers, Raising Ire." *Los Angeles Times*, November 23, 2021. https://www.latimes.com/california/story/2021-11-23/the-new-breed-of-takeover-robbers-hitting-luxury-retailers.

15   Smith, Steven. "Criminals Respond to Incentives Just as Consumers Do." *Right by the Bay*, Pacific Research Institute, December 1, 2021. https://www.pacificresearch.org/criminals-respond-to-incentives-just-as-consumers-do/.

16   Ibid.

17   Smith, Steven. Issue brief. *Paradise Lost: Crime in the Golden State 2011-2021*. Pacific Research Institute, February 2023. https://www.pacificresearch.org/wp-content/uploads/2023/02/ParadiseLost_CrimeStudy2022_Final_Web.pdf.

18   Ibid.

19   Smith, Steven. "Why Is In-N-Out Closing in Oakland? Out of Control Crime in the 'Crime Triangle.'" *Right by the Bay* (blog). Pacific Research Institute, January 23, 2024. https://www.pacificresearch.org/why-is-in-n-out-closing-in-oakland-out-of-control-crime-in-the-crime-triangle/.

20   Valinsky, Jordan. "In-N-Out Has Never Closed a Location, until Now. It Cites Crime as the Problem ." *CNN.Com*, January 24, 2024. https://www.cnn.com/2024/01/23/food/in-n-out-oakland-closure-crime/index.html.

21   Jackson, Kerry. *Living in Fear in California: How Well-Meaning Policy Mistakes Are Undermining Safe Communities and What Can Be Done to Restore Public Safety*. San Francisco, CA: Pacific Research Institute, 2019, 66.

22   California Department of Corrections and Rehabilitation Board of Parole Hearings, "Calendar Year 2021 Suitability Results," Accessed December 19, 2022, https://www.cdcr.ca.gov/bph/2021/03/15/calendar-year-2021-suitability-results/; California Department of Corrections and Rehabilitation Board of Parole Hearings, "Calendar Year 2020 Suitability Results," Accessed December 19, 2022, https://www.cdcr.ca.gov/bph/2020/03/04/cy-2020-suitability-results/; California Department of Corrections and Rehabilitation Board of Parole Hearings, "Calendar Year 2019 Suitability Results," Accessed December 19, 2022, https://www.cdcr.ca.gov/bph/2019/10/24/cy-2019-suitability-results/; California Department of Corrections and Rehabilitation, "Overview of Parole Hearings and Statistics," February 2020, https://www.cdcr.ca.gov/bph/wp-content/uploads/sites/161/2020/08/Parole-Hearings-Overview-Stats-Feb-2020-final-2.pdf; and "Suitability Hearing Summary, Calendar Year 1978 through Calendar Year 2021," California Department of Corrections and Rehabilitation Board of Parole Hearings, accessed December 19, 2022, https://www.cdcr.ca.gov/bph/2020/01/09/suitability-hearing-summary-cy-1978-through-cy-2018/

23   "Calendar Year 2022 Suitability Results." Board of Parole Hearings, California Department of Corrections and Rehabilitation, March 20, 2024. https://www.cdcr.ca.gov/bph/2022/03/16/calendar-year-2022-suitability-results/.

24   "Calendar Year 2023 Suitability Results." Board of Parole Hearings, California Department of Corrections and Rehabilitation, April 17, 2024. https://www.cdcr.ca.gov/bph/2023/02/22/calendar-year-2023-suitability-results/.

25 Smith, Steven. "Crimes, Punishment, and Parole – Mass Releases and Mass Victimization." *Right by the Bay* (blog). Pacific Research Institute, July 25, 2023. https://www.pacificresearch.org/crimes-punishment-and-parole-mass-releases-and-mass-victimization/.

26 "The Issue Is . . . CDCR Accountability." *Truth and Justice Journal* (blog). Placer County District Attorney's Office. Accessed May 4, 2024. https://www.placer.ca.gov/9060/The-issue-is-CDCR-accountability.

27 Rushford, Michael. "Prop. 57 Does Not Reduce Recidivism." Criminal Justice Legal Foundation, August 24, 2023. https://californiaglobe.com/fr/criminal-justice-legal-foundation-report-prop-57-does-not-reduce-recidivism/.

28 "The Issue Is . . . CDCR Accountability." *Truth and Justice Journal* (blog). Placer County District Attorney's Office. Accessed May 4, 2024. https://www.placer.ca.gov/9060/The-issue-is-CDCR-accountability.

29 Ibid.

30 Smith, Steven. Issue brief. *Paradise Lost: Crime in the Golden State 2011-2021*. Pacific Research Institute, February 2023. https://www.pacificresearch.org/wp-content/uploads/2023/02/ParadiseLost_CrimeStudy2022_Final_Web.pdf.

31 Smith, Steven. "The Mythical Crime Reduction Dividend." *Right by the Bay* (blog). Pacific Research Institute, April 3, 2023. https://www.pacificresearch.org/the-mythical-crime-reduction-dividend/.

32 Imai, Dr. Kent. "Analysis of 2020 California Correctional Health Care Services Inmate Mortality Reviews," California Prison Receivership, December 22, 2021. https://cchcs.ca.gov/wp-content/uploads/sites/60/MS/2020-CCHCS-Mortality-Review.pdf

33 "CDCR Announces Additional Actions to Reduce Population and Maximize Space Systemwide to Address COVID-19." California Department of Corrections and Rehabilitation, July 10, 2020, https://www.cdcr.ca.gov/news/2020/07/10/cdcr-announces-additional-actions-to-reduce-population-and-maximize-space-systemwide-to-address-covid-19/

34 Thompson, Don. "76,000 California Prison Inmates Could Be Released Earlier with Good Behavior." *Associated Press*, May 1, 2021. https://www.latimes.com/world-nation/story/2021-05-01/76-000-california-inmates-now-eligible-for-earlier-releases.

35 Lofstrom, Magnus, and Brandon Martin. "California's Major Cities See Increases in Homicides and Car Thefts ." Public Policy Institute of California, April 27, 2021. https://www.ppic.org/blog/californias-major-cities-see-increases-in-homicides-and-car-thefts/.

36 Koseff, Alexei. "Will Coronavirus Pandemic Free California Prisoners? Gavin Newsom Says No." *San Francisco Chronicle*, March 30, 2020. https://www.sfchronicle.com/politics/article/Will-coronavirus-pandemic-free-California-15165261.php.

37 Anaya, Tim. "Is Coronavirus Triggering De-Facto Early Release for Thousands of Offenders?" *Right by the Bay* (blog). Pacific Research Institute, April 7, 2020. https://www.pacificresearch.org/is-coronavirus-triggering-de-facto-early-release-for-thousands-of-offenders/.

38 Ibid.

CHAPTER 2

1   Fears, J. Wayne. *The Scouting Guide to Survival: More Than 200 Essential Skills for Staying Warm, Building a Shelter, and Signaling for Help.* New York, NY: Skyhorse Publishing, 2018.

2   "History of California Wildfires." Western Fire Chiefs Association, November 17, 2022. https://wfca.com/wildfire-articles/history-of-california-wildfires/.

3   Miltimore, Jon. "3 Inconvenient Truths 60 Minutes Forgot to Mention in Its Story on California Wildfires and Climate Change." *Foundation for Economic Education* (blog), October 7, 2020. https://fee.org/articles/3-inconvenient-truths-60-minutes-forgot-to-mention-in-its-story-on-california-wildfires-and-climate-change/.

4   "History of California Wildfires." Western Fire Chiefs Association, November 17, 2022. https://wfca.com/wildfire-articles/history-of-california-wildfires/.

5   Moon, Sarah. "California's Second-Largest Wildfire Was Sparked When Power Lines Came in Contact with a Tree, Cal Fire Says ." *CNN.Com*, January 5, 2022. https://www.cnn.com/2022/01/05/us/dixie-fire-power-lines-cause-pge/index.html.

6   "History of California Wildfires." Western Fire Chiefs Association, November 17, 2022. https://wfca.com/wildfire-articles/history-of-california-wildfires/.

7   "Wildfires." California Office of Environmental Health Hazard Assessment, August 23, 2023. https://oehha.ca.gov/climate-change/epic-2022/impacts-vegetation-and-wildlife/wildfires.

8   "History of California Wildfires." Western Fire Chiefs Association, November 17, 2022. https://wfca.com/wildfire-articles/history-of-california-wildfires/.

9   Brian Isom. "Burning down the house." Medium, May 2, 2019. https://medium.com/cgo-benchmark/burn-down-the-house-d43c63d885e4

10   Ibid, 9.

11   Jackson, Kerry. "California's Blackouts: How Did We Get Here and What Can We Do to Keep the Lights On?". *Capital Ideas* (blog). Pacific Research Institute, November 2019. https://www.pacificresearch.org/wp-content/uploads/2019/11/CapIdeas_CA_Jackson_Vol5_No11_NovF.pdf.

12   Jackson, Kerry. "Bad Policy Could Make Canada's Recent Fires Regular Occurrence in California." *Right by the Bay* (blog). Pacific Research Institute, July 6, 2023. https://www.pacificresearch.org/bad-policy-could-make-canadas-recent-fires-regular-occurrence-in-california/.

13   Ibid.

14   "Record 129 Million Dead Trees in California," USDA Forest Service, December 11, 2017. https://www.fs.usda.gov/Internet/FSE_DOCUMENTS/fseprd566303.pdf

15   "Let's Fight Fire with Fire." The Nature Conservancy, July 15, 2022. https://www.nature.org/en-us/about-us/where-we-work/united-states/california/stories-in-california/californias-wildfire-future/.

16   Jackson, Kerry. "California Wildfires Being Used by Greens to Promote Global

Warming Agenda." *Right by the Bay* (blog). Pacific Research Institute, October 20, 2020. https://www.pacificresearch.org/california-wildfires-being-used-by-greens-to-promote-global-warming-agenda/.

17 Kolkey, Dan. "Saving California." Speech presented at the Pacific Research Institute 2022 California Ideas in Action Conference, February 17, 2022. https://www.youtube.com/watch?v=o_Q4YPVdtp8&list=PLF-p_SwXSCouH8CYWtNtJEC98IFL51t-j5&index=6

18 Regan, Shawn. "Fanning the Flames." *City Journal.* 2023. https://www.city-journal.org/article/fanning-the-flames.

19 Jackson, Kerry. "California Wildfires Being Used by Greens to Promote Global Warming Agenda." *Right by the Ba y* (blog). Pacific Research Institute, October 20, 2020. https://www.pacificresearch.org/california-wildfires-being-used-by-greens-to-promote-global-warming-agenda/.

20 Ring, Edward. "Environmentalists Destroyed California's Forests." California Policy Center, September 10, 2020. https://californiapolicycenter.org/environmentalists-destroyed-californias-forests/.

21 Gallagher, James. "Saving California." Speech presented at the Pacific Research Institute 2022 California Ideas in Action Conference, February 17, 2022. https://www.youtube.com/watch?v=o_Q4YPVdtp8&list=PLF-p_SwXSCouH8CYWtNtJEC98I-FL51tj5&index=6

22 Ibid.

23 Office of California Gov. Gavin Newsom, Proclamation of a State of Emergency § (2019). https://www.gov.ca.gov/wp-content/uploads/2019/03/3.22.19-Wildfire-State-of-Emergency.pdf.

24 Chediak, Mark. "Facing $17 Billion in Fire Damages, a CEO Blames Climate Change." *Bloomberg*, August 13, 2018. https://www.bloomberg.com/news/articles/2018-08-13/facing-17-billion-in-fire-damages-a-ceo-blames-climate-change.

25 Jackson, Kerry. "California's Blackouts: How Did We Get Here and What Can We Do to Keep the Lights On?" Web log. *Capital Ideas* (blog). Pacific Research Institute, November 2019. https://www.pacificresearch.org/wp-content/uploads/2019/11/CapIdeas_CA_Jackson_Vol5_No11_NovF.pdf.

26 Ibid.

27 Ibid.

CHAPTER 3

1   Grylls, Bear. *Do your best: How to be a scout.* London: Hodder Faith, 2024.

2   California Senate Bill 100, Chapter 312, Statutes of 2018, https://leginfo.legisla-ture.ca.gov/faces/billTextClient.xhtml?bill_id=201720180SB100

3   California State Senate Rules Committee, Senate Floor Analysis of Senate Bill 100 (Amended 8/20/2018), August 28, 2018, https://leginfo.legislature.ca.gov/faces/billAnalysisClient.xhtml?bill_id=201720180SB100

4   California State Senate Democratic Caucus. FAQs on SB 100, September 7, 2017. https://focus.senate.ca.gov/sb100/faqs#:~:text=SB%20100%20requires%20that%20at,fuel%20cells%20using%20renewable%20fuels).

5   California State Senate Rules Committee, Senate Floor Analysis of Senate Bill 100 (Amended 8/20/2018), August 28, 2018, https://leginfo.legislature.ca.gov/faces/billAnalysisClient.xhtml?bill_id=201720180SB100

6   Pemberton, Pat. "California's Last Nuclear Plant Gets Lifeline amid Search for More Clean Energy." *Courthouse News Service*, March 15, 2024. https://www.court-housenews.com/californias-last-nuclear-plant-gets-lifeline-amid-search-for-more-clean-energy/.

7   "New Data Shows Investments to Build California's Clean Energy Grid of the Future Are Paying Off," May 9, 2024. California Energy Commission. https://www.energy.ca.gov/news/2024-05/new-data-shows-investments-build-californias-clean-ener-gy-grid-future-are-paying.

8   Issue brief. *Land Needs for Wind, Solar Dwarf Nuclear Plant's Footprint.* National Energy Institute, July 9, 2015. https://www.nei.org/news/2015/land-needs-for-wind-solar-dwarf-nuclear-plants?__cf_chl_tk=4a.j.G4KZ7uP6JJPNdZO2TlElyNC0D-MckKTZq44Bpm8-1715829705-0.0.1.1-1599.

9   Jackson, Kerry, and Wayne Winegarden. Rep. *Sapping California's Energy Future: Current Energy Mandates Are Incompatible with a Modern, Reliable Energy System*, June 2023. https://www.pacificresearch.org/wp-content/uploads/2023/05/Califor-niaSappedStudy_F.pdf and Goble, Gere. "Crawford County Voters Uphold Ban on Industrial Wind Farm." *Bucyrus Telegraph-Forum*, November 8, 2022. https://www.bucyrustelegraphforum.com/story/news/politics/elections/2022/11/08/crawford-voters-decide-on-wind-farm-development-in-ohio-election-2022/69497527007/ and Ellison, Garret. "Voters Defeat Michigan Wind Energy Project, Toss Supportive Officials." *MLive.Com*, November 9, 2022. https://www.mlive.com/public-inter-est/2022/11/voters-defeat-michigan-wind-energy-project-toss-supportive-officials.html?outputType=amp.

10   Willsher, Kim. "French Couple Who Said Windfarm Affected Health Win Le-gal Fight." *The Guardian*, November 8, 2021. https://www.theguardian.com/world/2021/nov/08/french-couple-wins-legal-fight-wind-turbine-syndrome-wind-farm-health.

11   Roth, Sammy. "California's San Bernardino County Slams the Brakes on Big Solar Projects." *Los Angeles Times*, February 28, 2019. https://www.latimes.com/business/la-fi-san-bernardino-solar-renewable-energy-20190228-story.html and Favot, Sarah. "L.A. County Supervisors to Ban Large Wind Turbines in Unincor-porated Areas." *Los Angeles Daily News*, July 14, 2015. https://www.dailynews.com/2015/07/14/la-county-supervisors-to-ban-large-wind-turbines-in-unincorpo-rated-areas/.

12   Olano, Maria Virginia. "California's Big Bet on Offshore Wind." *Canary Media*, September 16, 2022. https://www.canarymedia.com/articles/wind/chart-californias-big-bet-on-offshore-wind.

13   Temple, James. "California's Coming Offshore Wind Boom Faces Big Engineering Hurdles." *MIT Technology Review*, December 5, 2022. https://www.technologyreview.com/2022/12/05/1064243/californias-coming-wind-boom-faces-big-engineering-hurdles/.

14   Ridley, Matt. "Electricity from Wind Isn't Cheap and It Never Will Be." *The Telegraph*, September 10, 2023. https://www.telegraph.co.uk/news/2023/09/10/electricity-from-wind-isnt-cheap-and-it-never-will-be/.

15   Jackson, Kerry. "California's Big Battery Bet." *Power Magazine*, April 22, 2021. https://www.powermag.com/blog/californias-big-battery-bet/.

16   Kisela, Rachel. "California Went Big on Rooftop Solar. Now That's a Problem for Landfills." *Los Angeles Times*, July 14, 2022. https://www.latimes.com/business/story/2022-07-14/california-rooftop-solar-pv-panels-recycling-danger.

17   Issue brief. *Lead Poisoning*. World Health Organization, August 11, 2023. https://www.who.int/news-room/fact-sheets/detail/lead-poisoning-and-health#:~:text=Lead%20is%20a%20naturally%20occurring,many%20parts%20of%20the%20world.

18   Desai, Jemin, and Mark Nelson. "Are We Headed for a Solar Waste Crisis?" *Environmental Progress*, June 21, 2017. https://environmentalprogress.org/big-news/2017/6/21/are-we-headed-for-a-solar-waste-crisis.

19   Ibid.

20   U.S. Department of Energy Office of Energy Efficiency and Renewable Energy, Solar-Plus-Storage 101 § (2019). https://www.energy.gov/eere/solar/articles/solar-plus-storage-101.

21   Mai, T., D. Sandor, R. Wiser, and T. Schneider. Rep. *Renewable Electricity Futures Study: Executive Summary*. National Renewable Energy Laboratory, 2012. https://www.nrel.gov/docs/fy13osti/52409-ES.pdf.

22   Bryce, Robert. "Out Of Transmission" *Substack* (blog), February 9, 2023. https://robertbryce.substack.com/p/out-of-transmission.

23   Jackson, Kerry. "How Are We Going to Build New Transmission Lines for Renewable Energy Transition?" *Right by the Bay* (blog). Pacific Research Institute, May 3, 2023. https://www.pacificresearch.org/how-are-we-going-to-build-new-transmission-lines-for-renewable-energy-transition/.

24   Bryce, Robert. "Rolls-Royce's SMR Needs 10,000 Times Less Land Than Wind Energy, Proves 'Iron Law of Power Density.'" *Forbes.Com*, May 27, 2022. https://www.forbes.com/sites/robertbryce/2022/05/27/rolls-royces-smr-needs-10000-times-less-land-than-wind-energy-proves-iron-law-of-power-density/?sh=3b1fb85398f0.

25   "Diablo Canyon Nuclear Power Plant." Pacific Gas and Electric. Accessed May 15, 2024. https://www.pge.com/en/about/pge-systems/nuclear-power.html.

26   "CEC Determines Diablo Canyon Power Plant Needed to Support Grid Reliability," February 28, 2023. California Energy Commission. https://www.energy.ca.gov/news/2023-02/cec-determines-diablo-canyon-power-plant-needed-support-grid-reliability#:~:text=Located%20in%20San%20Luis%20Obispo,9%20percent%20of%20total%20electricity.

27   DiCamillo, Mark. Issue brief. *Majority Support for the State's All-Electric Car Mandate - New Vehicle Buying Intentions Align with Views about the Mandate.* UC Berkeley Institute of Governmental Studies, October 7, 2022. https://escholarship.org/uc/item/6fm432sb.

28   DiCamillo, Mark. Issue brief. *Majorities See the State's Changing Climate As Serious Health and Safety Threats.* UC Berkeley Institute of Governmental Studies, April 19, 2022. https://escholarship.org/uc/item/73c708p0#main.

29   Roth, Sammy. "Angelenos Are Alarmed by Air Pollution and Extreme Heat. Poll Finds They Want Action." *Los Angeles Times*, April 19, 2022. https://www.latimes.com/environment/story/2022-04-19/angelenos-alarmed-air-pollution-extreme-heat-poll-finds-want-action.

30   California Energy Commission, California Public Utilities Commission, Chie Hong Yee Yang, and Sarah Goldmuntz, Joint Agency Reliability Planning Assessment Covering the Requirements of SB 846 (First Quarterly Report for 2024) and SB 1020 (Annual Report) § (2024). https://www.cpuc.ca.gov/-/media/cpuc-website/divisions/energy-division/documents/summer-2021-reliability/tracking-energy-development/first-quarterly-joint-agency-reliability-planning-assessment-sb846.pdf.

31   Jackson, Kerry. "Latest Anti-Nuclear Lawsuit Threatens Progress on California's Clean Energy Goals." *Power Magazine*, May 1, 2023. https://www.powermag.com/blog/latest-anti-nuclear-lawsuit-threatens-progress-on-californias-clean-energy-goals/.

32   Jackson, Kerry, and Wayne Winegarden. Rep. *Sapping California's Energy Future: Current Energy Mandates Are Incompatible with a Modern, Reliable Energy System*, June 2023. https://www.pacificresearch.org/wp-content/uploads/2023/05/CaliforniaSappedStudy_F.pdf.

33   Jackson, Kerry. "Latest Anti-Nuclear Lawsuit Threatens Progress on California's Clean Energy Goals." *Power Magazine*, May 1, 2023. https://www.powermag.com/blog/latest-anti-nuclear-lawsuit-threatens-progress-on-californias-clean-energy-goals/.

34   Chandler, David. "Q&A: Options for the Diablo Canyon Nuclear Plant." *MIT News* (blog), November 8, 2021. https://news.mit.edu/2021/diablo-canyon-nuclear-plant-1108.

CHAPTER 4

1   "Award and Badge Explorer: Girl Scouts." Girl Scouts of the USA. Accessed May 16, 2024. https://www.girlscouts.org/en/members/for-girl-scouts/badges-journeys-awards/badge-explorer.html.

2   Ibid.

3   Rothstein, Robin, and Chris Jennings. "Examining the Cost of Living by State in 2024." Forbes, May 14, 2024. https://www.forbes.com/advisor/mortgages/cost-of-living-by-state/.

4   Woodrow, Christy. "The Most Beautiful Road Trips in California + Where To Stay." *Ordinary Traveler* (blog), April 8, 2024. https://ordinarytraveler.com/best-road-trips-california.

5   Ibid.

6   Jackson, Kerry. "California's High Gas Prices Go on Trial." *Center Square*, February 24, 2023. https://www.thecentersquare.com/california/article_28bd-1f3c-b47a-11ed-af05-d37a9e20f5a7.html.

7   Anaya, Tim. "No Investigation Needed – Government Energy Policy Fuels Record-High Gas Prices ." *Right by the Bay* (blog). Pacific Research Institute, June 22, 2022. https://www.pacificresearch.org/no-investigation-needed-government-energy-policy-fuels-record-gas-prices/ and Beam, Adam. "California Democrats to Investigate Cause of High Gas Prices." *Associated Press*, June 20, 2022. https://apnews.com/article/california-sacramento-government-and-politics-ecb-3c836bf3fb45d05b77bc676246362.

8   Cornett, Sarah. Issue brief. *California's Cap-and-Trade Program: Frequently Asked Questions*. California Legislative Analyst's Office, October 24, 2023. https://lao.ca.gov/Publications/Report/4811.

9   California Energy Commission. Estimated gasoline price breakdown and margins. Accessed May 15, 2024. https://www.energy.ca.gov/estimated-gasoline-price-breakdown-and-margins.

10   Stillwater Associates. *Stillwater's Projected Costs of the Approved HB 1091 Clean Fuels Standard*, June 15, 2021. https://stillwaterassociates.com/stillwaters-projected-costs-of-the-approved-hb-1091-clean-fuels-standard/.

11   California Energy Commission. Estimated gasoline price breakdown and margins. Accessed May 15, 2024. https://www.energy.ca.gov/estimated-gasoline-price-breakdown-and-margins.

12   Ibid.

13   Ibid.

14   Ibid.

15   California Air Resources Board, Low Carbon Fuel Standard 2023 Amendments: Standardized Regulatory Impact Assessment (SRIA) § (2023). https://ww2.arb.ca.gov/sites/default/files/2023-09/lcfs_sria_2023_0.pdf and Jackson, Kerry. "As Gas Prices Rise in California, Could Even More Pain at the Pump Be Coming?" *Times of San Diego*, March 8, 2024. https://timesofsandiego.com/opinion/2024/03/08/as-gas-prices-rise-in-california-could-even-more-pain-at-the-pump-be-coming/#google_vignette.

16   Ibid.

17   Winegarden, Wayne. Rep. *Legislating Energy Prosperity*. Pacific Research Institute and Power the Future, May 2020. https://www.pacificresearch.org/wp-content/uploads/2020/05/CAEnergyOpportunities_New_final_web.pdf.

18   Ibid.

19   Jackson, Kerry, and Wayne Winegarden. "More Regulations Are Not the Answer to California's High and Volatile Gas Prices." *Bakersfield Californian*, February 23, 2024. https://www.bakersfield.com/opinion/community-voices/community-voices-more-regulations-are-not-the-answer-to-california-s-high-and-volatile-gas/article_296c0dcc-d1c9-11ee-b13a-eb28abc6044a.html.

20   Ibid.

21   Ibid.

22   Ibid.

23   Jones, Jonathan. "States with the Most Oil Reserves [2024]." Construction Coverage, March 1, 2024. https://constructioncoverage.com/research/states-with-the-most-oil-reserves.

24   Valle, Sabrina. "California and Big Oil Are Splitting after Century-Long Affair." *Reuters*, January 29, 2024. https://www.reuters.com/sustainability/climate-energy/california-big-oil-are-splitting-after-century-long-affair-2024-01-29/.

25   "Governor Newsom Takes Action to Phase Out Oil Extraction in California," April 23, 2021. Office of Gov. Gavin Newsom. https://www.gov.ca.gov/2021/04/23/governor-newsom-takes-action-to-phase-out-oil-extraction-in-california/.

26   Yeager, Joshua. "Appeals Court Orders Kern County to Rewrite Oil Permit Ordinance – Again." *Valley Public Radio*, March 11, 2024. https://www.kvpr.org/local-news/2024-03-11/appeals-court-orders-kern-county-to-rewrite-oil-permit-ordinance-again.

27   Ibid.

28   Jackson, Kerry. "The California War On Gas Stations." *Right by the Bay* (blog). Pacific Research Institute, September 2, 2021. https://www.pacificresearch.org/the-california-war-on-gas-stations/.

29   Carleton, Audrey. "California Wine Country Towns Are Banning New Gas Stations." *Vice*, August 19, 2021. https://www.vice.com/en/article/m7ewp4/california-wine-country-towns-are-banning-new-gas-stations.

30   Mossalgue, Jennifer. "This Major US City Wants to Ban New Gas Stations." *Electrek*, February 15, 2024. https://electrek.co/2024/02/15/this-major-us-city-wants-to-ban-new-gas-stations/.

31   Ibid.

32   Kotkin, Joel. "The Killing of Kern County." *RealClearEnergy*, June 15, 2021. https://www.realclearenergy.org/articles/2021/06/15/the_killing_of_kern_county_781600.html.

33   Rep. *2021 Kern County Market Overview and Member Directory*. Kern Economic Development Corporation. Accessed May 15, 2024. https://kernedc.com/wp-content/uploads/2021/01/2021-Kern-EDC-Market-Overview.pdf.

34   Kotkin, Joel. "The Killing of Kern County." *RealClearEnergy*, June 15, 2021. https://www.realclearenergy.org/articles/2021/06/15/the_killing_of_kern_county_781600.html.

35   Jackson, Kerry. Issue brief. *Capital Ideas: Cracking Down on Fracking in California—Is It The Smart Thing to Do?* Pacific Research Institute, May 15, 2019. https://www.pacificresearch.org/capital-ideas-cracking-down-on-fracking-in-california-is-it-the-smart-thing-to-do/.

36   Ibid.

37   Rep. *Statistical Review of World Energy, 70th Ed.* BP, 2021. https://www.bp.com/content/dam/bp/business-sites/en/global/corporate/pdfs/energy-economics/statistical-review/bp-stats-review-2021-full-report.pdf.

38   Sanders, Jon. "The Green Real Deal: Cheap, Plentiful Natural Gas from Fracking." *John Locke Foundation* (blog), March 26, 2019. https://www.johnlocke.org/the-green-real-deal-cheap-plentiful-natural-gas-from-fracking/ and Flynn, Phil. "US Energy Independence Is on the Way Out." *Fox Business*, January 13, 2021. https://www.foxbusiness.com/energy/us-energy-independence-on-way-out.

39   "Electricity Rates for Every State." EnergyBot. Accessed May 16, 2024. https://www.energybot.com/electricity-rates/.

40   Winegarden, Wayne. Rep. *Zapped! How California's Punishing Energy Agenda Hurts the Working Class.* Pacific Research Institute, February 2, 2022. https://www.pacificresearch.org/wp-content/uploads/2022/02/CAElectrictyCostsByDistrict_F.pdf.

41   Brown, Marilyn A, Anmol Soni, Melissa V Lapsa, Katie Southworth, and Matt Cox. "High Energy Burden and Low-Income Energy Affordability: Conclusions from a Literature Review." *Progress in Energy* 2, no. 4 (October 31, 2020): 042003. https://doi.org/10.1088/2516-1083/abb954.

42   Domonoske , Camila. "California Sets Goal Of 100 Percent Clean Electric Power By 2045." *National Public Radio*, September 10, 2018. https://www.npr.org/2018/09/10/646373423/california-sets-goal-of-100-percent-renewable-electric-power-by-2045.

43   "California Cap and Trade." Center for Climate and Energy Solutions, August 24, 2021. https://www.c2es.org/content/california-cap-and-trade/.

44   Winegarden, Wayne. Rep. *Costly Subsidies for the Rich Quantifying the Subsidies Offered to Battery Electric Powered Cars.* Pacific Research Institute, February 2018. https://www.pacificresearch.org/wp-content/uploads/2018/02/CarSubsidies_final_web.pdf.

45   Maurer, Joanna, Andrew deLaski, and Marianne DiMascio. Rep. *States Go First: How States Can Save Consumers Money, Reduce Energy and Water Waste, and Protect the Environment with New Appliance Standards.* American Council for an Energy-Efficient Economy, July 25, 2017. https://www.aceee.org/research-report/a1702.

46   Winegarden, Wayne. Rep. *Zapped! How California's Punishing Energy Agenda Hurts the Working Class.* Pacific Research Institute, February 2, 2022. https://www.pacificresearch.org/wp-content/uploads/2022/02/CAElectrictyCostsByDistrict_F.pdf

47   Ibid.

48   Ibid.

49   Jackson, Kerry. "Power And Higher Prices To The People." *Right by the Bay* (blog). Pacific Research Institute, January 2, 2024. https://www.pacificresearch.org/power-and-higher-prices-to-the-people/.

50   Medina, Madilynne. "Here's What Your Pacific Gas and Electric Bill Will Look like next Year." *SF Gate*. December 14, 2023. https://www.sfgate.com/bayarea/article/here-s-pg-e-bill-look-next-year-18555114.php.

51   Jackson, Kerry. "Power And Higher Prices To The People." *Right by the Bay* (blog). Pacific Research Institute, January 2, 2024. https://www.pacificresearch.org/power-and-higher-prices-to-the-people/.

52   Ibid.

53   Christopher, Ben. "Californians Will See Lower Electricity Rates and a New Fee That Won't Vary with Power Use ." *CalMatters*, May 9, 2024. https://calmatters.org/housing/2024/05/californians-electricity-rates/.

54   California Public Utilities Commission. Care/FERA program. Accessed May 15, 2024. https://www.cpuc.ca.gov/industries-and-topics/electrical-energy/electric-costs/care-fera-program.

55   Christopher, Ben. "Californians Will See Lower Electricity Rates and a New Fee That Won't Vary with Power Use ." *CalMatters*, May 9, 2024. https://calmatters.org/housing/2024/05/californians-electricity-rates/.

56   Ibid.

57   Jackson, Kerry. "Sacramento Does an About Face on Electricity Bills Based on Income." *Right by the Bay* (blog). Pacific Research Institute, February 12, 2024. https://www.pacificresearch.org/sacramento-does-an-about-face-on-electricity-bills-based-on-income/.

58   St. John, Jeff. " Bill Would End California Experiment with Income-Based Electric Bills." *Canary Media*, February 7, 2024. https://www.canarymedia.com/articles/utilities/bill-would-end-california-experiment-with-income-based-electric-bills#:~:text=Under%20the%20utilities'%20joint%20proposal,pay%20%2485%20to%20%24128 and Jackson, Kerry. "Sacramento Does an About Face on Electricity Bills Based on Income." *Right by the Bay* (blog). Pacific Research Institute, February 12, 2024. https://www.pacificresearch.org/sacramento-does-an-about-face-on-electricity-bills-based-on-income/.

59   Jackson, Kerry. "Sacramento Does an About Face on Electricity Bills Based on Income." *Right by the Bay* (blog). Pacific Research Institute, February 12, 2024. https://www.pacificresearch.org/sacramento-does-an-about-face-on-electricity-bills-based-on-income/ and Wiener, Scott, Catherine Blakespear, Bill Dodd, Richard Roth, Ben Allen, Anna Caballero, Monique Limon, Marie Alvarado-Gil, Aisha Wahab, and Dave Cortese. Letter to Letter to California Public Utilities Commission president Alice Busching Reynolds. "Letter from Senate and Assembly Democrats Re Utility Fixed Charge Rate Increase Proposal," January 30, 2024. https://gvwire.s3.us-west-1.amazonaws.com/wp-content/uploads/2024/01/30150404/1-30-24-Income-Graduated-Fixed-Charge-Senate-Letter.pdf.

60   La, Lynn. "Whatmatters: Who Killed California Utility Bill Legislation?" *CalMatters*, April 26, 2024. https://calmatters.org/newsletter/california-utility-bills-legislature/.

61   Jones, Brian, Brian Dahle, Roger Niello, Shannon Grove, Scott Wilk, Rosilicie Ochoa Bogh, Kelly Seyarto, and Janet Nguyen. Letter to California Public Utilities Commission president Alice Busching Reynolds. "Senate Republican Caucus Letter on CPUC Rate Increase Proposal." *California Senate Republican Caucus*, May 7, 2024. https://src.senate.ca.gov/sites/src.senate.ca.gov/files/2024%20Caucus%20Flat%20Rate%20PUC%20Letter%20May%209%20Vote.pdf.

62   Nieves, Alex. "California lawmakers reject bill to add sunset date on $24 utility charge." *E&E News*, May 20, 2024, https://www.eenews.net/articles/california-lawmakers-reject-bill-to-add-sunset-date-on-24-utility-charge/.

CHAPTER 5

1   Fears, J. Wayne, J. Wayne Fears, and Rod Walinchus. *The Scouting Guide to Survival: More Than 200 essential skills for staying warm, building a shelter, and signaling for help*. New York: Skyhorse Publishing, 2018.

2   Killough, Kevin. "Stranded EV Pickup From California A Warning For Others Crossing Wyoming's Challenging Landscape." *Cowboy State Daily*, April 24, 2023. https://cowboystatedaily.com/2023/04/24/stranded-ev-pickup-from-california-a-warning-for-others-crossing-wyomings-challenging-landscape/.

3   Kenton, Luke. "'Bet They Wish They Had Gas!' Chaos in California as Tesla Drivers Are Stranded for Hours in a Half-a-Mile-Long Line to Charge Their Cars on Black Friday." *DailyMail.Com*, December 4, 2019. https://www.dailymail.co.uk/news/article-7755753/Chaos-California-Tesla-drivers-stranded-hours-half-mile-long-line-charge.html.

4   Jackson, Kerry. "California Is Throwing Kids, Parents and Taxpayers Under The E-Bus." *GV Wire*, October 23, 2023. https://gvwire.com/2023/10/23/california-is-throwing-kids-parents-and-taxpayers-under-the-e-bus/.

5   Jackson, Kerry. "Hey, Californians, How Do You Like the Governor's EV Mandate Now?" *Capital Ideas* (blog). Pacific Research Institute, April 1, 2024. https://www.pacificresearch.org/capital-ideas-hey-californians-how-do-you-like-the-governors-ev-mandate-now/.

6   "Governor Newsom Announces California Will Phase Out Gasoline-Powered Cars & Drastically Reduce Demand for Fossil Fuel in California's Fight Against Climate Change." Press release. Office of Governor Gavin Newsom. State of California. Accessed May 22, 2024. https://www.gov.ca.gov/2020/09/23/governor-newsom-announces-california-will-phase-out-gasoline-powered-cars-drastically-reduce-demand-for-fossil-fuel-in-californias-fight-against-climate-change/.

7   Becker, Rachel. "Newsom Orders Ban of New Gas-Powered Cars by 2035." *CalMatters*, September 25, 2020. https://calmatters.org/environment/2020/09/california-ban-gasoline-powered-cars-in-2035/.

8   Fink, Greg S. "Ford Lost $130,000 on Every EV It Sold in the First Quarter." *Car And Driver*, April 26, 2024. https://www.caranddriver.com/news/a60621256/ford-ev-revenue-losses-q1-2024/.

9   "California Moves to Accelerate to 100% New Zero-Emission Vehicle Sales by 2035." *California Air Resources Control Board*, August 25, 2022. State of California. https://ww2.arb.ca.gov/news/california-moves-accelerate-100-new-zero-emission-vehicle-sales-2035.

10   Supporting Dealerships. Letter to President Joe Biden. "Letter #1." *EV Voice of the Customer*, March 20, 2024. https://44308654.fs1.hubspotusercontent-na1.net/hubfs/44308654/EV%20Letter%201.pdf.

11   Catenacci, Thomas. "Dem Governor Withdraws Electric Vehicle Mandate in Stunning Blow to Environmentalists." *Fox News*, November 28, 2023. https://www.foxnews.com/politics/dem-governor-withdraws-electric-vehicle-mandate-stunning-blow-environmentalists.

12   Guillén, Alex. "Biden Targets 50 Percent Clean Car Sales by 2030." *Politico*, August 5, 2021. https://www.politico.com/news/2021/08/05/biden-clean-car-sales-2030-target-502548.

13   Frazin, Rachel. "Biden Administration Finalizes Rule Expected to Require Significant Shift to EVs." *The Hill*, March 20, 2024. https://thehill.com/policy/energy-environment/4544240-electric-vehicle-shift-rule-biden-administration-finalizes/.

14   "Ricketts: Biden EPA's EV Mandate 'Completely Delusional.'" Press Release. Office of Sen. Pete Ricketts, March 20, 2024. https://www.ricketts.senate.gov/news/press-releases/ricketts-biden-epas-ev-mandate-completely-delusional/.

15   "Sullivan, Ricketts, James, Fulcher Introduce Bipartisan Legislation to Overturn Biden's EV Mandates." Press Release. Office of Sen. Dan Sullivan, May 1, 2024. https://www.sullivan.senate.gov/newsroom/press-releases/sullivan-ricketts-james-fulcher-introduce-bipartisan-legislation-to-overturn-bidens-ev-mandates.

16   Winegarden, Wayne. Issue brief. *Costly Subsidies for the Rich*. Pacific Research Institute, February 2018. https://www.pacificresearch.org/wp-content/uploads/2018/02/CarSubsidies_final_web.pdf.

17   Cochrane, Emily, and Lisa Friedman. "What's in the Climate, Tax and Health Care Package?" *New York Times*, August 7, 2022. https://www.nytimes.com/2022/08/07/us/politics/climate-tax-health-care-bill.html.

18   Hirsch, Jerry. "EV Sales Start to Fall in California, an Industry Bellwether." *Automotive News*, January 31, 2024. https://www.autonews.com/retail/ev-bellwether-sales-start-drop-california?utm_medium=social&utm_source=twitter&utm_term=automotive_news&utm_content=8302510f-08db-4786-a8da-f351973afc5f.

19   Naughton, Nora. "Firefighters Are Still Learning How to Fight EV Fires. Here's Everything You Need to Know to Stay Safe." *Business Insiders*, November 9, 2023. https://www.businessinsider.com/electric-vehicle-fires-what-to-know-2023-11.

20   Hawley, Dustin. "How Much Do EV Batteries Cost?" *J.D. Power*, May 10, 2023. https://www.jdpower.com/cars/shopping-guides/how-much-do-ev-batteries-cost.

21   Brady, Ryan. "Electric Car Insurance: What To Know Before You Buy." *Nerd Wallet*, July 7, 2023. https://www.nerdwallet.com/article/insurance/electric-car-insurance.

22   Flex Alert, California ISO extends Flex Alert for today, 4-9 p.m. § (2022). https://www.flexalert.org/news.

23   Alejandro, Melissa, Mickey Francis, and Melissa Lynes, California leads the United States in electric vehicles and charging locations § (2023). https://www.eia.gov/todayinenergy/detail.php?id=61082.

24   Mitchell, Russ. "Broken Chargers, Lax Oversight: How California's Troubled EV Charging Stations Threaten Emission Goals." *Los Angeles Times*, January 24, 2024. https://www.latimes.com/environment/story/2024-01-24/california-ev-charging-stations-broken.

25   "Report Shows California Needs 1.2 Million Electric Vehicle Chargers by 2030." *California Energy Commission*. The State of California, June 9, 2021. California Energy Commission. https://www.energy.ca.gov/news/2021-06/report-shows-california-needs-12-million-electric-vehicle-chargers-2030.

26   Smith, Abby. "California Infrastructure Cannot Meet Gavin Newsom's 2035 Deadline for Emission-Free Automobiles." *Washington Examiner*, October 2, 2020. https://www.washingtonexaminer.com/news/511872/california-infrastructure-cannot-meet-gavin-newsoms-2035-deadline-for-emission-free-automobiles/.

27   Jackson, Kerry. "The Latest Buzz on Newsom's Electric Car Mandate." *Right by the Bay* (blog). Pacific Research Institute, October 8, 2020. https://www.pacificresearch.org/the-latest-buzz-on-newsoms-electric-car-mandate/.

28   Energy Innovation: Policy and Technology. "California Won't Achieve Its New
      Zero-Emission Vehicle Goal Until Multi-Unit Dwellers Can Access Electric Vehicle
      Charging." *Forbes*, September 28, 2020. https://www.forbes.com/sites/energyinno-
      vation/2020/09/28/california-wont-achieve-its-new-zero-emission-vehicle-goal-un-
      til-multi-unit-dwellers-can-access-ev-charging/?sh=19bbc9a95ff2.

29   Winegarden, Wayne, and Kerry Jackson. "Sapping California's Energy Future."
      Pacific Research Institute, June 2023. https://www.pacificresearch.org/wp-content/
      uploads/2023/05/CaliforniaSappedStudy_F.pdf.

30   Winegarden, Wayne, and Kerry Jackson. "Sapping California's Energy Future."
      Pacific Research Institute, June 2023. https://www.pacificresearch.org/wp-content/
      uploads/2023/05/CaliforniaSappedStudy_F.pdf.

31   Ben Fordham, "Electric vehicle owners ask neighbours to ration their power," 2GB
      Sydney, October 13, 2022 https://www.2gb.com/electric-vehicle-owners-ask-neigh-
      bours-to-ration their-power/

32   Wolfe, Ireland. "The Californian Diet." Healthfully, September 6, 2022. https://
      healthfully.com/the-californian-diet-8311397.html.

33   Ibid.

34   Kotkin, Joel. "A 'Diet' to Give California Drivers Indigestion." *Orange County Regis-
      ter*, May 29, 2016. https://www.ocregister.com/2016/05/29/a-diet-to-give-califor-
      nia-drivers-indigestion/.

CHAPTER 6

1   Fears, J. Wayne, J. Wayne Fears, and Rod Walinchus. *The Scouting Guide to Survival: More Than 200 essential skills for staying warm, building a shelter, and signaling for help*. New York: Skyhorse Publishing, 2018.

2   Grylls, Bear. *Do your best: How to be a scout*. London: Hodder Faith, 2024.

3   Greenhut, Steven, ed. *Saving California: Solutions to the State's Biggest Policy Problems*. Pasadena, CA: Pacific Research Institute, 2021.

4   California, State of. "Drought." Department of Water Resources, May 23, 2024. https://water.ca.gov/drought/#:~:text=California%20is%20no%20stranger%20to,in%20the%201920s%20and%201930s

5   Ibid.

6   Greenhut, Steven, ed. *Saving California: Solutions to the State's Biggest Policy Problems*. Pasadena, CA: Pacific Research Institute, 2021.

7   Ibid.

8   Ibid.

9   Ibid.

10   Lewison, Pam. "Water Fines for Farmers Will Not Keep the Wells from Running Dry." Web log. *Right by the Bay* (blog). Pacific Research Institute, March 3, 2023. https://www.pacificresearch.org/water-fines-for-farmers-will-not-keep-the-wells-from-running-dry/.

11   Jackson, Kerry. "One State, Under Water." *City Journal*, April 21, 2017. https://www.city-journal.org/article/one-state-under-water.

12   Peterson, Caitlin, Alvar Escriva-Bou, Josué Medellín-Azuara, and Spencer Cole. Issue brief. *Water Use in California's Agriculture*. Public Policy Institute of California, April 2023. https://www.ppic.org/publication/water-use-in-californias-agriculture/

13   Jackson, Kerry. "Farmers Flush With Water Now, But State Still Hasn't Prepared for the Next Drought." *GV Wire*, August 29, 2023. https://gvwire.com/2023/08/29/farmers-flush-with-water-now-but-state-still-hasnt-prepared-for-the-next-drought/.

14   California State Assembly. Assembly Bill 460. 2023-24 Legislative Session. As Amended in Assembly May 18, 2023. https://leginfo.legislature.ca.gov/faces/billTextClient.xhtml?bill_id=202320240AB460

15   Becker, Rachel. "California Ranchers Intentionally Violated an Emergency Water Order. Now Lawmakers Want to Triple the Fines." *CalMatters*, June 9, 2023. https://calmatters.org/environment/water/2023/06/california-water-fines/.

16   California State Assembly. Assembly Bill 460. 2023-24 Legislative Session. As Amended in Assembly May 18, 2023. https://leginfo.legislature.ca.gov/faces/billTextClient.xhtml?bill_id=202320240AB460

17   Greenhut, Steven, ed. *Saving California: Solutions to the State's Biggest Policy Problems*. Pasadena, CA: Pacific Research Institute, 2021.

18   Jackson, Kerry. "Farmers Flush With Water Now, But State Still Hasn't Prepared for the Next Drought." *GV Wire*, August 29, 2023. https://gvwire.com/2023/08/29/farmers-flush-with-water-now-but-state-still-hasnt-prepared-for-the-next-drought/.

19   Gonzalez, Vicki. "Sites Reservoir Project Finally Gets Green Light, Construction Expected to Begin in 2024." CapRadio, November 24, 2023. https://www.capradio.org/articles/2023/11/24/sites-reservoir-project-finally-gets-green-light-construction-expected-to-begin-in-2024/.

20   California, State of. "Sites Project." California Water Commission. Accessed May 28, 2024. https://cwc.ca.gov/Water-Storage/WSIP-Project-Review-Portal/All-Projects/Sites-Project.

21   Willis, Natalie. "Revised State Budget Cuts $500 Million for Water Storage, Sites Reservoir Slowly Inching Forward." *Valley Ag Voice*, May 13, 2024. https://www.valleyagvoice.com/revised-state-budget-cuts-500-million-for-water-storage-sites-reservoir-slowly-inching-forward/#:~:text=According%20to%20its%20website%2C%20construction,for%20%24875.4%20million%20of%20Prop.

22   Ibid.

23   "Temperance Flat Reservoir - What You Need to Know." Friant Water Authority. Accessed May 28, 2024. https://static1.squarespace.com/static/58c2eccc15d5db46200ea426/t/59e51a98ccc5c5f1c5766518/1508186777125/Temprance+jpg.pdf.

24   "Temperance Flat Dam." The Conservation Alliance, October 27, 2022. https://conservationalliance.com/success/temperance-flat-dam/.

25   Ibid.

26   Greenhut, Steven, ed. *Saving California: Solutions to the State's Biggest Policy Problems*. Pasadena, CA: Pacific Research Institute, 2021.

27   Ibid.

28   Mount, Jeffrey, and Ellen Hanak. Issue brief. *Just the Facts: Water Use in California*. Public Policy Institute of California Water Policy Center, May 2019. https://cwc.ca.gov/-/media/CWC-Website/Files/Documents/2019/06_June/June2019_Item_12_Attach_2_PPICFactSheets.pdf.

29   Lewison, Pam. "Water Fines for Farmers Will Not Keep the Wells from Running Dry." Web log. *Right by the Bay* (blog). Pacific Research Institute, March 3, 2023. https://www.pacificresearch.org/water-fines-for-farmers-will-not-keep-the-wells-from-running-dry/.

30   California State Senate. Senate Bill 1157. 2021-22 Legislative Session. Chapter 679, Statutes of 2022. https://leginfo.legislature.ca.gov/faces/billTextClient.xhtml?bill_id=202320240AB460

31   Greenhut, Steven, ed. *Saving California: Solutions to the State's Biggest Policy Problems*. Pasadena, CA: Pacific Research Institute, 2021.

32   Ibid.

CHAPTER 7

1   Fears, J. Wayne, J. Wayne Fears, and Rod Walinchus. *The Scouting Guide to Surviv-al: More Than 200 essential skills for staying warm, building a shelter, and signaling for help.* New York: Skyhorse Publishing, 2018.

2   Jackson, Kerry. "Plastics Fight Would Inconvenience Californians, Not Do Much to Help the Planet." *Orange County Register*, June 22, 2022. https://www.ocregister.com/2022/06/22/plastics-fight-would-inconvenience-californians-not-do-much-to-help-the-planet/?clearUserState=true.

3   "California Proposition 67, Plastic Bag Ban Veto Referendum (2016)." Ballotpedia. Accessed June 1, 2024. https://ballotpedia.org/California_Proposition_67,_Plas-tic_Bag_Ban_Veto_Referendum_(2016)#:~:text=The%20California%20Plastic%20Bag%20Ban,It%20was%20approved.

4   "Legislation To Ban Plastic Bags Passes Senate." Office of Sen. Catherine Blakespear, May 21, 2024. https://sd38.senate.ca.gov/news/legislation-ban-plas-tic-bags-passes-senate.

5   Ibid.

6   Sokolow, Louis, Celeste Meiffren-Swango, and Jenn Engstrom. Rep. *Plastic Bag Bans Work: Well-Designed Single-Use Plastic Bag Bans Reduce Waste and Litter.* Environment America Research and Policy Center, U.S. Public Interest Research Group Education Fund, and Frontier Group, January 2024. https://publicinterest-network.org/wp-content/uploads/2024/01/Plastic-Bag-Bans-Work-January-2024.pdf.

7   Ibid.

8   Jackson, Kerry. "The Data Is In: California No Better Off Under Plastic Bag Ban." *Right by the Bay* (blog). Pacific Research Institute, May 10, 2022. https://www.pacificresearch.org/the-data-is-in-california-no-better-off-under-plastic-bag-ban/.

9   Morris, Julian, and Lance Christensen. Issue brief. *An Evaluation of the Effects of California's Proposed Plastic Bag Ban*, July 2014. https://reason.org/wp-content/uploads/2014/06/california_plastic_bag_ban-1.pdf.

10   Jackson, Kerry. "The Data Is In: California No Better Off Under Plastic Bag Ban." *Right by the Bay* (blog). Pacific Research Institute, May 10, 2022. https://www.pacificresearch.org/the-data-is-in-california-no-better-off-under-plastic-bag-ban/.

11   Ibid.

12   Edwards, Chris, and Jonna Meyhoff Fry. Rep. *Life Cycle Assessment of Supermarket Carrier Bags: A Review of the Bags Available in 2006.* U.K. Environment Agency, February 2011. https://assets.publishing.service.gov.uk/government/uploads/sys-tem/uploads/attachment_data/file/291023/scho0711buan-e-e.pdf.

13   University of Georgia. "Plastic Bag Bans May Unintentionally Drive Other Bag Sales." *Science Daily*, March 29, 2022. https://www.sciencedaily.com/releas-es/2022/03/220329142327.htm#:~:text=Summary%3A,where%20they%20are%20in%20place.

14   California State Assembly. Assembly Bill 1346. 2021-22 Legislative Session. Chap-ter 753, Statutes of 2021. https://leginfo.legislature.ca.gov/faces/billTextClient.xhtml?bill_id=202320240AB460

15   State of California Executive Department. Executive Order N-79-20. September 23, 2020. https://www.gov.ca.gov/wp-content/uploads/2020/09/9.23.20-EO-N-79-20-Climate.pdf

16   Anaya, Tim. "Gas-Powered Lawn Equipment Ban Another Major Burden on Minority Entrepreneurs." *Right by the Bay* (blog). Pacific Research Institute, October 18, 2021. https://www.pacificresearch.org/gas-powered-lawn-equipment-ban-another-major-burden-on-minority-entrepreneurs/.

17   Ibid.

18   Willon, Phil. "California Moves toward Ban on Gas Lawn Mowers and Leaf Blowers." *Los Angeles Times*, October 9, 2021. https://www.latimes.com/california/story/2021-10-09/california-moves-toward-ban-on-gas-lawnmowers-and-leaf-blowers.

19   Anaya, Tim. "Banning Gas-Powered Leaf Blowers Could Have Unintended Consequences in Next Power Outage." *Right by the Bay* (blog). Pacific Research Institute, September 15, 2021. https://www.pacificresearch.org/banning-gas-powered-leaf-blowers-could-have-unintended-consequences-in-next-power-outage/.

20   Willon, Phil. "California Moves toward Ban on Gas Lawn Mowers and Leaf Blowers." *Los Angeles Times*, October 9, 2021. https://www.latimes.com/california/story/2021-10-09/california-moves-toward-ban-on-gas-lawnmowers-and-leaf-blowers.

21   Ibid.

22   Anaya, Tim. "Banning Gas-Powered Leaf Blowers Could Have Unintended Consequences in Next Power Outage." *Right by the Bay* (blog). Pacific Research Institute, September 15, 2021. https://www.pacificresearch.org/banning-gas-powered-leaf-blowers-could-have-unintended-consequences-in-next-power-outage/.

23   Anaya, Tim. "Gas-Powered Lawn Equipment Ban Another Major Burden on Minority Entrepreneurs." *Right by the Bay* (blog). Pacific Research Institute, October 18, 2021. https://www.pacificresearch.org/gas-powered-lawn-equipment-ban-another-major-burden-on-minority-entrepreneurs/.

24   Ibid.

25   Anaya, Tim. "Banning Gas-Powered Leaf Blowers Could Have Unintended Consequences in Next Power Outage." *Right by the Bay* (blog). Pacific Research Institute, September 15, 2021. https://www.pacificresearch.org/banning-gas-powered-leaf-blowers-could-have-unintended-consequences-in-next-power-outage/.

26   "CARB Approves Updated Regulations Requiring Most New Small Off-Road Engines Be Zero Emission by 2024," December 9, 2021. State of California, Air Resources Board. https://ww2.arb.ca.gov/news/carb-approves-updated-regulations-requiring-most-new-small-road-engines-be-zero-emission-2024.

27   Anaya, Tim. "Banning Gas-Powered Leaf Blowers Could Have Unintended Consequences in Next Power Outage." *Right by the Bay* (blog). Pacific Research Institute, September 15, 2021. https://www.pacificresearch.org/banning-gas-powered-leaf-blowers-could-have-unintended-consequences-in-next-power-outage/.

28   "Portable Generator Manufacturers' Association Fights California Ban." *Business Wire*, August 16, 2021. Portable Generator Manufacturers' Association. https://www.businesswire.com/news/home/20210816005039/en/Portable-Generator-Manufacturers'-Association-Fights-California-Ban.

29   California State Senate. Floor Analysis of Assembly Bill 1346. 2021-22 Legislative Session. September 1, 2021. https://leginfo.legislature.ca.gov/faces/billAnalysisClient.xhtml?bill_id=202120220AB1346

30   Jackson, Kerry. "Natural Gas Ban and a Flame Out of Five-Star Dining in California?" *Right by the Bay* (blog). Pacific Research Institute, June 5, 2023. https://www.pacificresearch.org/natural-gas-ban-and-a-flameout-of-five-star-dining-in-california/.

31   Plautz, Jason, and Niina Farah. "Berkeley Plans to Repeal First US Gas Ban." *E&E News*, May 26, 2024. https://www.eenews.net/articles/berkeley-plans-to-repeal-first-us-gas-ban/.

32   Markind, Daniel. "Palo Alto Drops Ban On Natural Gas - Will New York And Other Places Follow?" *Forbes.Com*, March 4, 2024. https://www.forbes.com/sites/daniel-markind/2024/03/04/palo-alto-drops-ban-on-natural-gaswill-new-york-and-other-places-follow/?sh=3d3c45bb15ca.

33   Shah, Elena. "Cities Try to Phase Out Gas Stoves—but Cooks Are Pushing Back." *Wall Street Journal*, July 17, 2021. https://www.wsj.com/articles/cities-try-to-phase-out-gas-stovesbut-cooks-are-pushing-back-11626514200.

34   Green, Miranda. "Bay Area Cities Go to War Over Gas Stoves in Homes and Restaurants." California Healthline, February 16, 2021. https://californiahealthline.org/news/article/bay-area-cities-go-to-war-over-gas-stoves-in-homes-and-restaurants/.

35   Jackson, Kerry. "Natural Gas Ban and a Flame Out of Five-Star Dining in California?" *Right by the Bay* (blog). Pacific Research Institute, June 5, 2023. https://www.pacificresearch.org/natural-gas-ban-and-a-flameout-of-five-star-dining-in-california/.

36   South Coast Air Quality Management District. Agenda Item #22 - Determine that Proposed Amended Rule 1153.1 – Emissions of Oxides of Nitrogen from Commercial Food Ovens, Is Exempt from CEQA, and Amend Rule 1153.1. Board Meeting of August 4, 2023. http://www.aqmd.gov/docs/default-source/Agendas/Governing-Board/2023/2023-Aug4-022.pdf?sfvrsn=6

37   Anaya, Tim. "Outlawing Commercial Gas Ovens Latest Government Hit on Minority Workers." *Right by the Bay* (blog). Pacific Research Institute, August 8, 2023. https://www.pacificresearch.org/outlawing-commercial-gas-ovens-latest-government-hit-on-minority-workers/.

38   "Fair Skies Ahead: Equitable Airport Security Screening Bill Passes Senate Transportation Committee With 8-4 Vote," April 23, 2024. Office of Sen. Josh Newman. https://sd29.senate.ca.gov/news/press-release/fair-skies-ahead-equitable-airport-security-screening-bill-passes-senate and Jackson, Kerry. "Sacramento Wants to 'CLEAR' Out Private Sector Convenience for Millions of Travelers." Capital Ideas. Pacific Research Institute, May 20, 2024. https://www.pacificresearch.org/capital-ideas-sacramento-wants-to-clear-out-private-sector-convenience-for-millions-of-travelers/.

39   Ibid.

40   Jackson, Kerry. "Sacramento Wants to 'CLEAR' Out Private Sector Convenience for Millions of Travelers." *Capital Ideas*. Pacific Research Institute, May 20, 2024. https://www.pacificresearch.org/capital-ideas-sacramento-wants-to-clear-out-private-sector-convenience-for-millions-of-travelers/.

41   Kingston, Jennifer. "Cities Are Starting to Ban New Gas Stations." *Axios*, March 1, 2021. https://www.axios.com/2021/03/01/cities-ban-gas-pollution and Jackson, Kerry. "The California War on Gas Stations." *Right by the Bay* (blog). Pacific Research Institute, September 2, 2021. https://www.pacificresearch.org/the-california-war-on-gas-stations/

42   Segura, Eleonor. "California City Bans New Gas Stations—Will Others Follow?" *Motor Trend*, March 5, 2021. https://www.motortrend.com/news/gas-station-ban-us-petaluma-california/ and Jackson, Kerry. "The California War on Gas Stations." *Right by the Bay* (blog). Pacific Research Institute, September 2, 2021. https://www.pacificresearch.org/the-california-war-on-gas-stations/

43   Carleton, Audrey. "California Wine Country Towns Are Banning New Gas Stations." *Vice*, August 19, 2021. https://www.vice.com/en/article/m7ewp4/california-wine-country-towns-are-banning-new-gas-stations?callback=in&code=NZCYZTJMYTETMTLKYI0ZOTCXLTG2N2ITODY1NZVLYTQYNJQ2&state=27f14f3e0d89447eb73b6a2a0ad25953.

44   Jackson, Kerry. "The California War on Gas Stations." *Right by the Bay* (blog). Pacific Research Institute, September 2, 2021. https://www.pacificresearch.org/the-california-war-on-gas-stations/.

45   U.S. Census bureau data

46   Jackson, Kerry. Interview with Todd Royal. Personal, August 20, 2021.

47   Ibid.

48   Ibid.

49   Yoder, Kate. "California Towns Are Banning New Gas Stations. Big Oil Is Paying Attention." *Grist*, February 28, 2024. https://grist.org/cities/california-cities-ban-new-gas-stations-big-oil-backlash/.

50   California State Assembly. Assembly Bill 1162. 2019-20 Legislative Session. Chapter 687, Statutes of 2019. https://leginfo.legislature.ca.gov/faces/billTextClient.xhtml?bill_id=201920200AB1162

51   Ibid.

52   McLaughlin, Robin. "Marriott's Win-Win Plastic Sustainability Initiative." *Lodging*, April 10, 2018. https://lodgingmagazine.com/marriotts-win-win-plastic-sustainability-initiative/ and Jackson, Kerry. "California Lawmakers Beat Back the Scourge of Hotel Shampoo Bottles." *Right by the Bay*(blog). Pacific Research Institute, April 23, 2019. https://www.pacificresearch.org/california-lawmakers-beat-back-the-scourge-of-hotel-shampoo-bottles/.

53   Anaya, Tim. "Don't Forget to Pack Your Own Shampoo Next Time You Stay at a California Hotel." *Right by the Bay* (blog). Pacific Research Institute, October 17, 2019. https://www.pacificresearch.org/dont-forget-to-pack-your-own-shampoo-next-time-you-stay-at-a-california-hotel/.

54   Ibid.

55   Zapka, Carrie A., Esther J. Campbell, Sheri L. Maxwell, Charles P. Gerba, Michael J. Dolan, James W. Arbogast, and David R. Making. "Bacterial Hand Contamination and Transfer after Use of Contaminated Bulk-Soap-Refillable Dispensers." *Applied and Environmental Microbiology* 77, no. 9 (May 2011): 2898–2904. https://www.ncbi.nlm.nih.gov/pmc/articles/PMC3126420/.

56   Jackson, Kerry. "California, Blinded by Plastic." *City Journal*, April 15, 2019. https://www.city-journal.org/article/california-blinded-by-plastic#:~:text=Only%20about%201%20percent%20of,notes%20Reason%20TV's%20Kristin%20Tate.

57   Anaya, Tim. "Don't Forget to Pack Your Own Shampoo Next Time You Stay at a California Hotel." *Right by the Bay* (blog). Pacific Research Institute, October 17, 2019. https://www.pacificresearch.org/dont-forget-to-pack-your-own-shampoo-next-time-you-stay-at-a-california-hotel/.

58   Borreani, Lisa. "Aseptic Packaging: Why Items like Milk Cartons Are Difficult to Recycle." RecycleMore, November 14, 2023. https://recyclemore.com/aseptic-packaging-why-items-like-milk-cartons-are-difficult-to-recycle/.

59   California State Senate. Senate Bill 54. 2021-22 Legislative Session. Chapter 75, Statutes of 2022. https://leginfo.legislature.ca.gov/faces/billTextClient.xhtml?bill_id=202120220SB54

60   California State Senate. Floor Analysis of Senate Bill 54. 2021-22 Legislative Session. June 29, 2022. https://leginfo.legislature.ca.gov/faces/billAnalysisClient.xhtml?bill_id=202120220SB54

61   Jackson, Kerry. "Could Milk and Juice Cartons Soon Be History in California? New Regulations Suggest Yes." *Right by the Bay* (blog). Pacific Research Institute, February 1, 2024. https://www.pacificresearch.org/could-milk-and-juice-cartons-soon-be-history-in-california-new-regulations-suggest-yes/.

CHAPTER 8

1   Anaya, Tim. "Newsom's Budget Plan Sinks in Deficit Quicksand." *Right by the Bay* (blog). Pacific Research Institute, February 22, 2024. https://www.pacificresearch.org/newsoms-budget-plan-sinks-in-deficit-quicksand/.

2   Winegarden, Wayne. "Gov. Newsom's Proposed Budget Fails the Moment." *Orange County Register*, January 10, 2024. https://www.ocregister.com/2024/01/10/gov-newsoms-proposed-budget-fails-the-moment/?clearUserState=true.

3   Winegarden, Wayne, and Tim Anaya. "Governor Newsom's Budget Crisis Is Déjà vu All Over Again." *Right by the Bay* (blog). Pacific Research Institute, April 8, 2024. https://www.pacificresearch.org/governor-newsoms-budget-crisis-is-deja-vu-all-over-again/.

4   McCann, Adam. "States with the Best School Systems." *WalletHub* (blog), July 24, 2023. https://wallethub.com/edu/e/states-with-the-best-schools/5335; Rep. *2019 Report Card for California's Infrastructure*. American Society of Civil Engineers, February 2023. https://infrastructurereportcard.org/state-item/california/; and "These Are the Safest States in America." US News and World Report. Accessed May 5, 2024. https://www.usnews.com/news/best-states/rankings/crime-and-corrections/public-safety.

5   Winegarden, Wayne. "Gov. Newsom's Proposed Budget Fails the Moment." *Orange County Register*, January 10, 2024. https://www.ocregister.com/2024/01/10/gov-newsoms-proposed-budget-fails-the-moment/?clearUserState=true.

6   "California Tax Data Explorer." Tax Foundation, February 16, 2024, accessed May 5, 2024. https://taxfoundation.org/location/california/.

7   Thom, Michael. Rep. *Nickel and Dimed: Cell Phone Fees to Mattress Fees - How Californians' Money Is Being Really Spent*. Pacific Research Institute, December 9, 2021. https://www.pacificresearch.org/wp-content/uploads/2022/08/NickelDimed_F_web.pdf.

8   Jackson, Kerry, and Wayne Winegarden. Rep. *California Migrating: Documenting the Causes and Consequences of California's Growing Exodus Problem*. Pacific Research Institute, September 23, 2021. https://www.pacificresearch.org/wp-content/uploads/2022/08/CA-Migration_F_web.pdf.

9   Walters, Dan. "California's Volatile Tax System Strikes Again." *CalMatters*, January 11, 2023. https://calmatters.org/commentary/2023/01/californias-volatile-tax-system-strikes-again/.

10   Jackson, Kerry. "Brown's Budget Underscores Need for Tax Reform." *Fox and Hounds Daily*, January 13, 2017. https://www.foxandhoundsdaily.com/2017/01/browns-budget-underscores-need-tax-reform/.

11   Skurk, Krystina. "Policy Experts: California Needs to Reform Its Tax System." *Center Square*, July 9, 2020. https://www.thecentersquare.com/california/article_7f0f0098-c149-11ea-a56b-af59d38b6c11.html.

12   Winegarden, Wayne. "Spending Watch: Too Much Government Spending and Volatile Tax Revenues Drive State's Budget Problem." *Right by the Bay* (blog). Pacific Research Institute, March 2024. https://www.pacificresearch.org/too-much-government-spending-and-volatile-tax-revenues-drive-states-budget-problem/.

13   Garosi, Justin. Issue brief. *Volatility of California's Personal Income Tax Structure.* California Legislative Analyst's Office, September 28, 2017. https://lao.ca.gov/ Publications/Report/3703.

14   Editorial Board. "California's Wall Street-Dependent Tax System Drives Budget Nightmares. That Must Change." *San Diego Union-Tribune*, December 14, 2023. https://www.sandiegouniontribune.com/opinion/editorials/story/2023-12-14/california-68-billion-deficit-volatile-revenue-capital-gains.

15   Winegarden, Wayne. "Spending Watch: Too Much Government Spending and Volatile Tax Revenues Drive State's Budget Problem." *Right by the Bay* (blog). Pacific Research Institute, March 2024. https://www.pacificresearch.org/too-much-government-spending-and-volatile-tax-revenues-drive-states-budget-problem/.

16   Nixon, Nicole. "How California Budget Rules Can Prevent Saving for a Rainy Day — and Why Newsom Wants to Change That." *CapRadio*, January 22, 2024. https://www.capradio.org/articles/2024/01/22/how-california-budget-rules-can-prevent-saving-for-a-rainy-day-and-why-newsom-wants-to-change-that/.

17   Fritts, Janelle. "Ranking Property Taxes on the 2022 State Business Tax Climate Index." *Tax Foundation* (blog), May 10, 2022. https://taxfoundation.org/data/all/state/ranking-property-taxes-2022/.

18   Jackson, Kerry. "Split Roll Would Hit Working Californians Hard." *San Diego Daily Transcript*, January 11, 2018. https://www.sdtranscript.com/common/login/?-source=news&sourceid=965631.

19   Laffer, Arthur, and Wayne Winegarden. "A Man's Home Is His Castle: The Legacy of Prop. 13." Essay. In *Eureka! How to Fix California*, 105. San Francisco, CA: Pacific Research Institute, 2012.

20   Jackson, Kerry. "Split Roll Would Hit Working Californians Hard." *San Diego Daily Transcript*, January 11, 2018. https://www.sdtranscript.com/common/login/?-source=news&sourceid=965631.

21   Laffer, Arthur, and Wayne Winegarden. "A Man's Home Is His Castle: The Legacy of Prop. 13." Essay. In *Eureka! How to Fix California*, 107. San Francisco, CA: Pacific Research Institute, 2012.

22   Coupal, Jon. "Prop. 13 Is Still Third Rail of California Politics." *Torrance Daily Breeze*, November 8, 2020. https://www.dailybreeze.com/2020/11/08/prop-13-still-third-rail-of-california-politics/.

23   Baldassare, Mark, Dean Bonner, Alyssa Dykman, and Lunna Lopes. Issue brief. *Proposition 13: 40 Years Later.* Public Policy Institute of California, June 2018. https://www.ppic.org/publication/proposition-13-40-years-later/.

24   Jackson, Kerry. "Split-Roll Forces Challenge Prop 13: How Will Californians React?" *Right by the Bay* (blog). Pacific Research Institute, August 26, 2019. https://www.pacificresearch.org/split-roll-forces-challenge-prop-13-how-will-californians-react/.

25   Ibid.

26   Ibid.

27   Jackson, Kerry. "Split Roll Would Hit Working Californians Hard." *San Diego Daily Transcript*, January 11, 2018. https://www.sdtranscript.com/common/login/?-source=news&sourceid=965631.

28   California Department of Finance, California State Budget, 2023-24 § (2023). https://ebudget.ca.gov/2023-24/pdf/Enacted/BudgetSummary/FullBudgetSummary.pdf.

29   Jackson, Kerry. "Split Roll Would Hit Working Californians Hard." *San Diego Daily Transcript*, January 11, 2018. https://www.sdtranscript.com/common/login/?source=news&sourceid=965631.

30   Ibid.

31   Zaremberg, Allan, and Rob Lapsley. "Proposition 13 Works and Remains Popular. So Why Are Special Interests Attacking It?" *CalMatters*, September 25, 2019. https://calmatters.org/commentary/split-roll-2/.

32   Jackson, Kerry. "Two Years After Voters Said No, Special Interests Try Again to Pass Split Roll." *Right by the Bay* (blog). Pacific Research Institute, October 8, 2021. https://www.pacificresearch.org/two-years-after-voters-said-no-special-interests-try-again-to-pass-split-roll/.

33   Anaya, Tim. "They're Baaack! Sacramento Liberals Once Again Propose a 'Wealth Tax.'" *Right by the Bay* (blog). Pacific Research Institute, February 7, 2023. https://www.pacificresearch.org/theyre-baaack-sacramento-liberals-once-again-propose-a-wealth-tax/.

34   "Tax on Extreme Wealth Introduced in California in Coordinated Effort with Seven Additional States." *Office of Assemblymember Alex Lee*. California State Assembly, January 23, 2023. Office of Assemblymember Alex Lee. https://a24.asmdc.org/press-releases/20230123-tax-extreme-wealth-introduced-california-coordinated-effort-seven.

35   Ibid.

36   Jackson, Kerry, and Wayne Winegarden. "Wealth Taxes Are Economic Failures." *Economic Standard*, March 11, 2022. https://theeconomicstandard.com/wealth-taxes-are-economic-failures/.

37   Ibid.

38   Rosalsky, Greg. "If a Wealth Tax Is Such a Good Idea, Why Did Europe Kill Theirs?" *National Public Radio*, February 26, 2019. https://www.npr.org/sections/money/2019/02/26/698057356/if-a-wealth-tax-is-such-a-good-idea-why-did-europe-kill-theirs.

39   Jackson, Kerry, and Wayne Winegarden. "Wealth Taxes Are Economic Failures." *Economic Standard*, March 11, 2022. https://theeconomicstandard.com/wealth-taxes-are-economic-failures/.

40   Jackson, Kerry. "Studies Show Wealth Tax Would Hurt California's Economy." *Right by the Bay* (blog). Pacific Research Institute, August 26, 2020. https://www.pacificresearch.org/studies-show-wealth-tax-would-hurt-californias-economy/.

41   Diamond, John W., and George R. Zodrow. Rep. *The Economic Effects of Wealth Taxes*. Center for Freedom and Prosperity, August 5, 2020. https://www.freedomandprosperity.org/files/White%20Paper/Diamond-Zodrow_Economic_Effects_of_Wealth_Taxes.pdf.

42   Jackson, Kerry. "Studies Show Wealth Tax Would Hurt California's Economy." *Right by the Bay* (blog). Pacific Research Institute, August 26, 2020. https://www.pacificresearch.org/studies-show-wealth-tax-would-hurt-californias-economy/.

43   California State Assembly, Committee Analysis of AB 259 (Lee) § (2024). https://leginfo.legislature.ca.gov/faces/billAnalysisClient.xhtml?bill_id=202320240AB259#.

44   Coupal, Jon. "California Is Not East Berlin. A Wealth Tax in California Would Expedite the Exodus." *Orange County Register*, January 12, 2024. https://www.ocregister.com/2024/01/12/california-is-not-east-berlin-a-wealth-tax-in-california-would-expedite-the-exodus/?clearUserState=true.

45   "Tax on Extreme Wealth Introduced in California in Coordinated Effort with Seven Additional States." *Office of Assemblymember Alex Lee.* California State Assembly, January 23, 2023. Office of Assemblymember Alex Lee. https://a24.asmdc.org/press-releases/20230123-tax-extreme-wealth-introduced-california-coordinated-effort-seven.

46   Ibid.

47   History.com Editors. "Gold Rush: California, Date & Sutter's Mill." History.com, April 6, 2010. https://www.history.com/topics/19th-century/gold-rush-of-1849.

48   Ibid

49   King, Hobart M. "Fool's Gold." Geology.com. Accessed May 2, 2024. https://geology.com/gold/fools-gold/.

50   "Stockton Mayor Who Started Guaranteed Income Program Concedes Defeat in Reelection Bid." *Associated Press*, November 18, 2020. https://ktla.com/news/politics/stockton-mayor-who-started-guaranteed-income-program-concedes-defeat-in-reelection-bid/.

51   Christie, Jim. "How Stockton Went Broke: A 15-Year Spending Binge." *Reuters*, July 3, 2012. https://www.reuters.com/article/us-stockton-bankruptcy-cause/how-stockton-went-broke-a-15-year-spending-binge-idUSBRE8621DL20120703/.

52   Itchon, Rowena. "Basic Income Comes to Stockton." *Right by the Bay* (blog). Pacific Research Institute, February 5, 2018. https://www.pacificresearch.org/basic-income-comes-to-stockton/.

53   Dunn, Damon. "The False Promise of Universal Basic Income." Essay. In *Punting Poverty: Breaking the Chains of Welfare*, 31. Pasadena, CA: Pacific Research Institute, 2020.

54   Ibid.

55   West, Dr. Stacia, Dr. Amy Castro Baker, Sukhi Samra, and Erin Coltrera. *Preliminary Analysis: SEED's First Year*. Stockton Economic Empowerment Demonstration, March 3, 2021. https://static1.squarespace.com/static/6039d612b-17d055cac14070f/t/603ef1194c474b329f33c329/1614737690661/SEED_Preliminary+Analysis-SEEDs+First+Year_Final+Report_Individual+Pages+-2.pdf.

56   Anaya, Tim. "Is Stockton's Basic Income Scheme Actually Working?" *Right by the Bay* (blog). Pacific Research Institute, March 10, 2021. https://www.pacificresearch.org/is-stocktons-basic-income-scheme-actually-working/.

57   "Heikki Hiilamo: 'Disappointing Results from the Finnish Basic Income Experiment.'" *University of Helsinki*, August 2, 2019. University of Helsinki. https://www.helsinki.fi/en/news/fair-society/heikki-hiilamo-disappointing-results-finnish-basic-income-experiment.

58   Jackson, Kerry. "Universal Basic Income — Just Another Welfare Program That Will Fail." *Fox and Hounds Daily*, May 5, 2020. https://www.foxandhoundsdaily.com/2020/05/universal-basic-income-just-another-welfare-program-that-will-fail/.

59   Anaya, Tim. "Other Countries Are Abandoning Basic Income – Will Stockton Learn from These Failures?" *Right by the Bay* (blog). Pacific Research Institute, August 23, 2018. https://www.pacificresearch.org/other-countries-are-abandoning-basic-income-will-stockton-learn-from-these-failures/.

60   Loriggio, Paola. "Ford Government Defends Move to Axe Basic Income Pilot Project." *Toronto Sun*, August 1, 2018. https://torontosun.com/news/provincial/ford-government-defends-move-to-axe-basic-income-pilot-project.

61   Ravani, Sarah. "Oakland's Guaranteed Income Program Caught up in Debate over Race and Equity." *San Francisco Chronicle*, April 7, 2021. https://www.sfchronicle.com/local-politics/article/Oakland-s-guaranteed-income-program-caught-up-16081715.php.

62   Smith, Dakota. "$1,000 a Month with No Strings Attached: Guaranteed Basic Income Could Be Coming to L.A." *Los Angeles Times*, April 20, 2021. https://www.latimes.com/california/story/2021-04-20/garcetti-la-guaranteed-basic-income-plan-what-to-know.

63   Jackson, Kerry. "Basic Income: High Praise but Poor Results." *Economic Standard*, June 9, 2021. https://theeconomicstandard.com/basic-income-high-praise-but-poor-results/.

64   Dunn, Damon. "The False Promise of Universal Basic Income." Essay. In *Punting Poverty: Breaking the Chains of Welfare*, 23. Pasadena, CA: Pacific Research Institute, 2020.

CHAPTER 9

1   Stainton, Hayley. "What Is Agritourism and Why Is It Growing So Fast?" Tourism Teacher, February 15, 2023. https://tourismteacher.com/agritourism/.

2   Vankin, Jonathan. "How California Agriculture Has Shaped the State and the Country." *California Local*, May 8, 2023. https://californialocal.com/localnews/statewide/ca/article/show/36707-california-agriculture-dairy-wheat-fruit-vegetables/.

3   Osborne, Margaret. "Millions of Sterile Fruit Flies Will Soon Be Dropped on Los Angeles." *Smithsonian Magazine*, November 2, 2023. https://www.smithsonianmag.com/smart-news/millions-of-sterile-fruit-flies-will-soon-be-dropped-on-los-angeles-180983176/.

4   Ibid.

5   Bailey, Pat. "Medfly and Other Fruit Flies Entrenched in California, Study Concludes." UC Davis, August 6, 2013. https://www.ucdavis.edu/news/medfly-and-other-fruit-flies-entrenched-california-study-concludes.

6   Karlamangla, Soumya. "California's Statewide Minimum Wage Is Now $16 an Hour." *New York Times*, January 2, 2024. https://www.nytimes.com/2024/01/02/us/california-minimum-wage.html.

7   Nagourney, Adam. "California Nears Deal to Adopt a $15 State Minimum Wage." *New York Times*, March 27, 2016. https://www.nytimes.com/2016/03/28/us/california-nears-deal-to-adopt-a-15-state-minimum-wage.html.

8   Karlamangla, Soumya. "California's Statewide Minimum Wage Is Now $16 an Hour." *New York Times*, January 2, 2024. https://www.nytimes.com/2024/01/02/us/california-minimum-wage.html.

9   Jackson, Kerry. "Reform Misguided Laws, Don't Raise Minimum Wage, to Address California's High Cost of Living." *GV Wire*, December 22, 2021. https://gvwire.com/2021/12/22/reform-misguided-laws-dont-raise-minimum-wage-to-address-californias-high-cost-of-living/.

10   Ibid.

11   Jackson, Kerry, and Wayne Winegarden. Rep. *California Migrating: Documenting the Causes and Consequences of California's Growing Exodus Problem*. Pacific Research Institute, September 2021. https://www.pacificresearch.org/wp-content/uploads/2021/09/CA-Migration_F_web.pdf.

12   Kuang, Jeanne. "Want to Vote on Raising California's Minimum Wage? Judge Says Not until 2024." *CalMatters*, July 22, 2022. https://calmatters.org/economy/2022/07/california-minimum-wage-november-ballot/.

13   Picchi, Aimee. "California's Fast-Food Workers Are Now the Highest Paid in U.S. with New $20 per Hour Wage." *MarketWatch (CBS News)*, April 1, 2024. https://www.cbsnews.com/news/california-fast-food-20-minimum-wage-law-prices/.

14   Ibid.

15   Sitori, Daniela, Eliyahu Kamisher, and Josh Eiderson. "How Panera Bread Ducked California's New $20 Minimum Wage Law." *Bloomberg.Com*, February 28, 2024. https://www.bloomberg.com/news/articles/2024-02-28/panera-bread-exempt-from-california-s-minimum-wage-increase-for-fast-food-worker?cmpid=socialflow-twitter-business&leadSource=uverify%20wall.

16   Ibid.

17   Zavala, Ashley. "What We Know about Panera, Gov. Newsom, California's New Fast Food Worker Law and NDAs." *KCRA.Com*, March 9, 2024. https://www.kcra.com/article/california-fast-food-law-panera-gov-gavin-newsom-controversy-ex-plained/60115774 and Jackson, Kerry. "California's Sourdough Politics." *Right by the Bay* (blog). Pacific Research Institute, March 19, 2024. https://www.pacificre-search.org/californias-sourdough-politics/.

18   Picchi, Aimee. "California's Fast-Food Workers Are Now the Highest Paid in U.S. with New $20 per Hour Wage." *MarketWatch (CBS News)*, April 1, 2024. https://www.cbsnews.com/news/california-fast-food-20-minimum-wage-law-prices/.

19   Kelso, Alicia. "Chipotle Proves Traffic Gains Are Possible in This Environment." *Nation's Restaurant News*, February 7, 2024. https://www.nrn.com/finance/chipot-le-proves-traffic-gains-are-possible-environment and Revell, Eric. "Fast-Food Prices Set to Rise at McDonald's, Chipotle and Others as California Minimum Wage Hike Looms." *Fox Business*, February 4, 2024. https://www.foxbusiness.com/markets/fast-food-prices-rise-mcdonalds-chipotle-california-minimum-wage-hike-take-ef-fect-this-spring and Picchi, Aimee. "California's Fast-Food Workers Are Now the Highest Paid in U.S. with New $20 per Hour Wage." *MarketWatch (CBS News)*, April 1, 2024. https://www.cbsnews.com/news/california-fast-food-20-minimum-wage-law-prices/.

20   Garcia, Karen. "Starbucks, Chipotle, McDonald's: Who's Raising Prices as Cali-fornia Fast-Food Law Starts Today." *Los Angeles Times*, March 28, 2024. https://www.latimes.com/california/story/2024-03-28/fast-food-workers-minimum-wage-is-going-up-which-chains-will-up-their-prices and Zilber, Ariel. "McDonald's Franchisee Raises Prices after Calif. Minimum Wage Law — but Won't Charge $20 for a Happy Meal." *New York Post*, April 2, 2024. https://nypost.com/2024/04/02/business/mcdonalds-franchisee-in-california-wont-charge-20-for-a-happy-meal/.

21   Garcia, Karen. "Starbucks, Chipotle, McDonald's: Who's Raising Prices as Cali-fornia Fast-Food Law Starts Today." *Los Angeles Times*, March 28, 2024. https://www.latimes.com/california/story/2024-03-28/fast-food-workers-minimum-wage-is-going-up-which-chains-will-up-their-prices.

22   Picchi, Aimee. "California's Fast-Food Workers Are Now the Highest Paid in U.S. with New $20 per Hour Wage." *MarketWatch (CBS News)*, April 1, 2024. https://www.cbsnews.com/news/california-fast-food-20-minimum-wage-law-prices/.

23   Jackson, Kerry. "Reform Misguided Laws, Don't Raise Minimum Wage, to Address California's High Cost of Living." *GV Wire*, December 22, 2021. https://gvwire.com/2021/12/22/reform-misguided-laws-dont-raise-minimum-wage-to-address-californias-high-cost-of-living/ and Kenton, Will. Issue brief. *Wage Push Inflation: Definition, Causes, and Examples*. Investopedia, January 5, 2024. https://www.investopedia.com/terms/w/wage-push-inflation.asp.

24   Ashenfelter, Orley, and Štěpán Jurajda. Rep. *Wages, Minimum Wages, and Price Pass-through: The Case of McDonald's Restaurants*, February 2021. https://docs.iza.org/dp14124.pdf.

25   Jackson, Kerry. "Reform Misguided Laws, Don't Raise Minimum Wage, to Address California's High Cost of Living." *GV Wire*, December 22, 2021. https://gvwire.com/2021/12/22/reform-misguided-laws-dont-raise-minimum-wage-to-address-californias-high-cost-of-living/.

26   Ashenfelter, Orley, and Štěpán Jurajda. Rep. *Wages, Minimum Wages, and Price Pass-through: The Case of McDonald's Restaurants*, February 2021. https://docs.iza.org/dp14124.pdf.

27   Federal Reserve Bank of St. Louis. There is no such thing as a free lunch - The
      Economic Lowdown Video series, April 30, 2024. https://www.stlouisfed.org/edu-
      cation/economic-lowdown-video-series/no-such-thing-free-lunch.

28   Miller, Daniel. "With Fewer Options, South L.A. Braces for Bigger Bills at Fast-Food
      Restaurants." *Los Angeles Times*, March 29, 2024. https://www.latimes.com/cali-
      fornia/story/2024-03-29/la-fast-food-south-la.

29   CorCom, Inc. Rep. Crisis in California: A Survey of Fast Food Employers' Responses
      to California's $20 Minimum Wage. Employment Policies Institute, July 26, 2024.
      https://epionline.org/app/uploads/2024/07/2024-06-California-Limited-Ser-
      vice-Restaurant-Operator-Survey-Final-Booklet.pdf.

30   Jackson, Kerry. Issue brief. *Capital Ideas: Should California Workers & Policy-
      makers Fear Flippy the Hamburger-Making Robot?*, May 14, 2018. https://www.
      pacificresearch.org/capital-ideas-should-california-workers-policymakers-fear-flip-
      py-the-hamburger-making-robot/.

31   Ibid.

32   Ibid.

33   Winegarden, Wayne. "Government-Mandated Hero Pay Fails to Achieve Its Lofty
      Goals." *Forbes.Com*, January 15, 2021. https://www.forbes.com/sites/waynewin-
      egarden/2021/01/15/government-mandated-hero-pay-fails-to-achieve-its-lofty-
      goals/?sh=ff0c16638156.

34   Ibid.

35   "'Hero Pay': LA City Council Votes to Finalize $5 an Hour Emergency Ordinance
      amid Pandemic." *City News Service*. March 3, 2021. https://abc7.com/los-angeles-
      hero-pay-la-city-council-grocery-workers/10385210/.

36   "Los Angeles County Passes Ordinance Requiring $5 'hero Pay' for Grocery Work-
      ers." *City News Service*, February 24, 2021. https://abc7.com/la-county-hero-pay-
      grocery-workers-board-of-supervisors/10365760/.

37   Ruiz, Jason. "Council Moves toward Mandating $4 an Hour 'Hero Pay' Boost for
      Grocery Workers." *Long Beach Post*, January 16, 2020. https://lbpost.com/news/
      grocery-worker-hero-hazard-pay-4-hour-raise-long-beach/.

38   "Los Angeles County Passes Ordinance Requiring $5 'hero Pay' for Grocery Work-
      ers." *City News Service*, February 24, 2021. https://abc7.com/la-county-hero-pay-
      grocery-workers-board-of-supervisors/10365760/.

39   Winegarden, Wayne. "Government-Mandated Hero Pay Fails to Achieve Its Lofty
      Goals." *Forbes.Com*, January 15, 2021. https://www.forbes.com/sites/waynewin-
      egarden/2021/01/15/government-mandated-hero-pay-fails-to-achieve-its-lofty-
      goals/?sh=ff0c16638156.

40   Ibid.

41   "Kroger To Close 3 Stores in Los Angeles in Response to Approval Of 'Hero Pay'
      Mandate." *CBS News Los Angeles*. March 12, 2021. https://www.cbsnews.com/
      losangeles/news/kroger-closing-3-stores-los-angeles-response-approval-hero-pay-
      mandate/.

42   Ibid.

43   Schrupp, Kenneth. "$25 Healthcare Minimum Wage to Cost California $4 Billion in
      First Year." *Center Square*, November 6, 2023. https://www.thecentersquare.com/
      california/article_a281213a-7cf5-11ee-ade1-437122f1b968.html.

44   Thompson, Don. "California Health Workers May Face Rude Awakening With $25 Minimum Wage Law." California Healthline, April 15, 2024. https://california-healthline.org/news/article/california-health-workers-25-dollar-wage-cuts/.

45   Jackson, Kerry. "$25 Hospital Minimum Wage Bill Would Boost Some Workers at Expense of Patients." *Times of San Diego*, June 13, 2023. https://timesofsandiego.com/opinion/2023/06/13/25-hospital-minimum-wage-bill-would-boost-some-workers-at-expense-of-patients/.

46   Schrupp, Kenneth. "$25 Healthcare Minimum Wage to Cost California $4 Billion in First Year." *Center Square*, November 6, 2023. https://www.thecentersquare.com/california/article_a281213a-7cf5-11ee-ade1-437122f1b968.html.

47   Beam, Adam. "California Democrats Agree to Delay Health Care Worker Minimum Wage Increase to Help Balance Budget." Associated Press, June 22, 2024. https://apnews.com/article/california-health-care-minimum-wage-delay-ba84849b7c0a8e96ed9d7da0c126395d

48   Schrupp, Kenneth. "$25 Healthcare Minimum Wage to Cost California $4 Billion in First Year." *Center Square*, November 6, 2023. https://www.thecentersquare.com/california/article_a281213a-7cf5-11ee-ade1-437122f1b968.html.

49   Pipes, Sally. "Wage Hikes Won't Fix US Healthcare." *Newsmax*, November 21, 2023. https://www.newsmax.com/sallypipes/healthcare-wages/2023/11/21/id/1143084/ and "Hospital Services at Risk Throughout California." California Hospital Association, April 13, 2023. https://www.kaufmanhall.com/sites/default/files/2023-04/CHA-Financial-Impact-Report.pdf.

50   "Hospital Services at Risk Throughout California." California Hospital Association, April 13, 2023. https://www.kaufmanhall.com/sites/default/files/2023-04/CHA-Financial-Impact-Report.pdf.

51   Thompson, Don. "California Health Workers May Face Rude Awakening With $25 Minimum Wage Law." *California Healthline*, April 15, 2024. https://california-healthline.org/news/article/california-health-workers-25-dollar-wage-cuts/.

CHAPTER 10

1   Rep. List of Professions That Have Been Negatively Impacted by AB 5. Freelancers Against AB 5 Facebook Group, March 2021. https://thelibreinitiative.com/
wp-content/uploads/2021/04/Freelancers-Against-AB5-List-of-600-Affected-Pro-
fessions-002.pdf.

2   Rochita, Ananda. "New Guidelines for Independent Contractors Forcing Businesses to Restructure." Video blog. *ABC 10 News (Sacramento, CA)* (TV news report),
September 6, 2018. https://web.archive.org/web/20180907001212/https://www.
abc10.com/amp/article?section=news&subsection=local&topic=sacramento
&headline=new-guidelines-for-independent-contractors-forcing-businesses-to-
restructure&contentId=103-591356619.

3   Palagashvili, Liya, Paola Suarez, Christopher Kaiser, and Vitor Melo. Issue brief.
*Assessing the Impact of Worker Reclassification: Employment Outcomes Post–Cali-
fornia AB5.* Mercatus Center at George Mason University, January 2024. https://
www.mercatus.org/research/working-papers/assessing-impact-worker-reclassifi-
cation-employment-outcomes-post.

4   Rep. List of Professions That Have Been Negatively Impacted by AB 5. Freelancers Against AB 5 Facebook Group, March 2021. https://thelibreinitiative.com/
wp-content/uploads/2021/04/Freelancers-Against-AB5-List-of-600-Affected-Pro-
fessions-002.pdf.

5   "State Level Legislation." American Society of Journalists and Authors, October
26, 2022. https://www.asja.org/what-we-do/advocacy/state-level-legislation/.

6   Dewey, Caitlin. "States and Cities Eye Stronger Protections for Gig Economy
Workers." *Stateline*, September 19, 2023. https://stateline.org/2023/09/19/
states-and-cities-eye-stronger-protections-for-gig-economy-workers/.

7   Jackson, Kerry. "California's War On Gig Work Is About To Devastate The Rest Of
The Country." *Daily Caller*, February 5, 2024. https://dailycaller.com/2024/02/05/
jackson-california-ab5-gig-workers-independent-contractors/.

8   Ibid.

9   Hebert, Tom. "Biden Labor Nominee Julie Su Is a Threat to Independent Contractors and Freelancers Nationwide." Web log. *Americans for Tax Reform Blog*
(blog). Americans for Tax Reform, February 28, 2023. https://www.atr.org/
biden-dol-nominee-julie-su-tax-hiker-mismanages-resources/.

10   Lin, Judy. "CA's Labor Chief Wants the Jobs of the Future — and She Wants
Them to Cut Inequality." *CalMatters*, October 16, 2019. https://calmatters.
org/economy/2019/10/california-labor-chief-jobs-future-income-inequality-ju-
lie-su-ab5-gig-economy-unions/.

11   California Department of Finance, California State Budget, 2020-21 § (2020).
https://ebudget.ca.gov/2020-21/pdf/Enacted/BudgetSummary/FullBudgetSum-
mary.pdf.

12   "Final Rule: Employee or Independent Contractor Classification under the Fair
Labor Standards Act, RIN 1235-AA43." U.S. Department of Labor. Accessed April
29, 2024. https://www.dol.gov/agencies/whd/flsa/misclassification/rulemaking.

13   House Committee on Education and the Workforce hearing, March 11, 2024, X
video, at https://twitter.com/EdWorkforceCmte/status/1770830484953563186

14   Winegarden, Wayne. "AB 5 Is Taking Away Opportunities for Communities of Color & Low-Income Communities." Web log. *Right by the Bay* (blog). Pacific Research Institute, March 9, 2022. https://www.pacificresearch.org/ab-5-is-taking-away-opportunities-for-communities-of-color-low-income-communities/.

15   Bhutto, Neil, Andrew C. Chang, Lisa J. Settling, Joanne W. Hsu, and Julia Hewitt. "Disparities in Wealth by Race and Ethnicity in the 2019 Survey of Consumer Finances." Web log. *FEDS Notes* (blog). Board of Governors of the Federal Reserve System, September 28, 2020. https://www.federalreserve.gov/econres/notes/feds-notes/disparities-in-wealth-by-race-and-ethnicity-in-the-2019-survey-of-consumer-finances-20200928.html.

16   Howard, Tiffiany. Rep. *The State of Black Entrepreneurship in America*. Congressional Black Caucus Foundation, April 2019. https://www.cbcfinc.org/wp-content/uploads/2019/05/CPAR-Report-Black-Entrepreneurship-in-America.pdf.

17   Crain, W. Mark, and Nicole V. Crain. Rep. *The Cost of Federal Regulation to the U.S. Economy, Manufacturing and Small Business*. National Association of Manufacturers, September 10, 2014. https://www.nam.org/wp-content/uploads/2019/05/Federal-Regulation-Full-Study.pdf.

18   "Most Independent Contractors Prefer Current Work Arrangement." Web log. *Spotlight on Statistics* (blog). U.S. Bureau of Labor Statistics, 2018. https://www.bls.gov/spotlight/2018/workers-in-alternative-employment-arrangements/home.htm#:~:text=%E2%80%8B%20Source%3A%20U.S.%20Bureau%20of%20Labor%20Statistics.,-View%20Chart%20Data&text=Independent%20contractors%20overwhelmingly%20favored%20their,evenly%20split%20in%20their%20preferences.

19   Osijek, Adam. "Freelance Forward Economist Report | Upwork." Upwork, December 8, 2021. https://www.upwork.com/research/freelance-forward-2021.

20   Publication. *The State of Independence in America 2020*. MBO Partners, December 9, 2020. https://info.mbopartners.com/rs/mbo/images/MBO_Partners_State_of_Independence_2020_Report.pdf.

21   "Independent Owner Operator Truck Driver Statistics for the United States." Web log. GlobeCon Freight Systems, June 18, 2016. https://web.archive.org/web/20160130133447/http://globeconfreight.com/blog/independent-owner-operator-truck-driver-statistics-united-states/.

22   Allderdice, Linda Auerbach, Jameson B. Rice, and Kristine Orozco Little. "Trucker Protest Over California Independent Contractor Law Shuts Down Port of Oakland." Web log. *Holland and Knight Transportation Blog* (blog). Holland and Knight, August 5, 2022. https://www.hklaw.com/en/insights/publications/2022/08/trucker-protest-over-california-independent-contractor-law-shuts-down.

23   Lewison, Pam. "To Protect Ag, Time for California to Roll Back AB 5." Web log. *Right by the Bay* (blog). Pacific Research Institute, July 28, 2022. https://www.pacificresearch.org/to-protect-ag-time-for-california-to-roll-back-ab-5/.

24   Ibid.

25   Hait, Andrew W., and Lynda Lee. "What's in That Truck I Just Passed on the Highway?" Web log. *America Counts: Stories* (blog). United States Census Bureau, February 24, 2021. https://www.census.gov/library/stories/2021/02/what-is-in-that-truck-i-just-passed-on-the-highway.html.

26   Eanet, Danielle G. "Judge Rules Against Trucking Industry on California Assembly Bill AB 5." Web log. *News & Insights* (blog). Eanet, PC, March 21, 2024. https://www.eanetpc.com/news-insights/2024/march/judge-rules-against-trucking-industry-on-califor/.

27   Kingston, John. "Groups Lose Latest Court Attempt to Block California's AB5 from State's Trucking Sector." *Freight Waves*, March 16, 2024. https://www.freightwaves.com/news/groups-lose-latest-court-attempt-to-block-californias-ab5-trucking-sector.

28   Board, Editorial. "9th Circuit Went Too Far with Homelessness Ruling." *Las Vegas Review Journal*, April 23, 2024. https://www.reviewjournal.com/opinion/editorials/editorial-9th-circuit-went-too-far-with-homelessness-ruling-3039257/.

CHAPTER 11

1   Fears, J. Wayne, J. Wayne Fears, and Rod Walinchus. *The Scouting Guide to Survival: More Than 200 essential skills for staying warm, building a shelter, and signaling for help.* New York: Skyhorse Publishing, 2018.

2   Koseff, Alexei. "Newsom Attended French Laundry Party with More Households than California Advises during Pandemic." *San Francisco Chronicle*, November 16, 2020. https://www.sfchronicle.com/politics/article/Newsom-attended-French-Laundry-party-with-more-15725393.php.

3   State of California, Executive Department. Executive Order N-33-20. March 19, 2020. https://www.gov.ca.gov/wp-content/uploads/2020/03/3.19.20-attested-EO-N-33-20-COVID-19-HEALTH-ORDER.pdf

4   Arango, Tim, and Jill Cowan. "Gov. Gavin Newsom of California Orders Californians to Stay at Home." *New York Times*, March 19, 2020. https://www.nytimes.com/2020/03/19/us/California-stay-at-home-order-virus.html.

5   California, State of. "California Public Health Experts: Mass Gatherings Should Be Postponed or Canceled Statewide to Slow the Spread of Covid-19." Governor of California, March 12, 2020. https://www.gov.ca.gov/2020/03/11/california-public-health-experts-mass-gatherings-should-be-postponed-or-canceled-statewide-to-slow-the-spread-of-covid-19/.

6   Cowan, Jill. "A Timeline of the Coronavirus in California." *New York Times*, June 15, 2021. https://www.nytimes.com/2021/06/15/us/coronavirus-california-timeline.html.

7   Cowan, Jill, and Priya Arora. "When Is California Reopening?" *New York Times*, April 7, 2021. https://www.nytimes.com/article/california-reopening-faq.html.

8   Willon, Phil, Hannah Fry, and Luke Money. "Californians Must Wear Face Masks in Public under Coronavirus Order Issued by Newsom." *Los Angeles Times*, June 18, 2020. https://www.latimes.com/california/story/2020-06-18/california-mandatory-face-masks-statewide-order-coronavirus-gavin-newsom.

9   Cowan, Jill. "Newsom Rolls Back Reopening in California." *New York Times*, July 14, 2020. https://www.nytimes.com/2020/07/14/us/california-counties-reopening.html.

10   Cano, Ricardo. "Nearly All California Schools Ordered to Shut down. Online Classes Mandatory." *CalMatters*, July 17, 2020. https://calmatters.org/education/2020/07/california-schools-shut-down-reopening/.

11   Pipes, Sally C. "The Illogical California Lockdown Orders." *San Francisco Chronicle*, December 28, 2020. https://www.sfchronicle.com/opinion/openforum/article/The-illogical-California-lockdown-orders-15830469.php.

12   Ibid.

13   Winegarden, Wayne, and McKenzie Richards. Issue brief. *No Solutions, Only Trade-Offs: An Evaluation of the Benefits and Consequences From COVID-19 Restrictions.* Pacific Research Institute, Center for Medical Economics and Innovation, September 26, 2023. https://www.pacificresearch.org/wp-content/uploads/2023/09/CMEI_Covid_FINAL.pdf.

14   "Unemployment Rate in California." Federal Reserve Economic Data (FRED), May 20, 2024. https://fred.stlouisfed.org/series/CAUR.

15   "California Budget Basics: Jobs & Small Businesses." Next 10, May 2021. https://www.next10.org/sites/default/files/2021-07/CBC-Jobs-May2021_0.pdf.

16   Walters, Dan. "COVID-19 Effects on California Will Linger for Years ." *CalMatters*, February 14, 2023. https://calmatters.org/commentary/2023/02/covid-effects-on-california-linger/.

17   Lansner, Jonathan. "California Suffers Largest Job-Growth Drop in US." *Orange County Register*, January 23, 2024. https://www.ocregister.com/2024/01/23/california-suffers-largest-job-growth-drop-in-us/?clearUserState=true.

18   "California Budget Basics: Jobs & Small Businesses." Next 10, May 2021. https://www.next10.org/sites/default/files/2021-07/CBC-Jobs-May2021_0.pdf.

19   Murphy, Maggie. "The Impact The Pandemic Has Had On California Businesses." *California Business Journal*. Accessed June 4, 2024. https://calbizjournal.com/the-impact-the-pandemic-has-had-on-california-businesses/.

20   Jackson, Kerry. "Local Businesses Shrug Off California's Strict COVID Restrictions." *Inside Sources*, January 5, 2021. https://insidesources.com/local-businesses-shrug-off-californias-strict-covid-restrictions/.

21   Ibid.

22   Ibid.

23   Best, Paul. "Some California Businesses Going Underground during Lockdowns." *Fox Business*, January 23, 2021. https://www.foxbusiness.com/economy/some-california-businesses-go-underground-during-lockdowns.

24   Jackson, Kerry. "Covid-19 Lockdowns Brings Rise in Black Market." *Right by the Bay* (blog). Pacific Research Institute, January 26, 2021. https://www.pacificresearch.org/covid-19-lockdowns-brings-rise-in-black-market/.

25   "The Impact of Covid-19 on Schools in California - UCLA Center for the Transformation of Schools." UCLA Center for the Transformation of Schools - UCLA Center for the Transformation of Schools, March 27, 2024. https://transformschools.ucla.edu/research/the-impact-of-covid-19-on-schools-in-california/.

26   Jones, Carolyn. "These Fed-up Parents Fought California's Pandemic Schooling and Won. Now What? ." *CalMatters*, February 16, 2024. https://calmatters.org/education/k-12-education/2024/02/student-learning-loss/.

27   Izumi, Lance. "New Research Shows Covid Impact on Student Learning Loss and Mental Health." *Capital Ideas* (blog). Pacific Research Institute, August 13, 2021. https://www.pacificresearch.org/new-research-shows-covid-impact-on-student-learning-loss-and-mental-health/.

28   Mays, Mackenzie. " Newsom Sends His Children Back to Private School Classrooms in California." *Politico*, October 30, 2020. https://www.politico.com/states/california/story/2020/10/30/newsom-sends-his-children-back-to-school-classrooms-in-california-1332811.

29   Mulligan, Casey B., and Robert D. Arnott. Working paper. *Non-COVID Excess Deaths, 2020-21: Collateral Damage of Policy Choices?* National Bureau of Economic Research, June 2022. https://www.nber.org/system/files/working_papers/w30104/w30104.pdf.

30   Ibid.

31   Jackson, Kerry. "California's Self-Inflicted Mental Health Crisis." *GV Wire*, December 21, 2020. https://gvwire.com/2020/12/21/opinion-californias-self-inflicted-mental-health-crisis/.

32   Pipes, Sally C. "The Illogical California Lockdown Orders." *San Francisco Chronicle*, December 28, 2020. https://www.sfchronicle.com/opinion/openforum/article/The-illogical-California-lockdown-orders-15830469.php.

33   Jackson, Kerry. "California's Self-Inflicted Mental Health Crisis." *GV Wire*, December 21, 2020. https://gvwire.com/2020/12/21/opinion-californias-self-inflicted-mental-health-crisis/.

34   Jackson, Kerry. "Local Businesses Shrug Off California's Strict COVID Restrictions." *Inside Sources*, January 5, 2021. https://insidesources.com/local-businesses-shrug-off-californias-strict-covid-restrictions/.

35   Pena, Luz. "Mental Health Experts Say COVID-19 Reopening, Closing Can Cause Anxiety, Depression." ABC 7 News (San Francisco, CA), July 13, 2020. https://abc7news.com/covid-19-anxiety-coronavirus-and-mental-health-suicide-rates-during/6315978/.

36   Polumbo, Brad. "Free States Faring Far Better Than Lockdown States in One Huge Way, New Data Show." *Foundation for Economic Education*. March 29, 2021. https://fee.org/articles/free-states-faring-far-better-than-lockdown-states-in-one-huge-way-new-data-show/.

37   Kerpen, Phil, Stephen Moore, and Casey Mulligan. Rep. *A Final Report Card on the States' Response to COVID-19*. Committee to Unleash Prosperity, April 11, 2022. https://committeetounleashprosperity.com/wp-content/uploads/2022/04/Which-States-Handled-the-Covid-Pandemic-Best.pdf.

38   Zinberg, Joel M., Brian Blase, Eric Sun, and Casey Mulligan. Rep. *Freedom Wins: States with Less Restrictive COVID Policies Outperformed States with More Restrictive COVID Policies*. Paragon Health Institute, February 2023. https://paragoninstitute.org/wp-content/uploads/2023/02/freedom-wins-policy-paper.pdf.

39   Ibid.

40   Bollyky, Thomas, Isabella Turilli, and Emma Castro. Rep. *Judging How U.S. States Performed in the COVID-19 Pandemic Depends on the Metric*. Council on Foreign Relations, July 13, 2023. https://www.cfr.org/article/judging-how-us-states-performed-covid-19-pandemic-depends-metric.

41   Committee to Unleash Prosperity. " Unleash Prosperity Hotline," February 23, 2021. https://mailchi.mp/83dcef0006ad/unleash-prosperity-hotline-865064?e=4b71f6033f.

42   Walters, Dan. "COVID-19 Effects on California Will Linger for Years ." *CalMatters*, February 14, 2023. https://calmatters.org/commentary/2023/02/covid-effects-on-california-linger/.

43   Jackson, Kerry. "Local Businesses Shrug Off California's Strict COVID Restrictions." *Inside Sources*, January 5, 2021. https://insidesources.com/local-businesses-shrug-off-californias-strict-covid-restrictions/.

44   Ibid.

CHAPTER 12

1   Fears, J. Wayne. *The Scouting Guide to Survival: More Than 200 Essential Skills for Staying Warm, Building a Shelter, and Signaling for Help.* New York, NY: Skyhorse Publishing, 2018.

2   Ibid.

3   Izumi, Lance. "New Research Shows Covid Impact on Student Learning Loss and Mental Health." *Capital Ideas* (blog). Pacific Research Institute, August 13, 2021. https://www.pacificresearch.org/new-research-shows-covid-impact-on-student-learning-loss-and-mental-health/

4   Dorn, Emma, Bryan Hancock, Jimmy Sarakatsannis, and Ellen Viruleg. Rep. *COVID-19 and Education: The Lingering Effects of Unfinished Learning.* McKinsey and Company, July 27, 2021. https://www.mckinsey.com/industries/public-sector/our-insights/covid-19-and-education-the-lingering-effects-of-unfinished-learning.

5   Fahle, Erin, Thomas J. Kane, Tyler Patterson, Sean F. Reardon, Douglas O. Staiger, and Elizabeth Stuart. Rep. *School District and Community Factors Associated With Learning Loss During the COVID-19 Pandemic.* Education Recovery Scorecard, Center for Education Policy Research at Harvard University, Stanford University Educational Opportunity Project, May 11, 2023. https://cepr.harvard.edu/sites/hwpi.harvard.edu/files/cepr/files/explaining_covid_losses_5.23.pdf.

6   Dorn, Emma, Bryan Hancock, Jimmy Sarakatsannis, and Ellen Viruleg. Rep. *COVID-19 and Education: The Lingering Effects of Unfinished Learning.* McKinsey and Company, July 27, 2021. https://www.mckinsey.com/industries/public-sector/our-insights/covid-19-and-education-the-lingering-effects-of-unfinished-learning.

7   Schwartz, Sarah. "How to Give Students the Confidence to Take on Rigorous Work." *Education Week*, February 8, 2022. https://www.edweek.org/teaching-learning/how-to-give-students-the-confidence-to-take-on-rigorous-work/2022/02.

8   McGahan, Jason. "Cecily Myart-Cruz's Hostile Takeover of L.A.'s Public Schools." *Los Angeles Magazine*, August 26, 2021. https://lamag.com/featured/cecily-myart-cruz-teachers-union.

9   Marzorati, Guy. "Newsom Proposes a Return to In-Person Learning Beginning Next School Year." *KQED*, May 14, 2021. https://www.kqed.org/news/11873813/newsom-proposes-a-return-to-in-person-learning-beginning-next-school-year.

10   California Department of Finance, Governor's Budget Summary, 2023-24 - K-12 Education § (2023). https://ebudget.ca.gov/2023-24/pdf/BudgetSummary/K-12Education.pdf.

11   National Center for Education Statistics, The Nation's Report Card: 2022 Mathematics State Snapshot, California §. Accessed May 8, 2024. https://nces.ed.gov/nationsreportcard/subject/publications/stt2022/pdf/2023011CA8.pdf.

12   Ibid.

13   Izumi, Lance. "Missing from Newsom's Ed Budget: Student Outcome Goals and Choice." *Right by the Bay* (blog). Pacific Research Institute, January 22, 2024. https://www.pacificresearch.org/missing-from-newsoms-ed-budget-student-outcome-goals-and-choice/ and California Department of Finance, Governor's Budget Summary, 2024-25 - K-123 Education § (2024). https://ebudget.

ca.gov/2024-25/pdf/BudgetSummary/K-12Education.pdf.

14   Fensterwald, John. "California Agrees to Target the Most Struggling Students to Settle Learning-Loss Lawsuit." *EdSource*, February 1, 2024. https://edsource.org/2024/california-agrees-to-target-most-struggling-students-to-settle-learning-loss-lawsuit/705088.

15   Izumi, Lance. "Lawsuit Settlement Forces Accountability on California's Spending for Student Learning Loss." *Right by the Bay* (blog). Pacific Research Institute, March 4, 2024. https://www.pacificresearch.org/lawsuit-settlement-forces-accountability-on-californias-spending-for-student-learning-loss/.

16   Fensterwald, John. "California Agrees to Target the Most Struggling Students to Settle Learning-Loss Lawsuit." *EdSource*, February 1, 2024. https://edsource.org/2024/california-agrees-to-target-most-struggling-students-to-settle-learning-loss-lawsuit/705088.

17   Fensterwald, John, and Daniel J. Willis. "California K-12 Enrollment Plunges Again, Falls below 6 Million." *EdSource*, April 11, 2022. https://edsource.org/2022/california-k-12-enrollment-plunges-again-falls-below-6-million/670111.

18   DiCamillo, Mark. Publication. *Updating Voter Views of the Public Schools*. Institute of Government Studies, University of California, Berkeley, February 25, 2022. https://escholarship.org/uc/item/1gz0n3nx.

19   Fears, J. Wayne. *The Scouting Guide to Survival: More Than 200 Essential Skills for Staying Warm, Building a Shelter, and Signaling for Help*. New York, NY: Skyhorse Publishing, 2018.

20   Ibid.

21   Gonzalez, Vicki. "KCRA 3 News." Broadcast. *Competing Rallies Held over Future of California Charter Schools*, May 22, 2019. https://www.kcra.com/article/competing-rallies-held-future-california-charter-schools/27562750.

22   Izumi, Lance. "A Return to Educational Excellence." Essay. In *Saving California: Solutions to the State's Biggest Policy Problems*, edited by Steven Greenhut, 79–94. Pasadena, CA: Pacific Research Institute, 2021.

23   Izumi, Lance. Issue brief. *New and Emerging Obstacles Facing Charter Schools*. Pacific Research Institute, January 5, 2021. https://www.pacificresearch.org/wp-content/uploads/2020/12/CharterSchoolBrief_f_web.pdf.

24   Izumi, Lance. "A Return to Educational Excellence." Essay. In *Saving California: Solutions to the State's Biggest Policy Problems*, edited by Steven Greenhut, 79–94. Pasadena, CA: Pacific Research Institute, 2021.

25   Izumi, Lance. Publication. "Supporting Charter Schools," Chapter in *Policy Manual for California School Board Members*. Pasadena, CA: Pacific Research Institute, 2023.

26   "Charters Up Close: Charter Schools Put Kids First." California Charter Schools Association. Accessed May 8, 2024. https://www.ccsa.org/charters-up-close/kids-first.

27   Izumi, Lance. Issue brief. *New and Emerging Obstacles Facing Charter Schools*. Pacific Research Institute, January 5, 2021. https://www.pacificresearch.org/wp-content/uploads/2020/12/CharterSchoolBrief_f_web.pdf.

28   Ibid.

29   Ibid.

30   Izumi, Lance. "A Return to Educational Excellence." Essay. In *Saving California: Solutions to the State's Biggest Policy Problems*, edited by Steven Greenhut, 79–94. Pasadena, CA: Pacific Research Institute, 2021.

31   Ibid.

32   Lake, Robin, Ashley Jochim, Paul Hill, and Sivan Tuchman. Rep. *Do the Costs of California Charter Schools Outweigh the Benefits?* Center on Reinventing Public Education, University of Washington Bothell, May 2019. https://files.eric.ed.gov/fulltext/ED595193.pdf and Izumi, Lance. "A Return to Educational Excellence." Essay. In *Saving California: Solutions to the State's Biggest Policy Problems*, edited by Steven Greenhut, 79–94. Pasadena, CA: Pacific Research Institute, 2021.

33   Johnson, Alison Heape, Josh B. McGee, Patrick J. Wolf, Jay F. May, and Larry D. Maloney. Rep. *Charter School Funding: Little Progress Towards Equity in the City.* University of Arkansas, Department of Education Reform, August 9, 2023. https://bpb-us-e1.wpmucdn.com/wordpressua.uark.edu/dist/9/544/files/2023/12/charter-school-funding-little-progress-towards-equity-in-the-city.pdf; and Izumi, Lance. "Los Angeles and Oakland Get 'F' Grades for Charter Funding Gaps." *Right by the Bay* (blog). Pacific Research Institute., August 21, 2023. https://www.pacificresearch.org/los-angeles-and-oakland-get-f-grades-for-charter-funding-gaps/.

34   "Award and Badge Explorer: Girl Scouts." Girl Scouts of the USA. Accessed May 9, 2024. https://www.girlscouts.org/en/members/for-girl-scouts/badges-journeys-awards/badge-explorer.html.

35   Ibid.

36   Izumi, Lance. "California's Woke Curricula Built on Research Quicksand." *Right by the Bay* (blog). Pacific Research Institute, April 21, 2022. https://www.pacificresearch.org/californias-work-curricula-built-on-research-quicksand/

37   Ibid.

38   Ibid.

39   Ibid.

40   National Center for Education Statistics. The Nation's Report Card: 2022 Reading State Snapshot: California. Accessed May 9, 2024. https://nces.ed.gov/nationsreportcard/subject/publications/stt2022/pdf/2023010CA4.pdf

41   Ellis, C., S. Holston, G. Drake, H. Putnam, A. Swisher, and H. Peske. Rep. *Teacher Prep: Strengthening Elementary Reading Instruction*. National Council on Teacher Quality, June 2023. https://www.nctq.org/dmsView/Teacher_Prep_Review_Strengthening_Elementary_Reading_Instruction

42   Bacigalupi, Megan. "California Gov. Gavin Newsom's Actions Don't Match His Words on Dyslexia." *San Francisco Chronicle*, December 8, 2021. https://www.sfgate.com/politics-op-eds/article/Gavin-Newsom-dyslexia-California-schools-16683003.php and Izumi, Lance. "Why Can't Children Read? Blame the Failed Way We Teach Reading." *RealClearEducation*, June 29, 2023. https://www.realcleareducation.com/articles/2023/06/29/why_cant_children_read_blame_the_failed_way_we_teach_reading_110882.html

43   Bacigalupi, Megan. "California Gov. Gavin Newsom's Actions Don't Match His Words on Dyslexia." *San Francisco Chronicle*, December 8, 2021. https://www.sfgate.com/politics-op-eds/article/Gavin-Newsom-dyslexia-California-schools-16683003.php

44   Ellis, C., S. Holston, G. Drake, H. Putnam, A. Swisher, and H. Peske. Rep. *Teacher Prep: Strengthening Elementary Reading Instruction*. National Council on Teacher Quality, June 2023. https://www.nctq.org/dmsView/Teacher_Prep_Review_Strengthening_Elementary_Reading_Instruction.

45   California State Parks. Emigrant Gap - Historical Landmark. Accessed May 9, 2024. https://ohp.parks.ca.gov/ListedResources/Detail/403

46   Ibid.

47   "2022–23 California Statewide Assessment Results and Chronic Absenteeism Rates Show Student Progress," October 18, 2023. California Department of Education. https://www.cde.ca.gov/nr/ne/yr23/yr23rel83.asp

48   Izumi, Lance. "California's Latest School Test Scores Are Nothing to Celebrate ." *Times of San Diego*, November 2, 2023. https://timesofsandiego.com/opinion/2023/11/02/californias-latest-school-test-scores-are-nothing-to-celebrate/

49   Ibid.

50   Ibid.

51   Poff, Jeremiah. "How Much Math and Reading Scores Fell in Every State during Pandemic." *Washington Examiner*, October 24, 2022. https://www.washingtonexaminer.com/news/223428/see-it-how-much-math-and-reading-scores-fell-in-every-state-during-pandemic/

52   Napolitano, Janet. Letter to Board of Regents, University of California. "Memo Re College Entrance Exam Use in University of California Undergraduate Admissions." *University of California*, May 21, 2020. https://regents.universityofcalifornia.edu/regmeet/may20/b4.pdf and Izumi, Lance. "Attempt to Overthrow Proposition 209 Ignores K-12's Responsibility." *Center Square*, June 4, 2020. https://www.thecentersquare.com/california/op-ed-attempt-to-overthrow-proposition-209-ignores-k-12-s-responsibility/article_28310898-a691-11ea-b551-7b675d960c40.html

53   Ibid.

54   Izumi, Lance. "SoCal NAACP Chapters Break with Unions Because Charter Schools Work ." *Times of San Diego*, May 10, 2019. https://timesofsandiego.com/opinion/2019/05/10/socal-naacp-chapters-break-with-unions-because-charter-schools-work/

55   NAACP San Diego Branch Counter-Resolution on Charter Schools, May 2019. https://s3.documentcloud.org/documents/5987162/190425-NAACP-RESOLUTION-CA-PUBLIC-SCHOOLS.pdf

56   Ibid.

57   Rep. *Urban Charter School Study Report on 41 Regions, 2015.* Stanford University Center for Research on Education Outcomes. Accessed May 9, 2024. https://urbancharters.stanford.edu/download/Urban%20Charter%20School%20Study%20Report%20on%2041%20Regions.pdf

58   "About Us." Fior d' Italia, April 28, 2023. https://fior.com/about-us/.

59   "Facts about English Learners in California." California Department of Education. Accessed May 10, 2024. https://www.cde.ca.gov/ds/ad/cefelfacts.asp.

60   Izumi, Lance. "California's Woke Curricula Built on Research Quicksand." *Right by the Bay* (blog). Pacific Research Institute, April 21, 2022. https://www.pacificresearch.org/californias-work-curricula-built-on-research-quicksand/.

61   Ibid.

62   Izumi, Lance. "New K-12 Ethnic Studies Opens the Door to Classroom Politiciza-
      tion." *Right by the Bay* (blog). Pacific Research Institute, October 13, 2024. https://
      www.pacificresearch.org/new-k-12-ethnic-studies-opens-the-door-to-classroom-
      politicization/.

63   Ibid.

64   Izumi, Lance. "How Ethnic Studies Opens the Door to CRT: Elina Kaplan, Lia
      Rensin and ACES." Essay. In *The Great Parent Revolt: How Parents and Grassroots
      Leaders Are Fighting Critical Race Theory in America's Schools*, 99–111. Pasadena,
      CA: Pacific Research Institute, 2022.

65   Salinas Union High School District, SUHSD History & Social Science Scope and Se-
      quence, Ethnic Studies Grade Levels 9th & 10th §. Accessed May 8, 2024. https://
      docs.google.com/document/d/1AwHKmV-Z9luVgsabQXg45X1bs7oJ7-w5_3TMdY-
      Dj8cs/edit.

66   Ibid.

67   Izumi, Lance. "How Ethnic Studies Opens the Door to CRT: Elina Kaplan, Lia
      Rensin and ACES." Essay. In *The Great Parent Revolt: How Parents and Grassroots
      Leaders Are Fighting Critical Race Theory in America's Schools*, 99–111. Pasadena,
      CA: Pacific Research Institute, 2022.

68   Ibid.

CHAPTER 13

1   "Come West and Be Cured (Clip)." PBS *The American Experience*. Accessed May 5, 2024. https://www.pbs.org/wgbh/americanexperience/features/plague-west/.

2   "The Land of Sunshine: Testimonials by W.C. Patterson and E.P. Johnson." PBS *The American Experience*. Accessed May 5, 2024. https://www.pbs.org/wgbh/american-experience/features/plague-sunshine/.

3   Ibid.

4   Ibid.

5   Kekatos, Mary. "California Becomes First State to Offer Health Insurance to All Undocumented Immigrants." *ABC News*, December 29, 2023. https://abcnews.go.com/Health/california-1st-state-of-fer-health-insurance-undocumented-immigrants/story?id=105986377.

6   Stremikis, Kristof. "Top Five Takeaways from CHCF's 2024 California Health Policy Poll." CHCF Blog. California Health Care Foundation, February 1, 2024. https://www.chcf.org/blog/top-takeaways-california-health-policy-poll/#relat-ed-links-and-downloads.

7   Coyle, Carmela. "New Report Confirms Depth of California's Health Care Crisis ." CEO Message (blog). California Health Care Foundation, April 13, 2023. https://calhospital.org/new-report-confirms-depth-of-californias-health-care-crisis/.

8   Winegarden, Wayne. "Just Say No to California's Drug-Making Plan." *San Francisco Chronicle*, February 24, 2020. https://www.sfchronicle.com/opinion/openforum/article/Just-say-no-to-California-s-drug-making-plan-15078104.php.

9   "Biosimilar Insulin Initiative." CalRx, April 27, 2024. https://calrx.ca.gov/biosimi-lar-insulin-initiative/.

10   "Why the Pelosi and Newsom Approaches to Prescription Drugs Won't Really Help Patients." Episode. *Next Round Podcast*. Pacific Research Institute, January 13, 2020. https://www.pacificresearch.org/wayne-winegarden-why-the-pelosi-and-newsom-approaches-to-prescription-drugs-wont-really-help-patients/.

11   Winegarden, Wayne. "Just Say No to California's Drug-Making Plan." *San Francisco Chronicle*, February 24, 2020. https://www.sfchronicle.com/opinion/openforum/article/Just-say-no-to-California-s-drug-making-plan-15078104.php.

12   Ibid.

13   Ibid.

14   Winegarden, Wayne. Issue brief. *Improving Market Efficiencies Will Promote Greater Drug Affordability*. Pacific Research Institute, January 8, 2020. https://medecon.org/wp-content/uploads/2020/01/DrugAffordability_F.pdf.

15   Van Nuys, Karen, Geoffrey Joyce, Rocio Ribero, and Dana Goldman. Rep. *Overpay-ing for Prescription Drugs: The Copay Clawback Phenomenon*. University of Southern California Leonard D. Schaeffer Center for Healthy Policy and Economics, March 12, 2018. https://healthpolicy.usc.edu/research/overpaying-for-prescription-drugs/.

16   Winegarden, Wayne. Issue brief. *Improving Market Efficiencies Will Promote Greater Drug Affordability*. Pacific Research Institute, January 8, 2020. https://medecon.org/wp-content/uploads/2020/01/DrugAffordability_F.pdf.

17   Ibid.

18   Pipes, Sally C. "California's Single-Payer Health Insurance Dream Remains a Fantasy." *Times of San Diego*, April 24, 2024. https://timesofsandiego.com/opinion/2024/04/25/californias-single-payer-health-insurance-fantasy-is-turning-to-ashes/#google_vignette.

19   "First Aid." First Aid Merit Badge, February 5, 2024. http://www.usscouts.org/usscouts/mb/mb008.asp.

20   Pipes, Sally C. "California's Single-Payer Health Insurance Dream Remains a Fantasy." *Times of San Diego*, April 24, 2024. https://timesofsandiego.com/opinion/2024/04/25/californias-single-payer-health-insurance-fantasy-is-turning-to-ashes/#google_vignette.

21   Pipes, Sally C. "California Single-Payer Bill Is Incremental Step to Disaster." *East Bay Times*, April 23, 2023. https://www.eastbaytimes.com/2023/04/19/opinion-california-single-payer-bill-is-incremental-step-to-disaster/.

22   Pipes, Sally C. "California's Single-Payer Health Insurance Dream Remains a Fantasy." *Times of San Diego*, April 24, 2024. https://timesofsandiego.com/opinion/2024/04/25/californias-single-payer-health-insurance-fantasy-is-turning-to-ashes/#google_vignette.

23   Pipes, Sally C. "California Single-Payer Bill Is Incremental Step to Disaster." *East Bay Times*, April 23, 2023. https://www.eastbaytimes.com/2023/04/19/opinion-california-sigle-payer-bill-is-incremental-step-to-disaster/.

24   Pipes, Sally C. "California's Single-Payer Health Insurance Dream Remains a Fantasy." *Times of San Diego*, April 24, 2024. https://timesofsandiego.com/opinion/2024/04/25/californias-single-payer-health-insurance-fantasy-is-turning-to-ashes/#google_vignette.

25   Zuckerman, Stephen, Laura Skopec, and Joshua Aarons. "Medicaid Physician Fees Remained Substantially below Fees Paid by Medicare in 2019." *Health Affairs* 40, no. 2 (February 1, 2021): 343–48. https://doi.org/10.1377/hlthaff.2020.00611 and Issue brief. *Medicaid Hospital Payment: A Comparison across States and to Medicare.* Medicaid and CHIP Payment and Access Commission, April 2017. https://www.macpac.gov/wp-content/uploads/2017/04/Medicaid-Hospital-Payment-A-Comparison-across-States-and-to-Medicare.pdf.

26   Winegarden, Wayne. "Spending Watch: Single Payer Will Worsen California's Healthcare System and Reduce Economic Growth." *Pacific Research Institute* (blog), March 2024. https://www.pacificresearch.org/single-payer-will-worsen-californias-healthcare-system-and-reduce-economic-growth/.

27   Winegarden, Wayne. "Spending Watch: Single Payer Will Worsen California's Healthcare System and Reduce Economic Growth." *Pacific Research Institute* (blog), March 2024. https://www.pacificresearch.org/single-payer-will-worsen-californias-healthcare-system-and-reduce-economic-growth/.

28   Walczak, Jared. Issue brief. *California Considers Doubling Its Taxes.* Tax Foundation, January 6, 2022. https://taxfoundation.org/blog/california-health-care-tax-proposal/.

29   Winegarden, Wayne. "Spending Watch: Single Payer Will Worsen California's Healthcare System and Reduce Economic Growth." *Pacific Research Institute* (blog), March 2024. https://www.pacificresearch.org/single-payer-will-worsen-californias-healthcare-system-and-reduce-economic-growth/.

30   Ibid.

31   Sosa, Anabel. "Single-Payer Healthcare Is a 'Tough, Tough Sell' as California Faces Massive Budget Shortfall." *Los Angeles Times*, February 21, 2024. https://www.latimes.com/california/story/2024-02-21/single-payer-healthcare-california-speaker-robert-rivas-budget-deficit-calcare.

32   Pipes, Sally C. "What I'd Tell California's Single-Payer Commission." *FoxNews.Com*. February 2, 2020. https://www.foxnews.com/opinion/sally-pipes-what-id-tell-californias-single-payer-commission.

33   Pipes, Sally C. "Don't Give Medicaid to Illegal Immigrants." *Washington Examiner*, January 15, 2024. https://www.washingtonexaminer.com/opinion/2793206/dont-give-medicaid-to-illegal-immigrants/.

34   *Medi-Cal Enrollment and Renewal*. Accessed May 5, 2024. https://www.dhcs.ca.gov/dataandstats/Pages/Medi-Cal-Eligibility-Statistics.aspx.

35   Pipes, Sally C. "Don't Give Medicaid to Illegal Immigrants." *Washington Examiner*, January 15, 2024. https://www.washingtonexaminer.com/opinion/2793206/dont-give-medicaid-to-illegal-immigrants/.

36   Kekatos, Mary. "California Becomes First State to Offer Health Insurance to All Undocumented Immigrants." *ABC News*, December 29, 2023. https://abcnews.go.com/Health/california-1st-state-offer-health-insurance-undocumented-immigrants/story?id=105986377.

37   Pipes, Sally C. "Don't Give Medicaid to Illegal Immigrants." *Washington Examiner*, January 15, 2024. https://www.washingtonexaminer.com/opinion/2793206/dont-give-medicaid-to-illegal-immigrants/.

38   Bollag, Sophia. "Undocumented Kids Can Get Health Care in California. Gavin Newsom Wants It for Young Adults, Too." *Sacramento Bee*. July 2, 2019. https://www.sacbee.com/news/politics-government/capitol-alert/article229743589.html.

39   Aguilera, Elizabeth. "CA Democrats Try Again to Provide Health Care to Needy Undocumented Seniors." *CalMatters*, September 9, 2019. https://calmatters.org/health/2019/09/free-health-care-undocumented-seniors-california-immigrants-medi-cal/.

CHAPTER 14

1   Kennedy, Mark. "Game Show 'The Price Is Right' Celebrates Its 50th Season." *Associated Press*, September 13, 2021. https://apnews.com/article/technology-entertainment-sports-arts-and-entertainment-new-york-393b3260f7b982bd925f16e-563a94b33.

2   Ibid.

3   Winegarden, Wayne. Issue brief. *Spending Watch: Reparations - A Financially Unrealistic Proposal That Will Bankrupt California*, February 2024. https://www.pacificresearch.org/spending-watch/.

4   Tran, Emi Tuyetnhi, and Curtis Bunn. "California's Reparations Report Excludes Payment Plan but Is Full of Program Proposals." *NBC News*. June 29, 2023. https://www.nbcnews.com/news/nbcblk/california-reparations-task-foce-read-final-report-rcna91452 and California Task Force to Study and Develop Reparation Proposals for African Americans, The California Reparations Report § (2023). https://oag.ca.gov/system/files/media/full-ca-reparations.pdf.

5   Itchon, Rowena. "How Much Could You Have to Pay in Reparations?" Right by the Bay (blog). Pacific Research Institute, March 31, 2023. https://www.pacificresearch.org/how-much-could-you-have-to-pay-in-reparations/.

6   Fry, Wendy. "Reparations Rift? California's Black Lawmakers Divided on How Far to Go." *CalMatters*, April 10, 2024. https://calmatters.org/california-divide/2024/04/reparations-california-legislature/.

7   California Task Force to Study and Develop Reparation Proposals for African Americans, The California Reparations Report § (2023). https://oag.ca.gov/system/files/media/full-ca-reparations.pdf and Fry, Wendy. "Reparations Panel Recommends Possible Millions for Eligible Black Californians." *CalMatters*, May 8, 2023. https://calmatters.org/california-divide/2023/05/california-reparations-approved/.

8   Winegarden, Wayne. Issue brief. Spending Watch: Reparations - A Financially Unrealistic Proposal That Will Bankrupt California, February 2024. https://www.pacificresearch.org/spending-watch/ and Fry, Wendy. "Reparations Panel Recommends Possible Millions for Eligible Black Californians." *CalMatters*, May 8, 2023. https://calmatters.org/california-divide/2023/05/california-reparations-approved/.

9   Winegarden, Wayne. Issue brief. Spending Watch: Reparations - A Financially Unrealistic Proposal That Will Bankrupt California, February 2024. https://www.pacificresearch.org/spending-watch/

10   Fry, Wendy. "'Just the Beginning': California Reparations Backers Applaud Bills, Even without Big Cash Payouts." *CalMatters*, January 31, 2024. https://calmatters.org/california-divide/2024/01/reparations-california-2/.

11   Fry, Wendy. "Reparations Rift? California's Black Lawmakers Divided on How Far to Go." *CalMatters*, April 10, 2024. https://calmatters.org/california-divide/2024/04/reparations-california-legislature/.

12   Ibid.

13   Ibid.

14   Ibid.

15   Fry, Wendy. "California Reparations Task Force to Recommend 'Down Payments' for Slavery, Racism." *CalMatters*, May 1, 2023. https://calmatters.org/california-divide/2023/05/reparations-payments-california/.

16   DiCamillo, Mark. "Majority of Voters Believe Black Californians Continue to Be Affected by the Legacy of Slavery, yet Cash Reparations Face Headwinds." UC Berkeley Institute for Governmental Studies, September 10, 2023. UC Berkeley Institute for Governmental Studies. https://escholarship.org/uc/item/5ks5g9f6?#-author.

17   Ibid.

18   California Task Force to Study and Develop Reparation Proposals for African Americans, The California Reparations Report § (2023). https://oag.ca.gov/system/files/media/full-ca-reparations.pdf.

19   Birle, Jack. "San Francisco Lawmakers Trying to Create $50 Million Reparations Office." *Washington Examiner*, March 23, 2023. https://www.washingtonexaminer.com/news/2752385/san-francisco-lawmakers-trying-to-create-50-million-reparations-office/.

20   Ibid.

21   Ohanian, Lee. Issue brief. *California On Your Mind: The Cost Of San Francisco's Reparations Proposal: Nearly $600,000 Per Household*. Hoover Institution at Stanford University, January 24, 2023. https://www.hoover.org/research/cost-san-franciscos-reparations-proposal-nearly-600000-household.

22   Beam, Adam. "11 U.S. Mayors Commit to Develop Reparations Pilot Projects." *Associated Press*, June 18, 2011. https://www.latimes.com/world-nation/story/2021-06-18/mayors-commit-to-develop-reparations-pilot-projects.

CHAPTER 15

1   Aydin, Rebecca. "How 3 Guys Turned Renting Air Mattresses in Their Apartment into a $31 Billion Company, Airbnb." Business Insider, September 20, 2019. https://www.businessinsider.com/how-airbnb-was-founded-a-visual-history-2016-2.

2   "About Us." Airbnb Newsroom, May 16, 2024. https://news.airbnb.com/about-us/.

3   "Shareholder Letter - Airbnb Investor." Airbnb. Accessed June 6, 2024. https://airbnb2020ipo.q4web.com/files/doc_financials/2023/q4/Airbnb_Q4-2023-Shareholder-Letter_Final.pdf.

4   Taylor, Mac, Chas Alamo, and Brian Uhler. Rep. Edited by Marianne O'Malley. *California's High Housing Costs: Causes and Consequences*. California Legislative Analyst's Office, March 17, 2015. https://www.lao.ca.gov/reports/2015/finance/housing-costs/housing-costs.pdf.

5   Ibid.

6   "April Home Sales and Price Report." California Association of Realtors, May 17, 2024. https://www.car.org/aboutus/mediacenter/newsreleases/2024-News-Releases/april2024sales.

7   "Existing-Home Sales Retreated 1.9% in April." National Association of Realtors, May 22, 2024. https://www.nar.realtor/newsroom/existing-home-sales-retreated-1-9-in-april#:~:text=Single-family%20home%20sales%20decreased,up%205.6%25%20from%20April%202023.

8   "KOA Campgrounds in California." KOA Campgrounds. Accessed June 6, 2024. https://koa.com/states-provinces/california/.

9   Lansner, Jonathan. "Southern Californians Need to Make $200,800 to Buy a Home ." *Orange County Register*, May 16, 2024. https://www.ocregister.com/2024/05/16/southern-californians-need-to-make-200800-to-buy-a-home/.

10   Jackson, Kerry. Issue brief. *Unaffordable: How Government Made California's Housing Shortage a Crisis and How Free Market Ideas Can Restore Affordability and Supply*. Pacific Research Institute, June 14, 2017. https://www.pacificresearch.org/wp-content/uploads/2017/06/CA_HousingBrief_Web.pdf.

11   Carr, Chris, Navi Dhillon, and Lucas Grunbaum. Rep. *The CEQA Gauntlet: How the California Environmental Quality Act Caused the State's Construction Crisis and How to Reform It*. Pacific Research Institute, February 27, 2022. https://www.pacificresearch.org/wp-content/uploads/2022/02/CEQA_Report_Final.pdf.

12   Ibid.

13   Ibid.

14   Seiler, John. "Enviro Law's Abusers Continue to Block Urban Housing." *Right by the Bay* (blog). Pacific Research Institute, October 20, 2022. https://www.pacificresearch.org/enviro-laws-abusers-continue-to-block-urban-housing/.

15   Carr, Chris, Navi Dhillon, and Lucas Grunbaum. Rep. *The CEQA Gauntlet: How the California Environmental Quality Act Caused the State's Construction Crisis and How to Reform It*. Pacific Research Institute, February 27, 2022. https://www.pacificresearch.org/wp-content/uploads/2022/02/CEQA_Report_Final.pdf.

16   Ibid.

17   Ibid.

18   Kaye, Loren. "What's Preventing New Housing In California? The Usual Suspects –
       Plus CEQA." *Eureka: California's Policy, Economics, and Politics* (blog). Hoover Institu-
       tion, May 15, 2015. https://www.hoover.org/research/whats-preventing-new-hous-
       ing-california-usual-suspects-plus-ceqa#:~:text=The%20usual%20suspects%20
       in%20California,to%20block%20a%20development%20project.

19   Taylor, Mac, Chas Alamo, and Brian Uhler. Rep. Edited by Marianne O'Malley.
       California's High Housing Costs: Causes and Consequences. California Legislative
       Analyst's Office, March 17, 2015. https://www.lao.ca.gov/reports/2015/finance/
       housing-costs/housing-costs.pdf.

20   Bruno, Carson. "NIMBY-Ism, and the California Housing Shortage." *RealClearMar-
       kets*, March 24, 2016. https://www.realclearmarkets.com/articles/2016/03/24/
       nimby-ism_and_the_california_housing_shortage_102078.html.

21   Jackson, Kerry. Issue brief. *Unaffordable: How Government Made California's Housing
       Shortage a Crisis and How Free Market Ideas Can Restore Affordability and Supply.*
       Pacific Research Institute, June 14, 2017. https://www.pacificresearch.org/wp-con-
       tent/uploads/2017/06/CA_HousingBrief_Web.pdf.

22   Ibid.

23   Mouzon, Steve. "How the NIMBY-YIMBY Debates Worsened the Housing Crisis."
       Common Edge, September 11, 2023. https://commonedge.org/how-the-yimby-nim-
       by-debate-worsened-the-housing-crisis/.

24   Lindbeck, Assar, and Paul A. Samuelson. *The political economy of the new left: An
       outsider's view.* New York: Harper & Row, 1977.

25   Diamond, Rebecca, Timothy McQuade, and Franklin Qian. Working paper. *The
       Effects of Rent Control Expansion on Tenants, Landlords, and Inequality: Evidence from
       San Francisco.* National Bureau of Economic Research, January 2018. https://www.
       nber.org/papers/w24181.

26   Brown Calder, Vanessa, and Ryan Bourne. "Rent Control: An Old, Bad Idea That
       Won't Go Away." *Governing*, November 5, 2018. https://www.cato.org/commen-
       tary/rent-control-old-bad-idea-wont-go-away#.

27   Murphy, Katy, and Angela Hart. "Rent Control: What We Can Learn from Berkeley
       and Santa Monica ." *Chico Enterprise-Record*, September 27, 2018. https://www.
       chicoer.com/2018/09/27/california-and-rent-control-what-we-can-learn-from-
       berkeley-and-santa-monica/?clearUserState=true.

28   Anderson, William. "Rent Control Is Destroying a City near You." *Right by the Bay*
       (blog). Pacific Research Institute, October 12, 2022. https://www.pacificresearch.
       org/rent-control-is-destroying-a-city-near-you/.

29   Staff. "California Solar Roof Mandate May Send New Home Prices through the
       Roof." NewHomeSource, May 13, 2024. https://www.newhomesource.com/learn/
       california-mandates-usage-of-solar-panels-on-all-new-homes-by-2020/.

30   Zart, Nicolas. "California Requires Solar Panels on New Homes 5 Years after
       1st California City Did." CleanTechnica, May 10, 2018. https://cleantechnica.
       com/2018/05/10/california-requires-solar-panels-on-new-homes-5-years-after-
       1st-california-city-did-thumbs-nose-at-washington-d-c/ and Jackson, Kerry. "Green
       Building Mandates Will Increase the Cost of Housing in California." *Times of San
       Diego*, August 24, 2021. https://timesofsandiego.com/opinion/2021/08/24/green-
       building-mandates-will-increase-the-cost-of-housing-in-california/.

31   Lozanova, Sarah. "California Solar Mandate for Installing Solar Panels." Green-
       Lancer, December 5, 2023. https://www.greenlancer.com/post/california-so-
       lar-mandate.

32   Artz, Kenneth. "California Solar Home Law Likely to Price Many Out of the Market." *Heartland Institute* (blog), January 22, 2020. https://heartland.org/opinion/california-solar-home-law-likely-to-price-many-out-of-the-market/.

33   Kisela, Rachel. "California Went Big on Rooftop Solar. Now That's a Problem for Landfills ." *Los Angeles Times*, July 14, 2022. https://www.latimes.com/business/story/2022-07-14/california-rooftop-solar-pv-panels-recycling-danger.

34   Ibid.

35   "An Inconvenient Truth: Solar Panels Wear out and They're a Potent Source of Hazardous Waste." Hazardous Waste Experts, February 16, 2024. https://www.hazardouswasteexperts.com/solar-panels-wear-out-hazardous-waste/.

36   Desai, Jemin, and Mark Nelson. "Are We Headed for a Solar Waste Crisis?" Environmental Progress, September 25, 2020. https://environmentalprogress.org/big-news/2017/6/21/are-we-headed-for-a-solar-waste-crisis.

37   O'Malley, Isabella. "As the First Generation of Solar Panels Begins Wearing out, a Recycling Industry Is Taking Shape." *Associated Press*. August 2, 2023. https://www.latimes.com/business/story/2023-08-02/as-solar-panels-wear-out-a-recycling-industry-takes-shape.

38   Staggs, Brooke. "Here's What Happens to Solar Panels When They're Retired." SiliconValley.com, January 23, 2024. https://www.siliconvalley.com/2024/01/23/heres-what-happens-to-solar-panels-when-theyre-retired/.

39   Meinch, Tree. "Solutions for Solar Panel Waste Are Just Beginning to Surface." *Discover*, August 2, 2023. https://www.discovermagazine.com/environment/solutions-for-solar-panel-waste-are-just-beginning-to-surface.

40   Jackson, Kerry. "A Delinquent Tenant's Paradise." *City Journal*, March 28, 2023. https://www.city-journal.org/article/californias-wrongheaded-eviction-moratoriums.

41   De Santiago Ayon, Ana, Winston Stromberg, and Matthew Friedrich. "Client Alert: Los Angeles City Council Dramatically Expands Permanent Renter Protections." Latham Watkins, February 10, 2023. https://www.lw.com/admin/upload/SiteAttachments/Alert-3067.pdf.

42   "Tenant Protections." Los Angeles City Attorney's Office. Accessed June 6, 2024. https://cityattorney.lacity.gov/tenant-protections.

43   Girod, Melanie. "The End of the Eviction Moratorium in San Francisco: What's Ahead?" Medium, October 15, 2023. https://medium.com/@mlngirod/the-end-of-the-eviction-moratorium-in-san-francisco-whats-ahead-3d4292d88215.

44   "California Eviction Moratorium 2023." Martinez Law Center, May 10, 2024. https://martinezlawcenter.com/california-eviction-moratorium-2023/#:~:text=The%20COVID%2D19%20pandemic%20led,extended%20well%20beyond%20that%20date.

45   Sisson, Paul. "Region Braces for Second Storm as County Approves Targeted 60-Day Eviction Ban." *San Diego Union-Tribune*, January 30, 2024. https://www.sandiegouniontribune.com/news/story/2024-01-30/region-braces-for-second-storm-as-county-approves-targeted-eviction-ban.

46   "Pandemic Eviction Bans Have Spawned a Renters'-Rights Movement." *The Economist*, February 16, 2023. https://www.economist.com/united-states/2023/02/16/pandemic-eviction-bans-have-spawned-a-renters-rights-movement.

CHAPTER 16

1   Wheeler, Micaiah, Colette Tano, Katherine Rush, Ed Prestera, Alyssa Andrichik, and Tanya de Sousa. "The 2023 Annual Homelessness Assessment Report (AHAR) to Congress." U.S. Department of Housing and Urban Development, Office of Community Planning and Development, December 2023. https://www.huduser.gov/portal/sites/default/files/pdf/2023-AHAR-Part-1.pdf.

2   Robertson, Nick. "Californians Often Struggle with Health, Trauma, Poverty before Losing Homes: Research ." *The Hill*, June 20, 2023. https://thehill.com/homenews/state-watch/4058093-californians-often-struggle-with-health-trauma-poverty/.

3   Kimberlin, Sara, and Monica Davalos. "Who Is Experiencing Homelessness in California?" California Budget and Policy Center, July 27, 2023. https://calbudget-center.org/resources/who-is-experiencing-homelessness-in-california/.

4   Wheeler, Micaiah, Colette Tano, Katherine Rush, Ed Prestera, Alyssa Andrichik, and Tanya de Sousa. "The 2023 Annual Homelessness Assessment Report (AHAR) to Congress." U.S. Department of Housing and Urban Development, Office of Community Planning and Development, December 2023. https://www.huduser.gov/portal/sites/default/files/pdf/2023-AHAR-Part-1.pdf.

5   Kendall, Marisa. "How Big Is California's Homelessness Crisis? Inside the Massive, Statewide Effort to Find Out ." *CalMatters*, January 26, 2024. https://calmatters.org/housing/homelessness/2024/01/california-homeless-point-in-time-count-2024/.

6   Wheeler, Micaiah, Colette Tano, Katherine Rush, Ed Prestera, Alyssa Andrichik, and Tanya de Sousa. "The 2023 Annual Homelessness Assessment Report (AHAR) to Congress." U.S. Department of Housing and Urban Development, Office of Community Planning and Development, December 2023. https://www.huduser.gov/portal/sites/default/files/pdf/2023-AHAR-Part-1.pdf.

7   Hehmeyer, Preeti, and Bruce Cain. "California's Population Drain." Stanford Institute for Economic Policy Research (SIEPR), October 2023. https://siepr.stanford.edu/publications/policy-brief/californias-population-drain#:~:text=California%20is%20still%20the%20largest,percent%20of%20the%20U.S.%20population.

8   Kendall, Marisa. "How Big Is California's Homelessness Crisis? Inside the Massive, Statewide Effort to Find Out ." *CalMatters*, January 26, 2024. https://calmatters.org/housing/homelessness/2024/01/california-homeless-point-in-time-count-2024/.

9   Wheeler, Micaiah, Colette Tano, Katherine Rush, Ed Prestera, Alyssa Andrichik, and Tanya de Sousa. "The 2023 Annual Homelessness Assessment Report (AHAR) to Congress." U.S. Department of Housing and Urban Development, Office of Community Planning and Development, December 2023. https://www.huduser.gov/portal/sites/default/files/pdf/2023-AHAR-Part-1.pdf.

10   Andrzejewski, Adam. "Updated! The San Francisco Poop Map by Openthebooks in Real Time." OpenTheBooks Substack, December 1, 2023. https://openthebooks.substack.com/p/updated-the-san-francisco-poop-map.

11   "Housing First (Fact Sheet)." Corporation for Supportive Housing. Accessed June 10, 2024. https://www.hcd.ca.gov/grants-funding/active-funding/docs/housing-first-fact-sheet.pdf.

12   Humpal, Emily. "A Lack of Mental Health Treatment, Not Money or Shelter Space, Is Contributing to Sacramento's Rising Homeless Numbers." *Right by the Bay* (blog). Pacific Research Institute, July 14, 2022. https://www.pacificresearch.org/a-lack-of-mental-health-treatment-not-money-or-shelter-space-is-contributing-to-sacramentos-rising-homeless-numbers/.

13   "Project Roomkey Fact Sheet." Los Angeles Department of Public Health, Substance Abuse Prevention and Control (SAPC), May 11, 2020. http://www.ph.la-county.gov/sapc/docs/providers/programs-and-initiatives/Project Roomkey Fact Sheet (May 2020).pdf.

14   California, State of. "During Digital Roundtable with Leaders from Rural Communities, Governor Newsom Announces Release of $30.7 Million in Fifth Round of Homekey Awards." Governor of California, October 16, 2020. https://www.gov.ca.gov/2020/10/16/during-digital-roundtable-with-leaders-from-rural-communities-governor-newsom-announces-release-of-30-7-million-in-fifth-round-of-home-key-awards/.

15   "Fact Sheet: Homelessness in California." California Senate Housing Committee, May 2021. https://shou.senate.ca.gov/sites/shou.senate.ca.gov/files/Homeless-ness in CA 2020 Numbers.pdf.

16   Jackson, Kerry, and Wayne Winegarden. Rep. *Project Homekey Provides No Way Home for California's Homeless*. Pacific Research Institute, July 2022. https://www.pacificresearch.org/wp-content/uploads/2022/07/Homekey_Final.pdf.

17   Ibid.

18   Anaya, Tim. "Where Is All the Money Going for Homeless in California?" *Right by the Bay* (blog). Pacific Research Institute, February 21, 2023. https://www.pacificresearch.org/where-is-all-the-money-going-for-homeless-in-california/.

19   Rep. *Homelessness in California: The State Must Do More to Assess the CostEffectiveness of Its Homelessness Programs*. Auditor of the State of California, April 9, 2024. https://information.auditor.ca.gov/reports/2023-102.1/index.html#section1.

20   Lambert, Hannah Ray, and Fox News. "'Where Do I Sign up?' San Diego Homeless Woman Says They're 'Spoiled' with Free Stuff, Phones." Fox News, June 13, 2023. https://www.foxnews.com/media/sign-san-diego-homeless-woman-says-spoiled-free-stuff-phones.

21   Matier, Phil, and Andrew Ross. "SF Mayor Vows to Clear out Homeless Tent Camps." *San Francisco Chronicle*, April 20, 2018. https://www.sfchronicle.com/bayarea/matier-ross/article/SF-mayor-vows-to-clear-out-homeless-tent-camps-12852701.php.

22   "San Francisco, California, Proposition C, Gross Receipts Tax for Homelessness Services (November 2018)." Ballotpedia. Accessed June 10, 2024. https://ballotpedia.org/San_Francisco,_California,_Proposition_C,_Gross_Receipts_Tax_for_Home-lessness_Services_(November_2018).

23   Jackson, Kerry. "Proposition C Makes San Francisco A 'Sanctuary City' For The Homeless." *Right by the Bay* (blog). Pacific Research Institute, December 3, 2018. https://www.pacificresearch.org/proposition-c-makes-san-francisco-a-sanctuary-city-for-the-homeless/.

24   Jarrett, Will. "SF Homeless Tally Drops – 'Investment Works'." *Mission Local*, May 17, 2022. https://missionlocal.org/2022/05/sf-homeless-drop-pit-count-sip-hotels/.

25   Angst, Maggie. "S.F. Homelessness Rises despite City Spending Hundreds of

Millions of Dollars, New Count Shows." *San Francisco Chronicle*, May 16, 2024. https://www.sfchronicle.com/sf/article/sf-homeless-count-shows-increase-tents-vehicles-19446549.php.

26   Ibid.

27   Greenhut, Steven, and Wayne Winegarden. *Giving Housing Supply a Boost.* Pasadena, CA : Pacific Research Institute, 91101. https://www.pacificresearch.org/reforms-to-increase-affordability-homebuilding-would-go-far-to-alleviate-states-housing-homeless-crises/.

28   Richards, Tori. "Gavin Newsom Invites World's Homeless to California." *Washington Examiner*, July 22, 2011. https://www.washingtonexaminer.com/news/2621221/gavin-newsom-invites-worlds-homeless-to-california/.

29   Ring, Edward. "Taxpayers and the Homeless Are Just Pawns in Scheme to Buoy Leftist Donors." *American Greatness*, January 12, 2021. https://amgreatness.com/2021/01/12/taxpayers-and-the-homeless-are-just-pawns-in-scheme-to-buoy-leftist-donors/.

30   McConnell, Eric. "Could The Cure For California's Insurance Crisis Be Worse Than The Disease?" *Benzinga*, April 8, 2024. https://finance.yahoo.com/news/could-cure-californias-insurance-crisis-170017805.html#:~:text=A%20Home%20Insurance%20Market%20In%20Chaos&text=It's%20no%20wonder%20that%20former,market%20is%20%22in%20chaos.%22.

31   Mitri, Lysée. "'I Feel Helpless': Homeowners Struggle to Find, Afford Insurance amid California's Crisis." *KCRA-TV Online (Sacramento, CA)*, February 26, 2024. https://www.kcra.com/article/california-homeowner-insurance-crisis-and-state-plan-for-problem/46913421.

32   Truong, Kevin. "'In Deep Doo-Doo': Policyholders Left Scrambling as State's Largest Home Insurer Retreats." *San Francisco Standard*, March 22, 2024. https://sfstandard.com/2024/03/22/state-farm-california-insurance-market-chaos-fair-plan/.

33   Chen, David. "'Not Sustainable': High Insurance Costs Threaten Affordable Housing." *New York Times*, June 7, 2024. https://www.nytimes.com/2024/06/07/us/home-insurance-homeless-affordable.html?unlocked_article_code=1.zE0.Vp2Z.MdlOQTuTvlTk&smid=url-share.

34   "Update on California." State Farm General Insurance Company, March 20, 2024. https://newsroom.statefarm.com/update-on-california/.

35   Parks, Kristine. "State Farm Cuts 72,000 California Home Insurance Policies: 'Decision Was Not Made Lightly.'" *Fox Business*, March 22, 2024. https://www.foxbusiness.com/media/state-farm-cuts-72000-california-home-insurance-policies-decision-was-not-made-lightly#:~:text=State%20Farm%20announced%20last%20year,to%20the%20San%20Francisco%20Chronicle.

36   "California New Business Update." State Farm General Insurance Company, May 26, 2023. https://newsroom.statefarm.com/state-farm-general-insurance-company-california-new-business-update/.

37   Kissell, Chris. "California Insurance Crisis: Why Are Insurance Companies Leaving California." Insurance.com, April 4, 2024. https://www.insurance.com/home-insurance/state-farm-stops-selling-home-insurance-in-california.

38   Shaheen, Perla. "Farmers Insurance Affiliate Drops 100,000 Customers in California." *10 News San Diego Online*, March 14, 2024. https://www.10news.com/news/

local-news/farmers-insurance-affiliate-drops-100-000-customers-in-california.

39   Mulkern, Anne. "California Weighs Use of Catastrophe Models in Home Insur-
      ance." *E&E News*, October 5, 2023. https://www.eenews.net/articles/califor-
      nia-weighs-use-of-catastrophe-models-in-home-insurance/.

40   Cabanatuan, Michael. "The Surprising Way California's Home Insurance Crisis Is
      Affecting Tahoe." *San Francisco Chronicle*, June 16, 2024. https://www.sfchronicle.
      com/california/article/insurance-crisis-spreading-nevada-tahoe-19513148.php.

41   Theodorou, Jerry. "California Is Dangerous for Insurers, but Not Due to Fires
      and Floods." *Orange County Register*, January 31, 2023. https://www.ocregister.
      com/2023/01/31/california-is-dangerous-for-insurers-but-not-due-to-fires-and-
      floods/?clearUserState=true.

42   California, State of. "Sustainable Insurance Strategy." CA Department of In-
      surance. Accessed June 19, 2024. https://www.insurance.ca.gov/01-consum-
      ers/180-climate-change/SustainableInsuranceStrategy.cfm.

43   Darmiento, Laurence. "State Regulators Identify Wildfire Neighborhoods Target-
      ed for Insurance Relief." *Los Angeles Times*, June 12, 2024. https://www.latimes.
      com/business/story/2024-06-12/california-homeowners-insurance-crisis-lara-wild-
      fire-risk-neighborhoods-newsom.

44   Sumagaysay, Levi. "Newsom Unveils Plan That Would Hasten Insurance-Rate
      Reviews — and Increases." *CalMatters*, May 30, 2024. https://calmatters.org/
      economy/2024/05/california-insurance-crisis-2/.

45   Greenhut, Steven. "California's Coming Insurance Crisis." *City Journal*, 2023 Special
      Issue. Accessed June 19, 2024. https://www.city-journal.org/article/californi-
      as-coming-insurance-crisis.

46   Greenhut, Steven. "State Is Deer in Headlights as Insurance Crisis Unfolds ." *Or-
      ange County Register*, March 22, 2024. https://www.ocregister.com/2024/03/22/
      state-is-deer-in-headlights-as-insurance-crisis-unfolds/.

CONCLUSION

1   Vranich, Joseph. Rep. *Why Companies Leave California*. Spectrum Location Services LLC, Accessed June 18, 2024. https://web.archive.org/web/20190518130448/ https://spectrumlocationsolutions.com/california/ and Jackson, Kerry. "Misguided State Policies Lead To More Companies Leaving California." *Fox and Hounds Daily*, April 7, 2017. https://www.foxandhoundsdaily.com/2017/04/misguided-state-poli-cies-lead-companies-leaving-california/.

2   Vranich, Joseph. Rep. *It's Time for Companies to Leave California's Toxic Business Climate*. Spectrum Location Services LLC, December 11, 2018 and Jackson, Kerry. "With Business Fleeing, California Doesn't Look So Golden." *Daily Caller*, January 7, 2019. https://dailycaller.com/2019/01/07/business-california-golden/.

3   Vranich, Joseph. Rep. *Why Companies Leave California*. Spectrum Location Services LLC, Accessed June 18, 2024. https://web.archive.org/web/20190518130448/ https://spectrumlocationsolutions.com/california/

4   Pacific Research Institute. *Survey: Why California's Most Coveted Industries Aren't Coming to the Golden State*, February 2018. https://www.pacificresearch.org/ wp-content/uploads/2018/02/SurveyDoc_F_NewWebLow.pdf.

5   Ibid.

6   Ibid.

7   Jones, Blake. "California Finally Reverses Its Population-Loss Streak ." *Politico*, April 30, 2024. https://www.politico.com/news/2024/04/30/california-popula-tion-grows-reversing-trend-00155069.

8   Pacific Research Institute. *Survey: Why California's Most Coveted Industries Aren't Coming to the Golden State*, February 2018. https://www.pacificresearch.org/ wp-content/uploads/2018/02/SurveyDoc_F_NewWebLow.pdf.

9   Cardone, Grant (@GrantCardone). "How California Lost $1B in Revenue with one tax payer." *X*, June 12, 2024. https://x.com/GrantCardone/sta-tus/1800880363234869377

10   Ibid.

11   Ibid and Jackson, Margaret. "Grant Cardone Claims California Lost $1 Billion After His 2012 Exodus To Florida." *Benzinga*, June 13, 2024. https://www.benzinga.com/ real-estate/24/06/39318291/grant-cardone-claims-california-lost-1-billion-after-his-2012-exodus-to-florida.

12   Cardone, Grant (@GrantCardone). "How California Lost $1B in Revenue with one tax payer." *X*, June 12, 2024. https://x.com/GrantCardone/sta-tus/1800880363234869377

13   Ibid.

14   Painter, Lora. "Understanding California's New Income Tax Rate and Who It Impacts." ABC 10 Sacramento, January 24, 2024. https://www.abc10.com/article/ money/california-new-income-tax-rate-explained/103-16bd54b0-d366-4f11-babf-1f7177de6b5f.

15   Yushkov, Andrey. "2024 State Individual Income Tax Rates and Brackets." Tax Foundation, February 20, 2024. https://taxfoundation.org/data/all/state/state-in-come-tax-rates-2024/.

16   Jackson, Kerry. "Misguided State Policies Lead To More Companies Leaving California." *Fox and Hounds Daily*, April 7, 2017. https://www.foxandhoundsdaily.com/2017/04/misguided-state-policies-lead-companies-leaving-california/ and Vranich, Joseph. Rep. *Why Companies Leave California*. Spectrum Location Services LLC, Accessed June 18, 2024. https://web.archive.org/web/20190518130448/https://spectrumlocationsolutions.com/california/

17   Jackson, Kerry, and Wayne Winegarden. "How to Slow, Reverse the California Exodus ." *Orange County Register*, October 4, 2021. https://www.ocregister.com/2021/10/04/how-to-slow-reverse-the-california-exodus/?clearUserState=true.

18   Buss, Dale. "Best & Worst States for Business 2024 Survey Finds Unsettled CEOS Ready to Roam." ChiefExecutive.net, April 23, 2024. https://chiefexecutive.net/best-worst-states-survey-shows-unsettled-ceos-are-ready-to-roam/.

19   Vranich, Joseph. Rep. *It's Time for Companies to Leave California's Toxic Business Climate*. Spectrum Location Services LLC, December 11, 2018 and Jackson, Kerry. "With Business Fleeing, California Doesn't Look So Golden." *Daily Caller*, January 7, 2019. https://dailycaller.com/2019/01/07/business-california-golden/.

20   Lansner, Jonathan. "California Critic's Ultimate Critique: He Moved to Pennsylvania! ." *Orange County Register*, April 18, 2018. https://www.ocregister.com/2018/04/18/california-business-critics-ultimate-critique-he-moved-to-pennsylvania/.

21   Vranich, Joseph, and Lee Ohanian. Working paper. *Why Company Headquarters Are Leaving California in Unprecedented Numbers*. Hoover Institution at Stanford University, September 14, 2022. https://www.hoover.org/sites/default/files/research/docs/21117-Ohanian-Vranich-4_0.pdf.

22   Ibid.

23   Ibid.

24   "Issues - Regulatory Reform." California Business Roundtable, April 5, 2012. https://www.cbrt.org/issues/regulatory-reform/#:~:text=By%20a%20large%20margin%2C%20California's,year%20between%201992%20and%202002.

25   Vranich, Joseph, and Lee Ohanian. Working paper. *Why Company Headquarters Are Leaving California in Unprecedented Numbers*. Hoover Institution at Stanford University, September 14, 2022. https://www.hoover.org/sites/default/files/research/docs/21117-Ohanian-Vranich-4_0.pdf.

26   Probasco, Jim. "7 States with No Income Tax." Investopedia, June 7, 2024. https://www.investopedia.com/financial-edge/0210/7-states-with-no-income-tax.aspx#:~:text=Which%20Are%20the%20Tax%2DFree,tax%20on%20certain%20high%20earners.

27   Stacker. "Where People in California Are Moving to Most." Stacker, March 28, 2024. https://stacker.com/california/where-people-california-are-moving-most.

28   Jackson, Kerry, and Wayne Winegarden. Rep. *California Migrating: Documenting the Causes and Consequences of California's Growing Exodus Problem*. Pacific Research Institute, September 23, 2021. https://www.pacificresearch.org/wp-content/uploads/2022/08/CA-Migration_F_web.pdf.

29   Ibid.

30   Ibid.

31   Ibid.

32   Ibid.

33   Oreskes, Benjamin. "4 in 10 California Residents Are Considering Packing up
      and Leaving, New Poll Finds." *Los Angeles Times*, June 23, 2023. https://www.
      latimes.com/california/story/2023-06-23/california-residents-considering-leav-
      ing-cost-new-poll.

34   Kotkin, Joel. "A 'Diet' to Give Drivers Indigestion." *Los Angeles Daily News*, May 17,
      2016. https://www.dailynews.com/2016/05/27/a-diet-to-give-drivers-indigestion-
      joel-kotkin/.

35   Smith, Steve. Rep. *Paradise Lost: Crime in the Golden State, 2011-2021*. Pacific
      Research Institute, February 7, 2023. https://www.pacificresearch.org/wp-content/
      uploads/2023/02/ParadiseLost_CrimeStudy2022_Final_Web.pdf.

36   Halper, Evan. "Make America California Again? That's Biden's Plan." *Los Angeles
      Times*, January 17, 2021. https://www.latimes.com/politics/story/2021-01-17/
      make-america-california-again-how-biden-will-try.

37   Harris, Kamala. "Remarks by Vice President Harris at the California State Legisla-
      ture Democratic Caucus Reception," January 25, 2024. https://www.whitehouse.
      gov/briefing-room/speeches-remarks/2024/01/25/remarks-by-vice-president-har-
      ris-at-the-california-state-legislature-democratic-caucus-reception-sacramento-ca/

ACKNOWLEDGMENTS

The authors wish to thank PRI President, CEO and Thomas W. Smith Fellow in Health Care Policy Sally Pipes for her support and encouragement of this important project.

Special thanks go to PRI Vice President of Development Ben Smithwick and Deputy Communications Director Emily Humpal, without whom this book project would not have become a reality.

We also wish to acknowledge the tremendous work of PRI's scholars and fellows past and present, whose work fill and inspire the pages of this book, particularly Wayne Winegarden, Lance Izumi, Steve Smith, Pam Lewison, Damon Dunn, Steven Greenhut, Bartlett Cleland, and PRI board member, the Hon. Dan Kolkey.

KERRY JACKSON

This book would not have been possible without the "work" of Gov. Gavin Newsom and a long parade of California policymakers going back decades whose coastal elite agenda has pushed this state toward a crisis. Had they followed a more judicious policy path, this guide would not have been written because there would have been no need for us to point the way out of the quagmire each contributed to.

TIM ANAYA

I wish to acknowledge several individuals who have been teachers, mentors, sounding boards, colleagues and friends: Speaker Kevin McCarthy; The Hon. Mike Villines, literally a profile in courage; Jeff Danzinger, Matt Cox and Walter von Huene, my colleagues from the most entertaining gubernatorial speechwriting office that ever existed; and "Team Conway" – Sabrina Lockhart, Erin Guerrero, Deborah Gonzalez, and "La Reina" herself, The Hon. Connie Conway.

You have all inspired me to, even with the odds seemingly insurmountable, fight for the California we want to see and the ideas we know are right.

I'd also like to recognize five important individuals to me who are no longer with us, but who would have gotten a kick of my co-writing this book – Ivan Altamura, Kris Lesher-Aring, Margi and David Bockweg and Betty Klein.

Most importantly, I'd like to salute my parents Bob and Jan Anaya – and my brother Daniel (who will be annoyed by every word he reads in this book, but maybe will learn something!)

BIOGRAPHIES

KERRY JACKSON

Kerry Jackson is the William Clement Fellow in California Reform at the Pacific Research Institute.

An independent journalist and opinion writer with extensive experience covering politics and public policy, he is a leading analyst and commentator on California's housing, poverty, and homeless problems.

Jackson is a co-author of the 2021 book *No Way Home* (Encounter Books), which was an Amazon.com number one new release for mental health law books and top 10 bestseller for urban planning and development books. The book examines the root causes of homelessness in California and whether current programs related to housing, social services and employment are actually making the problem worse.

His 2023 study, "Project Homekey is Providing No Way Home for the State's Homeless" (co-authored with Dr. Wayne Winegarden), provided the first evidence that, despite spending billions of dollars on Gov. Newsom's Project Homekey initiative, California's homeless problem was growing worse than ever, receiving national media coverage from the Associated Press.

His 2018 brief on poverty in California, "Good Intentions: How California's Anti-Poverty Programs Aren't Delivering and How the Private Sector Can Lift More People Out of Poverty," garnered national attention for his *Los Angeles Times* op-ed asking, "Why is liberal California the poverty capital of America?" In addition, his 2017 brief on California's housing crisis, "Unaffordable," drew bipartisan praise from then-Gov. Jerry Brown's housing policy director.

Jackson is also the author of *Living in Fear in California*, a book that explores sweeping changes to California's public safety laws that have undermined safe communities; "Sapping California's Energy Future" (with Winegarden), which documents how state government green mandates are increase the energy burdens of Californians; and "Enriching Lawyers" (also with Winegarden), which documents how lawsuit abuse hurts taxpayers and consumers.

His commentaries have been published in the *Los Angeles Times, New York Post, FoxNews.com, San Francisco Chronicle, San Diego Union-Tribune, CalMatters, City Journal, Daily Caller,* the *New York Observer, Orange County Register, Bakersfield Californian, San Francisco Examiner, Fresno Bee, Ventura County Star,* and *Forbes,* among others.

He regularly appears on radio and television programs commenting on the problems affecting California. Jackson has been a past guest on National Public Radio, One America News Network, Newsmax TV, and "The Dr. Drew Show," among others.

Before coming to PRI, Jackson spent 18 years writing editorials on domestic and foreign policy for *Investor's Business Daily* (IBD) and three years as the assistant director of public affairs for the American Legislative Exchange Council. He has written for the American Media Institute and Real Clear Investigations and edited "The Growth Manifesto" for the Committee to Unleash Prosperity.

A graduate of Georgia State University, Kerry has also served as a public affairs consultant for the George Mason University School of Law and worked as a reporter and editor for local newspapers in the metro Atlanta and northern Virginia regions.

TIM ANAYA

Tim Anaya is Pacific Research Institute's Vice President of Marketing and Communications.

In his role, he oversees PRI's media relations activities, serves as PRI's media spokesperson, and coordinates outreach to policymakers and opinion leaders. Under his leadership, PRI was awarded a prestigious Communications Excellence Award from State Policy Network.

In 2018, he launched PRI's "California Ideas in Action" policy conference in Sacramento, which annually brings together speakers from across the political spectrum advocating for free-market policy reforms to undo the policy-driven burdens faced by Californians every day. He is co-host of PRI's Next Round podcast, which has released over 300 episodes featuring politicians, policy wonks, authors, and other interesting people sharing their thoughts on current events and free market ideas. He has interviewed an eclectic array of guests ranging from the the Speaker of the U.S. House of Representatives and Pulitzer Prize winners to Academy Award nominees and golf legend Dottie Pepper.

He is also the editor and a regular columnist for PRI's *Right by the Bay* blog, which features new content daily from PRI scholars on California politics and policy.

His comments on California politics and policy have appeared in numerous media outlets in California and nationally. Anaya is a regular guest panelist at the Commonwealth Club's "Week to Week Political Roundtable" events in San Francisco.

Throughout a career spanning more than 25 years, Anaya has had a front row seat to politics and policymaking in Sacramento.

He held a variety of positions in nearly two decades working at the State Capitol. He served as communications director for then-Assembly Minority Leader and future Congresswoman Connie Conway, managing the staff and operations of the Assembly Republican communications department.

He was a senior communications advisor to 9 Assembly Republican Leaders from 2003-16, including former Leader and future House Speaker Kevin McCarthy. He also worked as a speechwriter for former California Gov. Arnold Schwarzenegger.

He is a graduate of Santa Clara University and the University of Southern California.

ABOUT PACIFIC RESEARCH INSTITUTE

The Pacific Research Institute (PRI) champions freedom, opportunity, and personal responsibility by advancing free-market policy solutions. It provides practical solutions for the policy issues that impact the daily lives of all Americans, and demonstrates why the free market is more effective than the government at providing the important results we all seek: good schools, quality health care, a clean environment, and a robust economy.

Founded in 1979 and based in San Francisco, PRI is a non-profit, non-partisan organization supported by private contributions. Its activities include publications, public events, media commentary, community leadership, legislative testimony, and academic outreach.

Center for Business and Economics
PRI shows how the entrepreneurial spirit—the engine of economic growth and opportunity—is stifled by onerous taxes, regulations, and lawsuits. It advances policy reforms that promote a robust economy, consumer choice, and innovation.

Center for Education
PRI works to restore to all parents the basic right to choose the best educational opportunities for their children. Through research and grassroots outreach, PRI promotes parental choice in education, high academic standards, teacher quality, charter schools, and school-finance reform.

Center for the Environment
PRI reveals the dramatic and long-term trend toward a cleaner, healthier environment. It also examines and promotes the essential ingredients for abundant resources and environmental quality: property rights, markets, local action, and private initiative.

Center for Health Care
PRI demonstrates why a single-payer Canadian model would be detrimental to the health care of all Americans. It proposes market-based reforms that would improve affordability, access, quality, and consumer choice.

Center for California Reform
The Center for California Reform seeks to reinvigorate California's entrepreneurial self-reliant traditions. It champions solutions in education, business, and the environment that work to advance prosperity and opportunity for all the state's residents.

Center for Medical Economics and Innovation
The Center for Medical Economics and Innovation aims to educate policymakers, regulators, health care professionals, the media, and the public on the critical role that new technologies play in improving health and accelerating economic growth.

Free Cities Center
The Free Cities Center cultivates innovative ideas to improve our cities and urban life based around freedom and property rights – not government.

AVAILABLE HOUSING

SAFE PARKS TO ENJOY